THE BOAT OWNER'S MAINTENANCE BOOK

by
Geoffrey O'Connell

Published by Ashford Press Publishing 1988
1 Church Road
Shedfield
Southampton
SO3 2HW

Text ©: Geoffrey O'Connell 1988
Illustrations ©: Geoffrey O'Connell and Ashford
Press Publishing, 1988

Printed in Great Britain

British Library Cataloguing in Publication Data

O'Connell, Geoffrey

The boat owner's maintenance book.
1. Boats and boating — Maintenance and repair —
Amateurs' manuals

I. Title
623.8'202'0288   VM351

ISBN 1-85253-012-X

Errors and omissions
Whilst great care has been taken in the compilation
of this book, it is regretted that neither author nor
publisher can accept responsibility for the use, or
consequences of the use of the information and
opinions expressed herein, nor for any inaccuracies
or mishaps arising from the work.

Disclaimer
The author has no commercial connection with any
business or firm listed herein, other than as a partner
of Willowbridge Enterprises, and no warranty or
guarantee is implied or given in their respect.
   That a business, firm or product, is not listed or
detailed does not imply any criticism. The impressions,
opinions and viewpoints expressed in this publication
are highly individualistic and readers must make their
own judgments on all the matters presented herein.

Illustrations by G.R. O'Connell and T. Spittles
Cover photographs by G.R. O'Connell
Cover design by Jonathon Duval
Printed and bound by Oxford University Press.

ACKNOWLEDGEMENTS

If I was listing my grateful thanks in chronological order then Bob Bingham of South Western Marine Factors would have to be first named. Years ago now, Bob set me off on the trials and trepidations of authorship by commissioning the progenitor of a companion book in this series. He has much for which to answer!

Viv Hitie pounded the word processor and Nick and Lynn Carter, my colleagues (and more importantly friends) at Willowbridge Enterprises assisted by smacking my hands over some of the worst grammatical errors. Colin Silvester, naval architect and another friend, read an early draft and made a number of very useful criticisms and Ted Spittles, although being 'reimbursed on earth', performed a magnificent job of translating my initial scrawlings into technical drawings and sketches more than worthy of this publication.

A number of manufacturers and firms associated with the marine industry were helpful in my preparation of the book, some far beyond the call of duty. The most co-operative included International Paints, Kemp Masts, Lucas Marine, Munster Sims Engineering and Ripaults Ltd. Their full title and respective addresses, as well as those of other companies who will be useful to the reader and who may have supplied information, are to be found at the back of Chapter Twelve.

As spelt out in the text, I have no commercial connection with any firm detailed in the book other than as a partner of a small, Inland Waterways boatyard.

ABOUT THE AUTHOR

Geoffrey O'Connell has a very wide experience of all aspects of boat building and marine engineering spanning some twenty seven years. A Mechanical Engineering apprenticeship was followed by a period of building up an Inland Waterway hire fleet in the early 1960s and setting up one of the first cabin cruiser production flow lines as well as a marine engineering works in the middle 1960s.

Later experience encompassed building steel and wooden inshore fishing vessels up to 55ft in length, yard repair work, marina management and custom boat building.

Production of competition and cruising yachts between 22ft and 34ft from the lamination of the GRP mouldings to the finished boat, completed a thorough technical and practical grounding in the marine trade.

Geoffrey O'Connell's highly personalised style of writing not only encompasses books on yacht building and maintenance but humour, a series of GROC's Greek island travel guides and a magnum opus concerning the history of Southwick village.

by the same author
BOAT BOOKS
The Boat Building Book

LOCAL HISTORY
Secretive Southwick — Domesday to D-Day
Southwick — The D-Day Village that went to War

GROC's CANDID GUIDE TO:
Corfu & The Ionian Islands including Athens
Crete, Athens & Piraeus
Rhodes, The Dodecanese Islands, Athens City & Piraeus
The Cyclades Islands, Athens & Piraeus
Samos & N.E. Aegean Islands, Athens & Piraeus
The Greek Mainland Islands including the Sporades & Argo-Saronic

HUMOUR
Divorce Without Remorse

THE BOAT OWNERS MAINTENANCE BOOK

CONTENTS

ILLUSTRATIONS

INTRODUCTION

The wonder is always new that any sane man can be a sailor. R.W. Emerson 1803-1882.

Owning a boat is a way of life which must take precedence over a job, marriage, social life and all other pursuits. The pleasure of boating must be paid for with labour and some money but then what enjoyment does not have to be balanced in the scales with toil and cash?

The idea behind this book is to help keep maintenance as painless as is possible, be it a perfunctory tidy-up or a major refit. Naturally, continuous summer running upkeep helps reduce the winter overhaul costs and time. On the other hand it may well be that a craft is one purchased with an extensive schedule of refurbishment allowed for or that, even if it was not the original intention, rather a lot becomes necessary. Let us hope not!

Whilst touching on the matter of purchase, prior to buying a boat it is absolutely essential to employ the services of a surveyor, remembering that an insurance or 'builder's condition' survey is not extensive enough to give any more than an indication of a boat's working order. And please steer clear of friends with 'knowledge'. The whole subject of purchasing a second-hand boat is to be dealt with by a companion book in this series.

It is much easier to schedule the winter tasks if, during the summer months, a 'Defects List' or log of faults has been kept. This will at least ensure a sound basis for the projected work.

Throughout this book it has been assumed that the basic structure of a craft is correct and no major alterations are envisaged. Owners fortunate enough to have little to do in any particular winter season must bear with those who have a large and detailed programme on their, and their family's hands — well, what are families for?

The following chapters should give the amateur a comprehensive guide to the work in hand and enough basic knowledge, if not skill, to save being bamboozled by the average boatyard and its employees.

1

WATER TO HARDSTANDING

Perhaps the first words of wisdom are that an owner must ensure the craft is comprehensively insured. And do advise the chosen company of any intention to lift or trail the boat. These 'activities' may result in an additional premium but if there is an accident at least, after the acrimonious debate as to who was to blame for what, an owner should not be out of pocket. Periods during which a boat is stored on hardstanding, be it in the open or under cover, may result in a lower premium, so do keep the insurer informed.

The extent of the winter programme determines if it is necessary to haul a craft out of the water. Even boats left afloat require some of the work detailed in the following chapters.

Where it is planned to leave a boat afloat for the winter season, certainly Inland Waterway craft benefit from the provision of winter leeboards. These should be heavy, waterlogged planks hung over the side to protect the hull from ice and drifting debris. (Illus. 1). Owners who have to get at a 'boat's bottom' have a choice of careening, a trailer and slipway, craning or a travel-hoist.

Careen

A word redolent of the 18th century. It describes the process of finding a suitable beach and inducing a boat to lay over on its side, on a falling tide, in order to carry out the necessary hull work during low water. After which the vessel is allowed to float upright on the incoming tide only to be laid over on the other side, on the next ebbing tide, to complete the job (Illus. 2). The trick is to ensure that nothing impedes the craft's self-righting moment, otherwise an embarrassing situation might develop! To aid the craft to 'lie down' without a hitch (and on the correct side) all the portable ballast and internal items should be moved to the side that is to take to the ground and the anchor chain be laid along the appropriate side-deck. As the tide floods, the above items must be moved to the other side, that is away from the laid over flank, in order to make refloating as faultless as possible.

All a bit unnecessary on the Inland Waterways where owners of the flat bottomed narrow boats can borrow a convenient lock sill. But they must be careful not to damage the rudder gear (Illus. 3).

Prior to careening do not forget to:-

close all the seacocks

move the contents of the (to be uppermost) lockers and shelves to the downside compartments

remember that any container holding liquid, but without a sealed lid, requires attention and

ensure the anchor chain is carefully secured if spread along the deck.

A further helping hand can be given with the use of warps to a convenient shore-based point. Owners of sailing craft may use a line to the far, main sheet winch and or a masthead halyard to 'aid' the process. For that matter, judicious use of a block and tackle or mini-hoist may well be of great assistance (Illus. 4). Once the craft is on its way over, the mooring chain, if used, may be judiciously re-stowed in the anchor locker, as long as the deck angle allows safe access.

Illustration 1 Winter leeboards

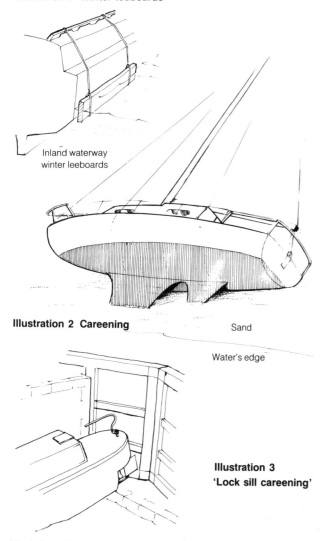

Inland waterway winter leeboards

Illustration 2 Careening

Sand

Water's edge

Illustration 3 'Lock sill careening'

Watch the rudder doesn't get caught in the lock gates!

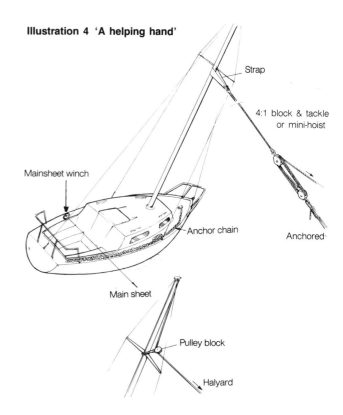

Illustration 4 'A helping hand'

Strap

4:1 block & tackle or mini-hoist

Mainsheet winch

Anchor chain

Anchored

Main sheet

Pulley block

Halyard

Trailers

Owners of trailered craft really need no advice. That is unless the trailer was not cleaned off after it was last used, especially if that was seven or eight months ago, in sea-water! Moreover, it rather depends if the intention is to trail the craft for some distance or leave it on hardstanding, close to where it is to be slipped.

If in doubt, check (Illus. 5):-

the brakes are not binding; the wheel bearings are not rusty and, conversely, are well packed with grease; the tyres have no nasty bulges in the side walls; that, if fitted, the inner tubes (and valves) have not moved in relation to the pressed steel rim and the valve hole (usually due to heavy braking or prolonged underinflation); the mudguards are securely fitted; there is a fully serviceable spare wheel; the ball hitch/ brake mechanism is working easily; the reverse lever override is operational; the jockey wheel is fully operable, including the quick release handle; the winch is in good order; the centre keel rollers, hull support tubes and rubber flats/ rollers are all movable and have not become deformed, rusted, or strained into an immobile position; the lighting set is fully operational and that the ball hitch on the tow vehicle is the same size as that on the trailer! Oh, and don't forget a jack and wheelbrace, just in case.

A paramount task, always promised but almost always left undone, is marking the craft and trailer with clear pointers to indicate the loading point for the best balance. How many times have I cursed not doing the job previously, having finally positioned a boat after hours of sweat and wet trousers.

The present trailer laws have been the subject of much legislation over the last five years or so.

Basic facts are as follows:-

1. a trailer and load weighing in excess of a gross maximum weight of 750kg must be braked.

2. the weight of the tow vehicle of an un-braked trailer must be double that of the combined weight of the trailer and its load.

3. un-braked trailers must be clearly marked with the maximum weight of the trailer and load. The marking can be in paint.

Illustration 5 Trailers

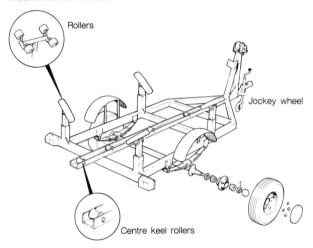

Rollers

Jockey wheel

Centre keel rollers

4. braked trailers must have hydraulically damped overrun couplings.

5. the minimum braking efficiency of a towing vehicle plus loaded, braked trailer must be 45%G (well, yes....!).

6. where trailer and load exceed 3500kg, vacuum or pressure brakes must be actuated from the towing vehicle, 50mm ball hitches are illegal and, technically, a tachograph should be fitted to the towing vehicle.

7. the maximum towing speed for any trailer, on any road, is 50 mph. Naturally, lower speed limits must be obeyed.

8. ball hitches are recommended to be between 350-420mm from the ground, with the fully laden load attached.

9. trailers should have a chain or cable fitted that activates the trailer handbrake if the tow vehicle and trailer become uncoupled.

10. trailers may not 'wear' a mix of radial and crossply tyres.

11. the usual maximum width of a load is 2.9m but this is subject to 2.3m and 2.5m rules.

The usual maximum trailer length, excluding coupling and drawbar, is 7m but dispensations can, in practical terms, allow a craft of up to 9m to be towed.

12. lighting sets are best fitted with the minimum of a yellow reflective number plate (matching the towing vehicles registration number), and at each side of the board, a combined stop/tail-light, an indicator light and an amber side reflector. The combined stop/tail-light clusters should have a clear side lens to illuminate the number plate.

Lighting sets, more especially the plugs, usually give trouble after they have been kicking about in the garage since they were last used. The following indicates the connections for a 7 pin plug and socket:-

Pin	Ref.No.	Colours	Function
1	L	Yellow	Left-hand indicator
2	54G	Blue	Rear fog lamp(s)
3	31	White	Earth
4	R	Green	Right-hand indicator
5	58R	Brown	Right-hand tail-light (and, if fitted, sidelight) as well as the rear number plate illuminating device
6	54	Red	Stop lights
7	58L	Black	Left-hand tail-light (and, if fitted, sidelight) and number plate illumination

Most trailer 'ills' would be averted if, after a dunking, the trailer was thoroughly hosed down with fresh water, wheel bearings re-packed with grease, springs and other movable parts treated with a water repellant spray, and all box section drain holes cleared out.

Annual trailer overhaul should include:-

removing outbreaks of rust with a wire brush and/or light hammering with the peen end of a hammer; repainting where necessary; replacement of rusted fastenings and checking wheel bearings for undue wear.

An invaluable hint is to fit a strap to secure the jockey wheel in the 'up position' when towing. On how many occasions has the wheel dropped down, unseen, whilst motoring along, with wearing results...! One last point is not to 'immerse' a trailer immediately after a long journey during which the wheel bearings will have warmed up, if not become very hot. Hot bearings soak up water like a sponge, so allow them to cool down first.

Craning

Prior to discussing the particular aspects concerning craning, it may not go amiss to mull over various points to bear in mind when selecting the site at which to overwinter. The choice should not only be guided by craning and bank storage fees, but exactly what services and facilities are available. Can the boat be chocked as high as is practical when requested; do bank storage fees include access to conveniently sited water and power points; is the electricity metered; will the yard loan an extension lead if required; is it the sort of place where the odd bit of timber machining goes uncharged; do the facilities and supplies to hand include, for instance, engineering, electricians and cover/hood/sail repairs; are sub-contractors, that an owner might wish to employ, allowed reasonable admission and, depending upon the craft's construction (i.e. GRP, steel, plywood, wood, ferrocement or aluminium), can the boatyard initiate the requisite specialist attention?

Additionally, try to assess the work-force's attitude to a job by observation and ascertain if a firm price can be extracted for a particular job. Be warned not to put in hand work without at least an estimate and, if the undertaking is of an unknown quantity, impose cash limits, requesting to be consulted when the cost reaches that level for further appraisal. Chat with other clients to try and reach a decision on the boatyard's business philosophy (co-operation — what's that?)

The success of craning a boat depends as much on the supplementary gear as on the crane itself. Does the equipment include a frame to keep the lifting load off the hull's gunwales, or more importantly the topsides, and are there 'good looking', wide, soft webbing lifting strops? (Illus. 6a). If so, fine. When a frame is not available consider making a pair of wooden spreaders (Illus. 6b).

6a

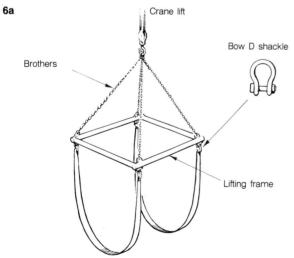

Crane lift

Brothers

Bow D shackle

Lifting frame

Illustration 6 Crane 'goodies'

Soft webbing lifting strops

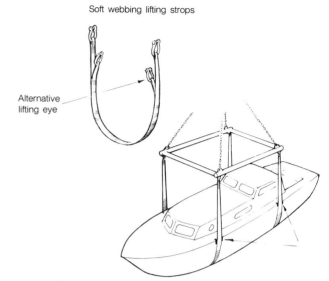

Alternative lifting eye

Once a craft is successfully lifted place marks on the hull so as not to loose the balance points

6b

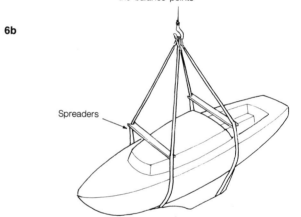

Spreaders

Travel Hoists

Their use usually proves comparatively costly, which is another reason to check out competing charges.

Whatever method is used to remove a craft from the water, when first ashore, facilities required may well include a high pressure wash-off, or sand-blasting in the case of a steel hull. And remember it is much easier to clean a 'ship's bottom' whilst still wet. Algae and fouling once dried-on can be 'fearsome' to remove. Some yards hire out the equipment, others insist on doing the job themselves — whatever, do not omit to have the job done prior to chocking up. Most 'self-respecting' firms — is this a synonym for expensive? — automatically clean off a boat's underside prior to storing ashore for the winter. The hull and deck should be completely washed down using a detergent. This is obviously very important where the vessel has been subject to salt water, but a little less so for an Inland Waterway boat.

Hardstanding

Hardstanding and the method of 'sitting' the craft very much depends on the type of vessel. For instance, trailered boats are obviously no problem. It may be that an owner has a permanent cradle — and very nice too, (Illus. 7). If not, and the boat is flat bottomed, shallow 'Vee'd' or twin keeled, then the arrangements are comparatively simple (Illus. 8a, b, c). On the other hand a fin keeled yacht or a motor sailer, with a long straight through keel, requires careful attention. Illustrations 9 a, b & c detail the necessary arrangements. The boatyard may be very professional in their approach but they may not . . . . ! Please forego oil drums and the odd length of unsupported timber prop without pads top and bottom (Illus. 10)!

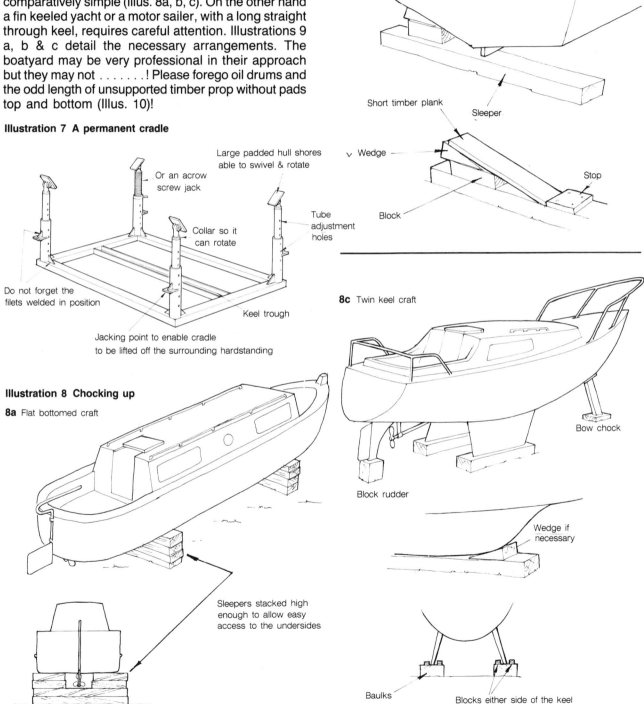

Illustration 7 A permanent cradle

Or an acrow screw jack

Large padded hull shores able to swivel & rotate

Collar so it can rotate

Tube adjustment holes

Do not forget the filets welded in position

Keel trough

Jacking point to enable cradle to be lifted off the surrounding hardstanding

Illustration 8 Chocking up

8a Flat bottomed craft

Sleepers stacked high enough to allow easy access to the undersides

8b 'Vee'd' hull craft

Short timber plank

Sleeper

Wedge

Block

Stop

8c Twin keel craft

Bow chock

Block rudder

Wedge if necessary

Baulks

Blocks either side of the keel

Illustration 9 Hardstanding cradles & cripples

9a Fin keeled yacht

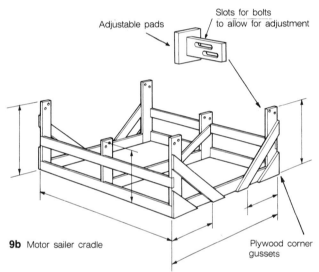

Adjustable pads

Slots for bolts
to allow for adjustment

9b Motor sailer cradle

Plywood corner
gussets

Material 150mm x 50mm (6″ x 2″) softwood to be doubled where the keel
sits on cross beams. The frame to be bolted together and angled braces
positioned as shown at the cross beams and carried as high as possible at
the uprights without interfering with the adjustable pads

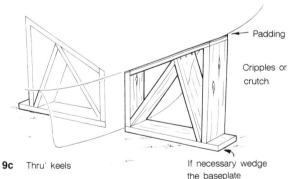

Padding

Cripples or
crutch

9c Thru' keels

If necessary wedge
the baseplate

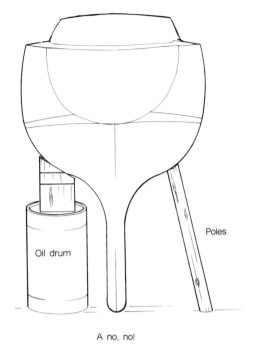

Oil drum

Poles

A no, no!

Illustration 10

Covering

As soon as the vessel is safely positioned, provision for covering must be made. There is absolutely no point in allowing the worst of the winter's depredations to collapse a cockpit hood, stain the topsides or, worse still, strip off varnish and paintwork. Before enveloping the topsides and decks, wash down with warm, soapy water and dry, (preferably with a chamois leather) as this task is difficult to carry out at a later date, amongst a tangle of frames, canvas and rope.

Cockpits covers, and their side curtains, or spray dodgers where fitted, are best not left in position over the winter, due to the rapid deterioration that can take place. Remove and store them complete with their frameworks, if necessary, placing the covers into a specialist's care for any repairs. Modern practice is to do away with as many fixed dot fasteners as possible and replace them with rubbers. These allow for some cover shrinkage, which fixed fasteners do not (Illus. 11a & b).

Before 'sealing up' the boat all bedding, mattresses, personal possessions, 'wet' and 'dry' stores, galley equipment and cockpit locker contents must be removed. If the mattress covers are PVC, have not been made with a zip and the vessel is, or has been, wet inside, consider unstitching a seam to allow the internal foam to fully dry out.

Apart from aiding ventilation throughout it is not a bad discipline to have an annual sort-out of the cruising season's various accumulations. Certainly the anchor chain and warp must be payed out and 'flaked off' beneath the bows. The exercise not only allows a thorough inspection of the mooring gear but dries off the chain and chain locker, allowing the latter to be cleaned out.

Illustration 11 Covers

11a Cockpit covers & side screens

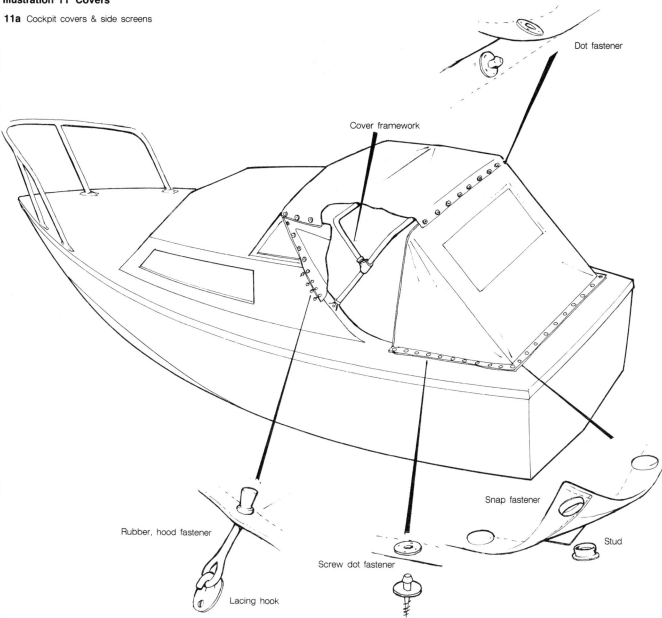

Dot fastener

Cover framework

Rubber, hood fastener

Lacing hook

Screw dot fastener

Snap fastener

Stud

11b Spray dodgers

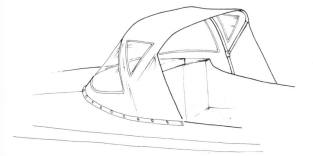

Illustration 12 Over winter cover framework

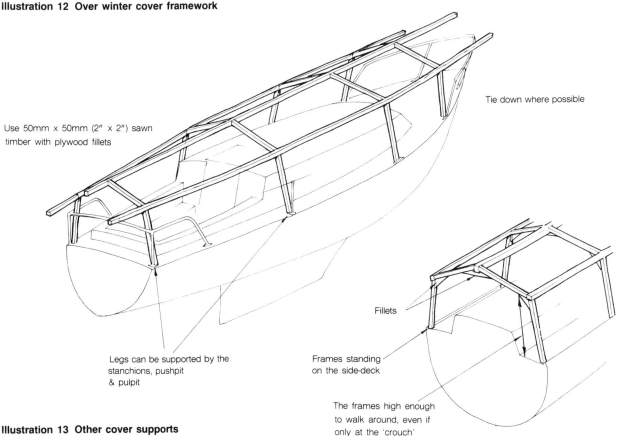

Use 50mm x 50mm (2" x 2") sawn
timber with plywood fillets

Tie down where possible

Legs can be supported by the
stanchions, pushpit
& pulpit

Fillets

Frames standing
on the side-deck

The frames high enough
to walk around, even if
only at the 'crouch'

Illustration 13 Other cover supports

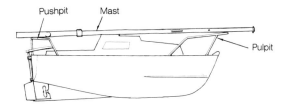

Pushpit   Mast

Pulpit

13a No, no for use of the mast to support a cover

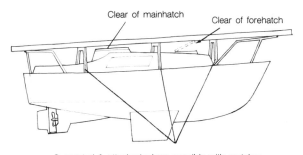

Clear of mainhatch   Clear of forehatch

Supported & attached where possible with crutches

13b Yes to a timber kingplank

In conjunction with covering, ventilation is an absolute must and the method used should allow an adequate through draught to the craft's interior. A framework can be constructed which sits on the side-deck but this might be considered a little elaborate unless extensive work is programmed (Illus. 12). The important thing is to keep the winter oversheets off the deck as much as is possible, allowing the fore and main hatches to be left off or at least propped open. Yachts are often to be seen with the mast used as the central support for a cover, the main spar being supported on the pulpit and pushpit (Illus. 13a). This may be an expeditious solution but is not to be advised because spars require special attention, as detailed in Chapter Four. A well supported timber should be used (Illus. 13b). This must extend over both the bow and stern sufficiently to allow the covers to do the same, especially when the craft is built of plywood or timber. It is essential that the covers and supports are kept off the deck as much as is possible, certainly in the way of the hatches. The main hatch may be left in the closed position but only if the companionway doors are left open or, if fitted, the dropboards are removed.

It is in the interest of an owner's pocket that covers are well made and reinforced with plentiful, adequately distributed eyelets. And do tie them down properly, bearing in mind that, given half-a-chance, the wind will rip them off in no time at all (Illus. 14a & b). Any false economies in this department must, yes must, result in the necessity to buy replacements after the first, or second winter gale. Ensure covers do not wear away on sharp corners and that getting on and into the boat does not necessitate a complete readjustment of the arrangements.

Illustration 14 The covers, fastening down and access steps

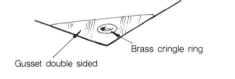

Cover

Long ties

14a

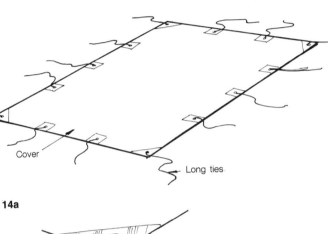

Brass cringle ring

Gusset double sided

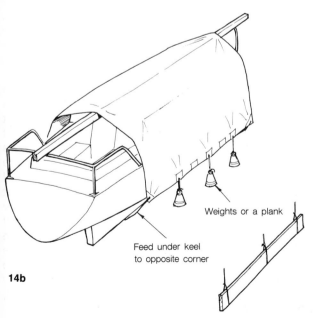

Weights or a plank

Feed under keel
to opposite corner

14b

14c A solid set of steps

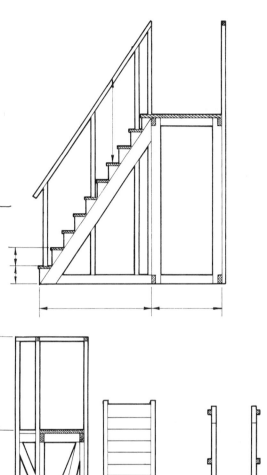

And, do make sure the access ladder is firmly secured both at the top and bottom. There is no point in spending months incapacitated due to torn or broken limbs caused by toppling off them. Why not acquire a solid pair of steps (Illus. 14c)?

Now the stage is set for winterizing.

2

WINTERIZING THE EXTERIOR - GENERAL

As a friend rather aptly put it, the information contained in this and Chapters Three and Four are the 3,000 mile service section. For more extensive, serious, specialist repairs and treatments, or the 12,000 mile service, please refer to Chapter Six.

If the vessel is a yacht, details in Chapter Four cover treatment of the mast, sails and rigging.

GENERAL

Hulls constructed of materials other than timber require the bilges completely drying out and kept that way. Any loose, internal ballast should be removed and stored and, after cleaning, reference numbered if the ballast is tailored to the shape of the hull. All internally framed craft must have the drain and limber holes cleared out and excess liquid mopped up.

It goes without saying that the lockers and cupboards have been emptied and berth cushions removed and stored, preferably in a dry place (under the beds at home if must be). As many as is possible of the locker tops, drawer fronts and cabin sole boards* should be

stored, thus allowing a free flow of ventilating air to keep sweet and fresh 'those parts that are not usually reached by . . . . .' And do not forget to clear out all food lockers.

Sole boards may well require plan referencing if they are fitted and shaped.

DECKS

Loose or suspect fittings must be removed, re-bedded on sealant and re-fastened (*See* **Brightwork** further on in this Chapter and Illus. 16). Incidentally, scaling steel decks is much more fiddly in the way of deck fittings that are welded to the deck.

Timber and plywood decks may have been overlaid with a proprietary deck covering. Tears must be re-glued and a small copper patch fitted, if really necessary, or a portion cut out and a similarly shaped piece let in (Illus. 15). Any suspicion that the timber beading trapping the deck material is not bedded down properly, or that the deck itself is showing signs of deterioration, and the covering must be completely

Illustration 16 Deck fitting fastenings & doublers

For suitable sealants *See* the relevant
paragraph in Chapter Ten

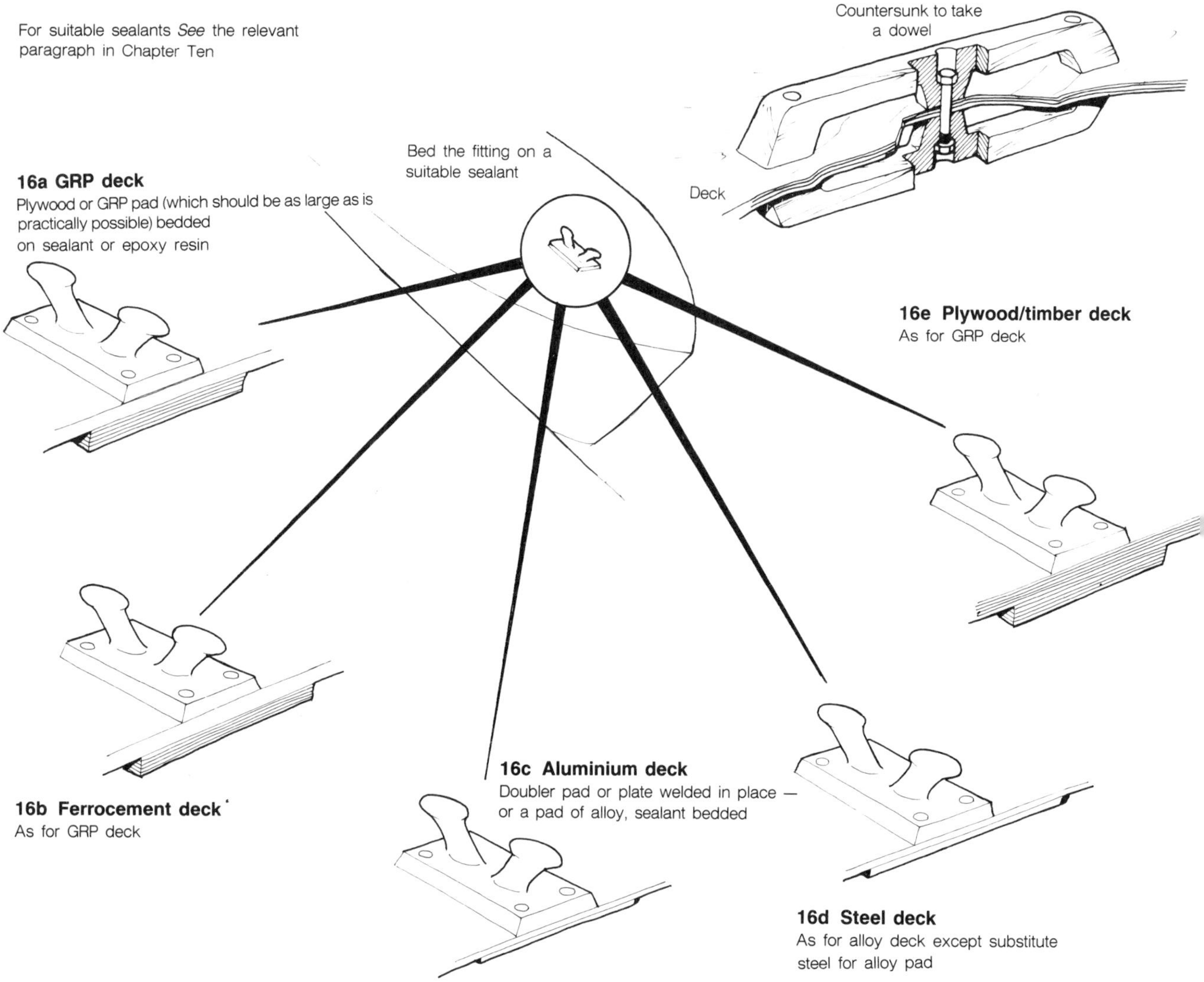

16f Handrails matched inside and out and thru' bolted

Countersunk to take
a dowel

Deck

Bed the fitting on a
suitable sealant

16a GRP deck
Plywood or GRP pad (which should be as large as is
practically possible) bedded
on sealant or epoxy resin

16e Plywood/timber deck
As for GRP deck

16b Ferrocement deck
As for GRP deck

16c Aluminium deck
Doubler pad or plate welded in place —
or a pad of alloy, sealant bedded

16d Steel deck
As for alloy deck except substitute
steel for alloy pad

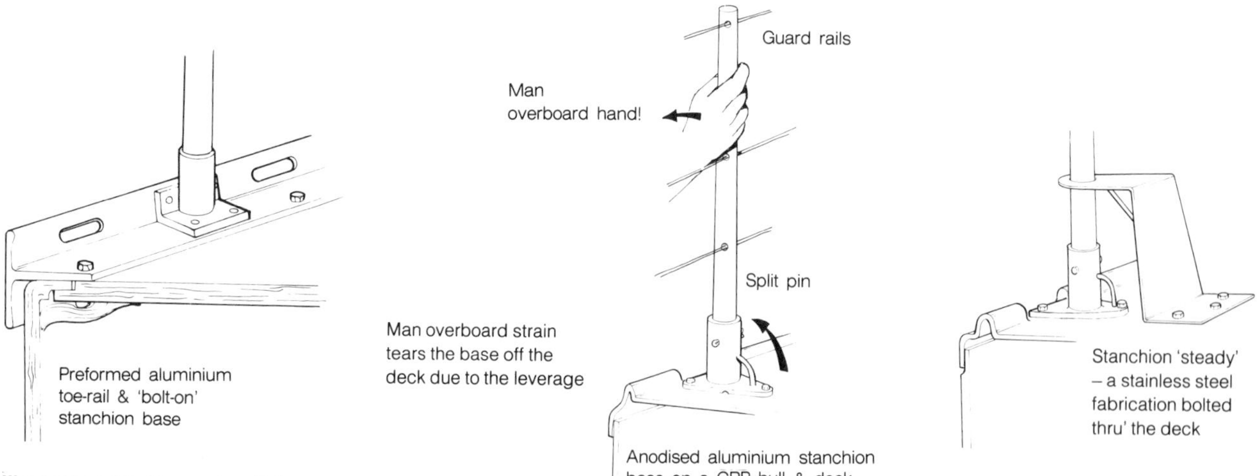

Guard rails

Man
overboard hand!

Split pin

Man overboard strain
tears the base off the
deck due to the leverage

Preformed aluminium
toe-rail & 'bolt-on'
stanchion base

Anodised aluminium stanchion
base on a GRP hull & deck

Stanchion 'steady'
– a stainless steel
fabrication bolted
thru' the deck

Illustration 17 Stanchion fixings

removed for further examination, but more of this in Chapter Six.

Illustration 15 Deck covering repairs

Note the backing off to the quadrant to pinch the cabin-side and deck and allow sufficient sealant to remain in situ

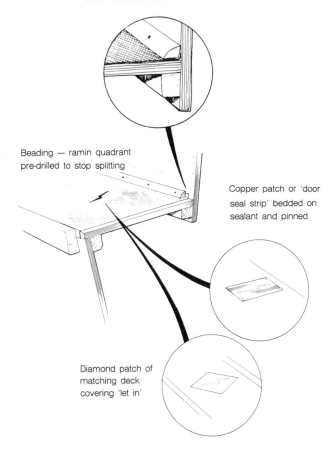

Beading — ramin quadrant pre-drilled to stop splitting

Copper patch or 'door seal strip' bedded on sealant and pinned

Diamond patch of matching deck covering 'let in'

Brightwork, Deck Fittings & Navigation Lights

Pushpit, pulpit, stanchions, bollards, cleats, fairleads and grabrails should be individually checked both for wear and that they are securely thru' fastened. (Winches, genoa tracks, rigging eyes and associated yacht fittings are dealt with in Chapter Four but the same rule applies.) Lightly spray deck fittings with inhibiting oil.

Apart from windows, deck fittings are probably the source of most leaks and the pushpit and pulpit are most likely to cause problems. This is due to the comparatively small bases on which they are often mounted, especially taking into account the leverage they experience.

Rather than leave an individual fitting loose, unfasten it, which may well be a two-handed job, re-seal and re-fasten ensuring that there is an adequate backing pad on to which to bolt down (Illus. 16a, b, c, d, e &

f). Murphy's Law dictates that these words of advice may well not be that easy to carry out! For instance, an inner cabin lining could preclude access to the internal fastenings but do not despair, this subject is dealt with in Chapter Six.

It is vital that stanchion bases are correctly tightened down, remembering that they may have to bear a person's total weight in adverse conditions. If there is any doubt on this score a modification worth considering is detailed in Illustration 17.

Navigation lights, where removable, should be stored off the boat for the winter, the deck plug fittings sprayed with inhibiting oil and capped with polythene bags held in place by elastic bands. Fittings that are not detachable should have the bulbs removed and the bulb mounting socket sprayed. (See Illus. 114).

Another 'favourite' leak point are the electric deck sockets. They quite often cause difficulties because the feed wires were originally fitted rather bunched up, thus tending to exert an upwards pressure. This would not matter if the deck sockets were not usually manufactured with such small bases that they cannot be pulled hard down.

Cockpit & Scupper Drains

The following are 'Musts' in respect of cockpit and scupper drains and, for that matter, any thru' the shell skin fitting:-

that the gate valves work easily; corroded pipe clips are replaced with stainless steel units and, where possible, are doubled up; clip-to-pipe-to-skin fitting connections are sound and there are no kinks in the pipe runs.

Naturally the backing pads should be large enough to adequately spread the load. This latter stricture is similar in application to that covered in Illustration 16. Are the drains large enough? Nothing less than 38mm (1 1/2″), but preferably 50mm (2″), should be fitted and if there is any doubt, it is not an insuperable job to fit a larger system. (Illus. 18).

THE CHAIN LOCKER

The drain holes, that ensure any water shipped can easily drain away, must be kept clear and the anchor chain fastening to the craft be inspected annually. Padding out the interior of the locker with headlining material can save chain wear, chafe and noise (Illus. 19).

Illustration 18 Cockpit drains

Illustration 19 — The chain locker

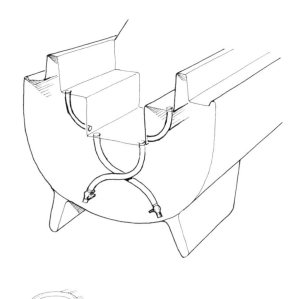

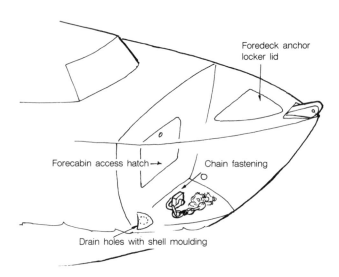

Foredeck anchor locker lid

Forecabin access hatch →

Chain fastening

Drain holes with shell moulding

Indent moulded in a GRP lay-up

This indent has to be enlarged to allow a larger skin fitting to sit 'flush' and not proud

Trepan out for the larger skin fitting

Glass in' place beneath the sole a (GRP) pad (temporarily held in place by a couple of self tappers) sealant bedded, on to which to 'nut-up' the skin fitting

Cockpit sole

Sealant bedded skin fitting

Laminations bonding in the pad

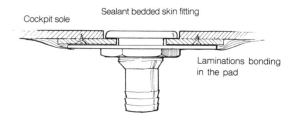

N.B. Other materials from which a craft may be constructed can be similarly treated, referring to Illustration 16 for 'suitable treatment' of the pad

GRP HULLS

Hulls constructed of glass reinforced plastic require high pressure washing-off externally with individual attention to those areas where fouling proves stubborn. Usually stiff brushing with a hard, nylon bristled brush or light scraping removes the most recalcitrant growth.

A thorough examination of the hull's external surface should take place, especially in the area of the wind and water-line in order to check that no straightforward blistering or less straightforward osmosis or wicking is present. Blisters are self-evident but can, initially, resemble osmosis. This latter, far more serious complaint, the AIDS of the GRP boat world, shows up at the outset as smallish, circular blisters and is caused by the differential between fluid that has found its way beneath the gelcoat and the surrounding water. Despite extensive research, the causes or more correctly the manufacturing defects that encourage the cancer of osmosis to gain a foothold cannot yet be precisely and exactly diagnosed. It has been established that lack of a second gelcoat, too fast an accelerated resin mix and an excess of styrene do not help matters.

It certainly appears that GRP craft continuously left afloat, more especially where the ambient temperature of the water is warmer than usual, are more prone to the dreaded blight, particularly in a band either side of the wind and water-line. Antifouling the hull up to 150mm (6″) above the water-line may well aid resistance to this scourge of fibreglass craft but specialist treatments now exist *(See* Chapter Six). Wicking is where capillary action has taken place with moisture passing along glassfibre strands which swell and show up as elongated blisters.

Illustration 20 Gelcoat repairs

20a Star crack

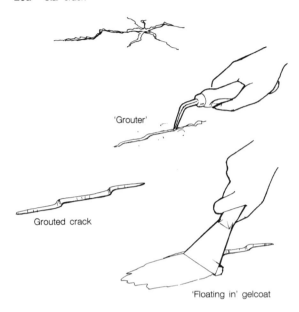

'Grouter'

Grouted crack

'Floating in' gelcoat

20b Holding the gelcoat in position with cellophane or 'upside down'

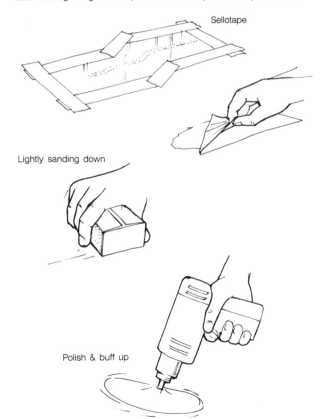

Sellotape

Lightly sanding down

Polish & buff up

If none, or very slight blistering is present here and there, then all is well. More extensive damage must be the subject of a closer, possibly professional examination. Details are set out in Chapter Six as are an explanation of the technical terms used in conjunction with GRP and details of the intricacies of working with the material.

Normal, everyday dullness, kick marks, scuffing and even minor scratches can be dealt with by old fashioned elbow grease. The surface can be T-Cut back and then polished. There are a number of proprietary rubbing, cutting and polishing compounds available from most chandlers.

Blemishes, star cracks, slight blisterings, chips or fractures may now be dealt with. The area requiring attention must be very lightly rubbed down with fine wet and dry paper and then cleaned off with some acetone. To treat star cracks or 'spiders webs', grout out the fracture lines and 'float-in' some gelcoat (Illus. 20a). Often repairs are positioned on a part of the craft's surface such that the gelcoat tends to droop out. If so it will be necessary to 'fix it' with a strip of sellotape placed smooth side downwards over the repair. If the area of damage is too wide for this simple dodge then tape into place a tightly spread portion of waxed oven paper or, preferably, part of a polycarbonate sheet (Illus. 20b). Small cratering over an area must be smoothed down with wet and dry paper, the little craters cleaned out and filled with gelcoat which, when set hard, can be lightly smoothed off, again with wet and dry (Illus. 20c). When blisters or voids are present it is best not to break the outer skin, but lance them, allow to dry out and then inject gelcoat, preferably with a hospital syringe (Illus 20d). Fortunately, there are a number of packaged GRP kits suitable for the more cosmetic repairs and available to the DIY owner either from chandlers or motor accessory shops.

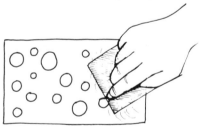

20c Small craters being sanded down prior to 'floating in' gelcoat

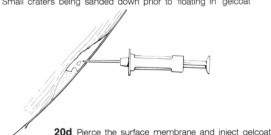

20d Pierce the surface membrane and inject gelcoat

STEEL HULLS

To remove fouling from steel there is the easy and the hard option. The difficult way involves hosing the hull down, scrubbing off with a long brush, scraping away with a palette knife followed by rotary and, finally, hand wire brushing. Any very stubborn rust or mill scale must be carefully ground off using a grindette and inaccessible nooks or crannies treated with an anti-rust solution. Ensure that goggles are worn during all these processes as flaked paint or metal that finds its way into the eyes can prove a work stopper! An alternative protector is a welder's mask fitted with clear lenses which don't steam up and can easily be pushed up out the way (Illus. 21).

Then there is the easy way .... sand or shot-blasting! After either treatment, which ought to result in thoroughly clean steel plates, any imperfections should be filled with a trowel filler followed by an overall application of two coats of steel paint primer.

PLYWOOD HULLS

The bilges require completely drying out, using a sponge to soak up the last bit of moisture, after which apply throughout a good quality bilge paint. Externally the treatment is as for timber craft but to ensure that delamination has not occurred important areas to check include the plywood sheet ends, especially in the way of the transom. It may be necessary to remove masking pieces to make the inspection (Illus. 22a, b & c). Prior to re-fastening them apply a coat of primer.

Illustration 22 Masking pieces (or quarter badging) & chine stringers

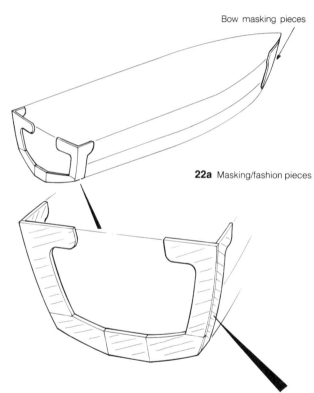

Bow masking pieces

22a Masking/fashion pieces

Transom plywood joints masked by hardwood fashion pieces, bedded on sealant, screwed & dowelled

22b

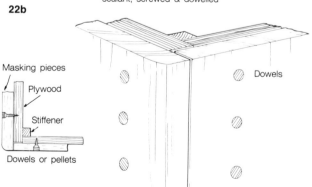

Masking pieces

Plywood

Stiffener

Dowels or pellets

Dowels

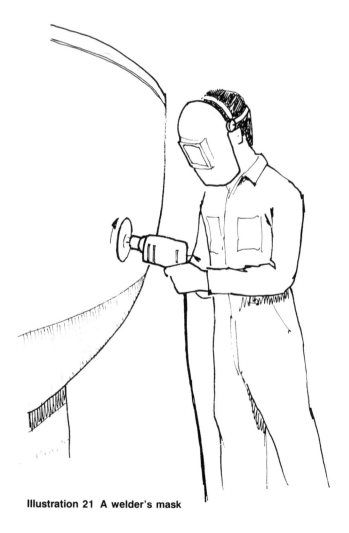

Illustration 21 A welder's mask

22c

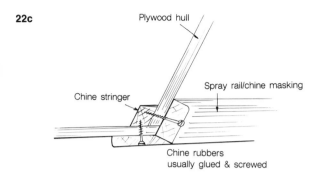

Plywood hull

Spray rail/chine masking

Chine stringer

Chine rubbers
usually glued & screwed

Check (1) the inner chine stringer is not holding water, being sloped the wrong
way i.e. not backed off
(2) the join of the spray rail/chine masking is effectively 'stopped up'

A no, no as forms a water trap

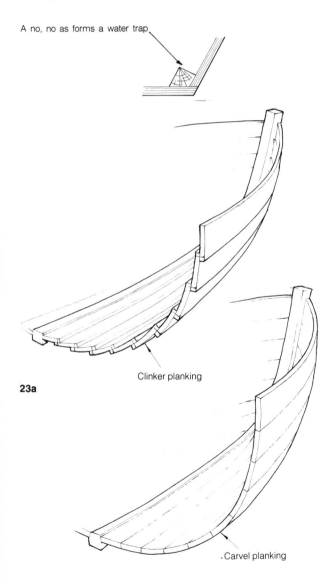

Clinker planking

23a

Carvel planking

Illustration 23 A timber hull's construction

TIMBER PLANKED HULLS

Only timber planked hulls 'benefit' from placing water in the bilges. This is often necessary after a long term sojourn ashore, prior to launching, and encourages the timbers to swell, thus reducing the amount of caulking and stopping. The drying properties of the winter winds really are amazing.

Clinker construction is usually only employed on small craft whilst the carvel method of planking is utilised for larger boats (Illus. 23a). Exceptions to this empirical rule include Yorkshire cobles. They are not only clinker built up to 30ft plus in length but, interestingly enough, are planked first (to pattern jigs) with the massive frames adzed to shape and fitted afterwards.

Probably the best procedure to winterize a timber vessel is to remove any internal ballast prior to bank storage, pump the bilges and, once on land, mop out, checking the timbers, more especially in the way of internal stringers, frames and limber holes (Illus. 23b). In fact anywhere in which bilge water may be trapped, ensuring that all the limber holes are absolutely clear. Any water placed in the bilges should be mixed with a proprietary anti-fungal solution.

Externally the surface should be high pressure washed off. If lucky, only the areas where the paint has chipped away or a seam has started will require rubbing down, fairing in, trowel cementing, sanding off and priming before winter's onset (See Chapter Ten). On the other hand . . . .

To test a timber hull's soundness, gentle, light tapping with the handle end of a hammer should result in a sound, ringing resilience. A soggy feel spells trouble, as do fastenings that have 'started' and lengths of missing or bulging seam stopping. Areas where the paint evinces signs of peeling or blistering may well indicate very wet, possibly rotten timber.

FERROCEMENT HULLS

As ferro hulls are usually painted, the initial treatment for a 'concrete' hull is very much the same as for GRP, it being necessary to high pressure wash off the fouling.

Slight abrasions or scoring can be treated with trowelling cement which, after application and hardening, should be sanded down. Flakes, small cracks, severe crazing, holes and dents must be ground back, grouted out, washed with fresh water and thoroughly dried, with the fervent hope that any penetration has not reached the reinforcing mesh. Localised patches can be treated with an epoxy resin filler. Larger areas require a quality building cement to be mixed in with the epoxy resin filler, making a putty, which is then applied after a brushing of epoxy resin. When the filler has set it must be sanded down and faired in after which a sealer, followed by a coat of primer, should be painted over the repair, leaving the completion of the painting until the spring (Illus. 24).

Where the size of the repair warrants an aggregate and cement mix, the aggregate should be no larger than 6mm (1/4'') (the usual 'path' size is 18mm (3/4'')) and it is preferable to apply a grouting agent prior to cementing up.

23b . . . and the detail

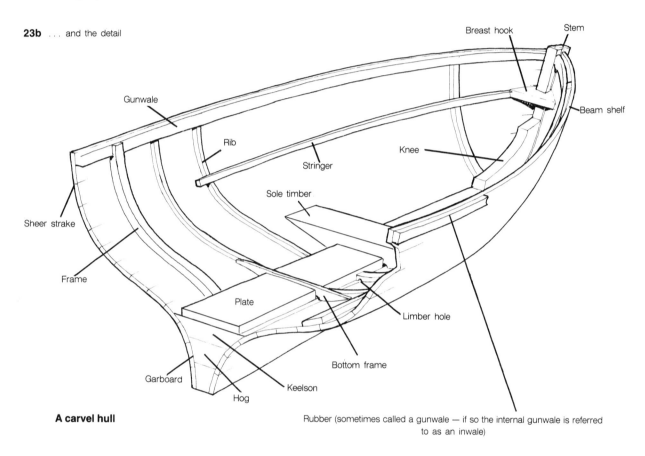

A carvel hull

Rubber (sometimes called a gunwale — if so the internal gunwale is referred to as an inwale)

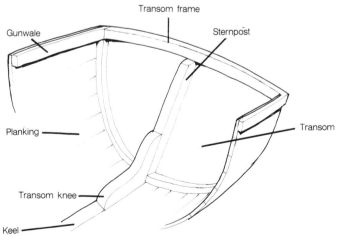

Illustration 25 Aluminium craft repairs

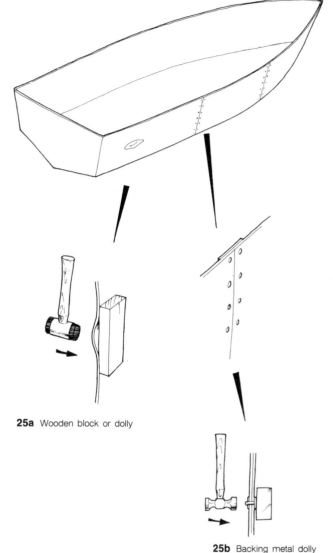

25a Wooden block or dolly

25b Backing metal dolly

Illustration 24 Ferro repairs

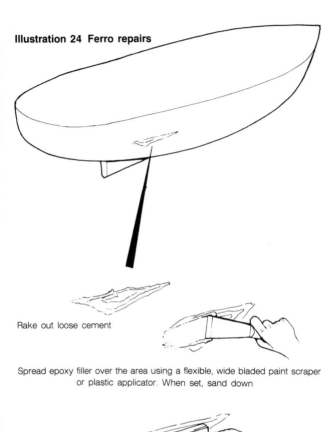

Rake out loose cement

Spread epoxy filler over the area using a flexible, wide bladed paint scraper or plastic applicator. When set, sand down

Sandpaper area & surround

ALUMINIUM HULLS

Aluminium should be cleaned with a high pressure wash and the surface very, very gently sanded down. Where paint needs to be completely removed, a paint remover and scraper must be carefully used followed by, if necessary, an exceedingly light sanding with a wet and dry paper. Care must be taken so as not to cut into the surface of the aluminium.

Dents may be removed by using a rubber hammer and a backing dolly or wooden block held on the other side to the hollow (Illus 25a). Nowadays there is very little riveting and most aluminium is welded but where rivets require tightening up, lightly hammer one side, holding a metal block against the other side (Illus 25b).

The surface must be painted almost immediately as untreated plates deteriorate very quickly. For painting details refer to Chapter Ten.

KEELS

External Cast Iron Keels

They require vigorous cleaning off, preferably with an electric powered rotary wire brush, followed by strenuous, hand wire brushing in local areas, as necessary, and sandpapering. Voids must be filled with trowel cement and the whole thoroughly treated with an anti-oxidisation liquid after which leave them (and the hull) until closer to the date of re-launching, when the coats of primer and antifouling should be applied.

Seeping and weeping up past a particular keel bolt might be cured by simply unfastening the particular bolt and sealing with caulking cotton, plenty of sealant and a large penny washer (Illus. 26a).

Every two or three years it is necessary to draw one or two of the keel bolts. That is, undo and completely withdraw them one at a time and closely inspect for signs of wasting. (Illus 26b). Murphy's Law dictates that the fastenings will be well and truly seized in place. If so, prior to the Herculean efforts that may be necessary, liberally dowse the fastenings with a freeing liquid (as for instance Plus-Gas), ideally a week prior to further labours. The toil might include tightening up (sic) ever so slightly (to break the thread joint), tapping the bolt head (to do the same), and heating, all of which help free-off a recalcitrant bolt or bolts. These measures, as well as a lot of patience, may well be required and do not assume because they will not budge that the bolts must be all right — the one does not follow the other. Chapter Five and Illustration 51 details some of the steps and tools that may be of assistance. For those prepared to shell out £125 or more, there is at least one firm who can X-Ray the wretched things, thus ascertaining if all the blood, sweat, skinned knuckles and tears is really necessary. Do not forget that, as stated in the Introduction, if the craft is recently acquired it must be assumed that a full survey was commissioned prior to purchasing, in the course of which examination a keel bolt or two should have been drawn!

Internally Encapsulated Ballast.

It is preferable that this type of ballast is cast-iron. On the other hand it may well be 'shot' or, worse still, other miscellanea. Whatever the material, it will have been placed into the hollow profile of the moulded keel and laminated into position. If the craft is GRP, the outside

Waisted keel bolt

26b

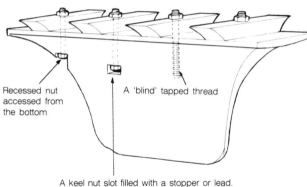

Recessed nut accessed from the bottom

A 'blind' tapped thread

A keel nut slot filled with a stopper or lead. The trick is to locate the sealed off slot . . .

Illustration 26 External keels & their fastenings

26a A weeping keel bolt

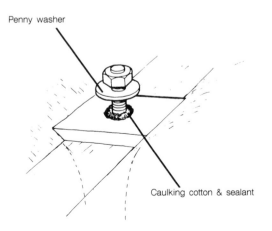

Penny washer

Caulking cotton & sealant

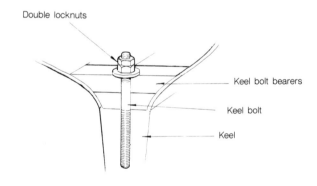

Double locknuts

Keel bolt bearers

Keel bolt

Keel

of the hull in the way of the keel should be tapped with the wooden handle end of a hammer, not the peen end please. Hopefully a solid, ringing sound will result, but any signs of panting or hollowness and further work will have to be put in hand as detailed in Chapter Six and Illustration 91.

3

WINTERIZING THE INTERIOR

Assuming all drawers, under bunk storage and cupboards have been emptied . . .

THE GALLEY

After a summer's hard use the cooker could probably do with removing from the boat for a thorough clean. At least it allows the congealed fat to be removed from the surrounds! More importantly it allows the pipework and gas tap, that should be adjacent to the cooker, to be inspected as well as the cooker compartment washed out. Assuming the cooker is 'driven' by low pressure bottled gas, the cast-iron, ring burners and the flame spreaders should be soaked in warm, soapy water, rinsed off, cleaned and dried, not forgetting to prick out the 'little holes' (Illus. 27a). The metal grill flame shields may have to be replaced — once they are a year or two old they seem to drop so much rust on the bacon!

Despite it appearing an obvious rejoinder, owners must clean food storage lockers and the fridge, if one is fitted. Wash out the cold locker and rod the locker drain tube — well there should be one. Boat- builders almost always fit stupidly small diameter copper pipe as a drain which inevitably gets blocked with mouldy food. I can never understand why they don't install a ½″ tube with a gas tap, that is if it is possible to gain access to the tap. A gas tap? Yes, to stop hot air rising up the pipe from the bilges. Leave the lid off the locker, and all other lockers for that matter, for the duration of the lay-up.

Water heaters (Illus. 27b), as well as galley and other fresh water pumps,should have the maker's instructions followed but, if not available, simply drain off any water in the unit. I prefer them 'unplumbed' and stored in the dry, away from the boat, for the duration of the winter. This avoids corrosion and possible frost damage if they have not, perchance, been completely drained. I suggest the airing cupboard, or adjacent to the central heating boiler (with all the other bits and pieces). One is aware that the family might have to forget the more mundane, domestic tasks of airing washing while a boat is out of commission!

Illustration 27 Gas 'driven' cookers and water heaters

27a A two burner ring and grill cooker

27b A water heater*

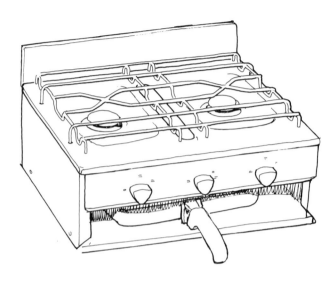

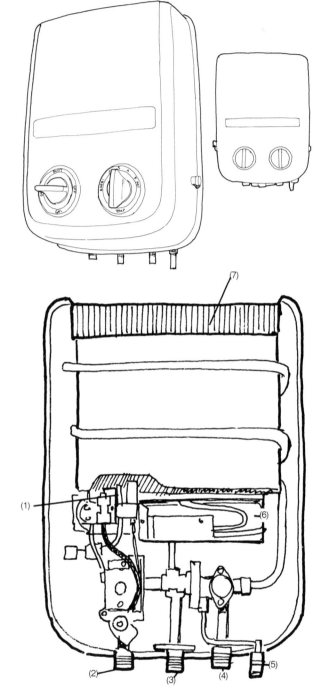

The metal grill flame spreaders should be thrown away when they start to disintegrate

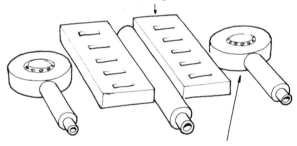

Clean out gas holes

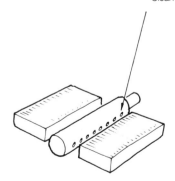

Underside view of the grill

(1) Pilot light   (5) Water drain plug

(2) Gas inlet   (6) Main burner

(3) Hot water outlet   (7) Heat exchanger

(4) Water inlet

* by courtesy of Morco Products Ltd.

Formica topped surfaces may well have to be cleaned up with a Jif type cleansing cream or T-Cut paste. Unsightly fractures, blemishes, scoring or bubbling, caused by hot pan bottoms, can be repaired by replacing the whole surface or by graving in a piece, rather similar to deck covering repairs in a way (See Illus. 15). The surface can be cut using a guide and a very, very sharp trimming knife. The cut-out should be a 'regular' shape thus enabling the piece to-be-let-in to be exactly the same shape. An impact adhesive coupled with heavy weights ensures the repair will not lift on setting off.

DOMESTIC WATER SYSTEM

The drinking water arrangements must be flushed through annually, starting at the water tank, using a proprietary brand of domestic water tank cleaner, a mild solution of bleach or Milton. The arrangement used to pump the water governs the attention needed and Illustration 28a details a representative fresh water plumbing system. A hand or foot pump may well require the valves or seals changed (Illus 28b) and electric pumps should have the contacts cleaned (Illus 28c). To save the injurious effects of frost damage, the whole system must be drained down, taps left open, plunger pumps have the plunger removed and flipper pumps be opened up (Illus 28d). Inspect, and spray with inhibiting oil, the sink waste and, if fitted, galley sea-water pump, seacock, gate valve and pipe clips.

Some readers might question the need to separate water pipes from their spigots but it does ensure they are completely drained and that the pipe clips are not only checked but are stainless steel. I am aware that

Illustration 28 Domestic water system

28a

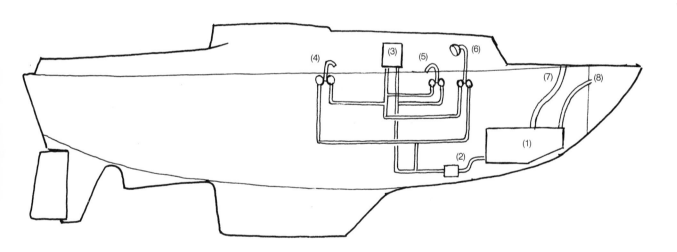

(1) Water tank   (2) In line, non-priming electric water pump

(3) Instant (gas) water heater

(4) Galley hot & cold running water with mixer, electric contact taps

(5) Vanitory unit with hot & cold running water with mixer, electric contact taps

(6) Shower unit with separate hot & cold water mixer, electric contact taps

(7) Filler pipe

(8) Vent pipe — why not into the top of the chain locker — as long as the locker is fitted with drains!

Where the water tank is not placed above the pump the following are possible alternative arrangements
(a) a priming foot-pump & one way valve
(b) a self-priming electric water pump

28b A foot pump*

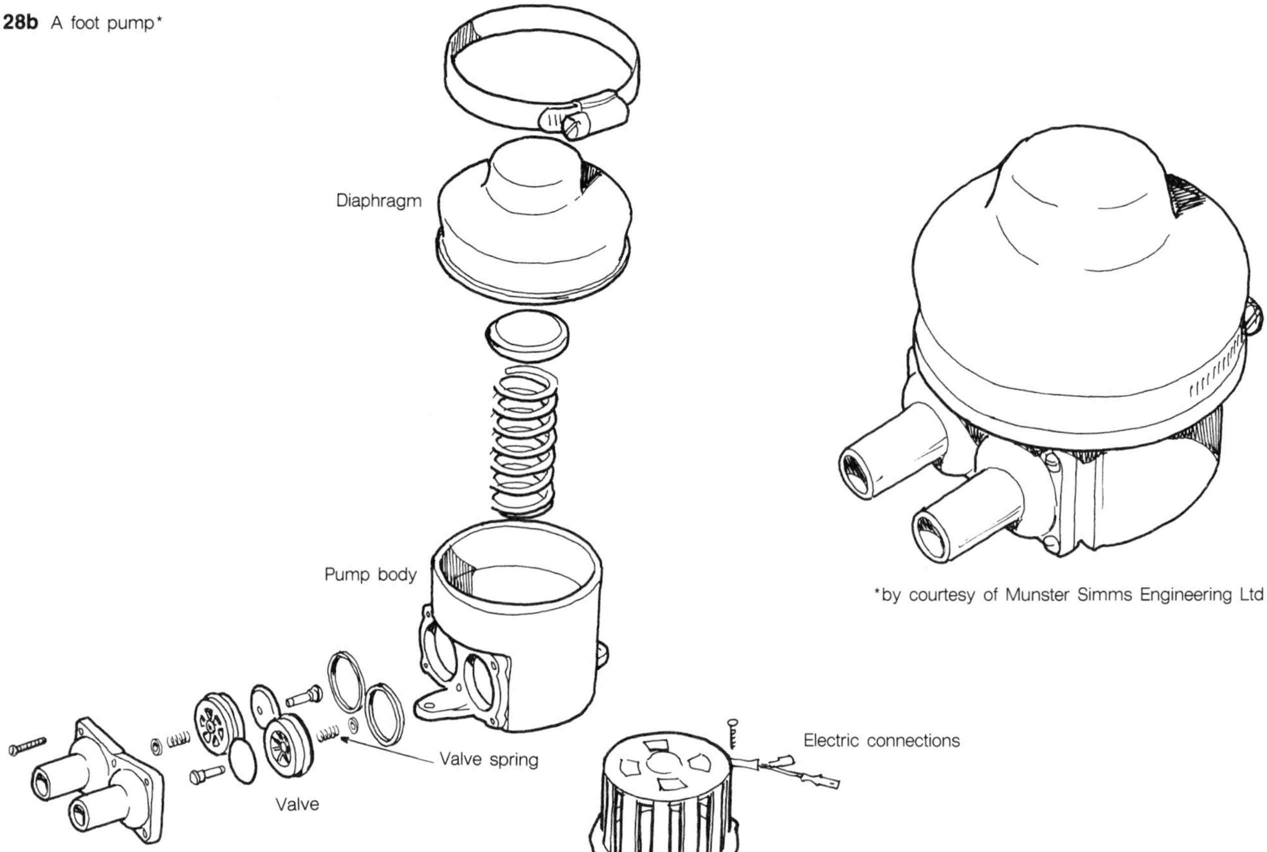

Diaphragm

Pump body

Valve spring

Valve

*by courtesy of Munster Simms Engineering Ltd

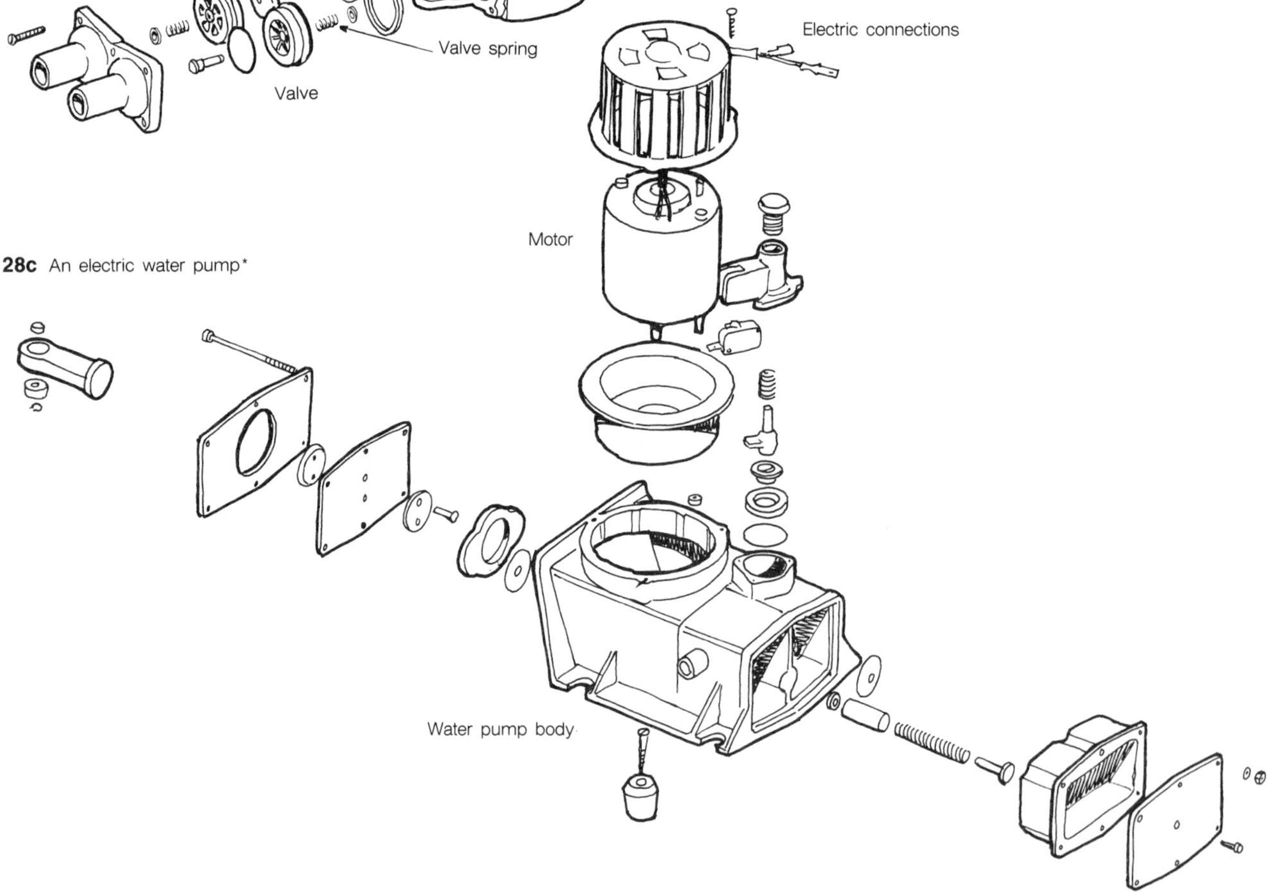

Electric connections

Motor

28c An electric water pump*

Water pump body

*by courtesy of Munster Simms Engineering Ltd

28d Hand operated water pumps*

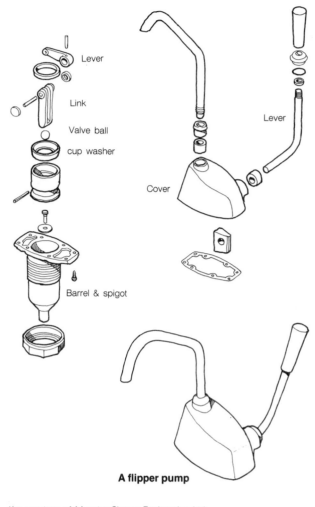

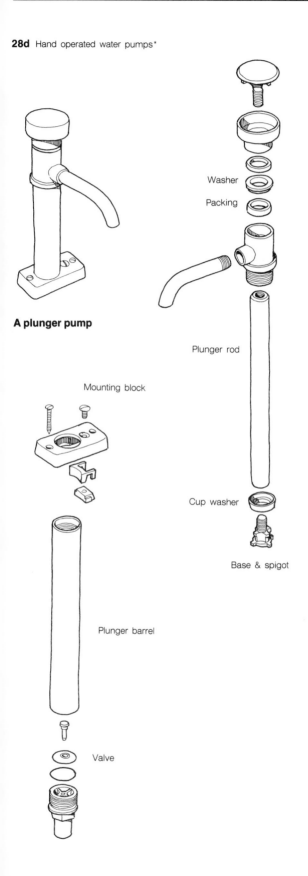

A plunger pump

Mounting block

Washer

Packing

Plunger rod

Cup washer

Base & spigot

Plunger barrel

Valve

Lever

Link

Valve ball

cup washer

Cover

Barrel & spigot

Lever

A flipper pump

*by courtesy of Munster Simms Engineering Ltd

I keep on about pipe clips but, apart from the thru' hull skin fittings, the dangers of which should be apparent, they are one of the most usual reasons for onboard problems. I once spent a thirsty last day or so towards the end of a Fastnet Race because a pipe clip had rotted through. Cleaning one's teeth in canned beer just isn't the same as good old 'aqua-pura'!

Where pipes are removed from a faucet or fitting, tie or tape them up so they do not drop into the bilges. If there is any chance of this happening, put a cork or stopper in the end to save possible contamination (Illus. 28e). When replacing the pipes remember to dip the ends in hot water to ease them over a tight spigot and fasten the clips whilst the pipe is still rubbery.

28e

Spigot

Water pipe

Put a cork in it!

BOTTLED GAS SYSTEMS

Low pressure bottled gas installations ought to be pressure tested annually, which is a specialist job. Soapy water can be used to check joints for leaks but this is a far from ideal procedure. One method NOT to be used, unless the perpetrator has an unfulfilled wish for the afterlife, is to apply a match to the various connections. There is now an aerosol spray that can be used to detect gas leaks, indicating the same by foaming on the spot!

Illustration 29 A bottled gas system & locker

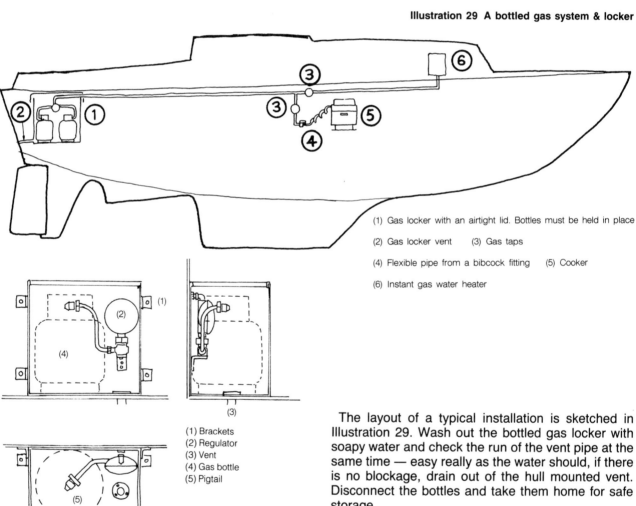

(1) Gas locker with an airtight lid. Bottles must be held in place

(2) Gas locker vent   (3) Gas taps

(4) Flexible pipe from a bibcock fitting   (5) Cooker

(6) Instant gas water heater

(1) Brackets
(2) Regulator
(3) Vent
(4) Gas bottle
(5) Pigtail

A 3.9kg propane bottle locker* 381mm high, 267mm deep & 381mm wide

* by courtesy of Calor Gas Ltd

The layout of a typical installation is sketched in Illustration 29. Wash out the bottled gas locker with soapy water and check the run of the vent pipe at the same time — easy really as the water should, if there is no blockage, drain out of the hull mounted vent. Disconnect the bottles and take them home for safe storage.

Where gas pipes are routed through a bulkhead, and not coupled via a bulkhead fitting, ensure that vibration has not resulted in friction with the resultant erosion of the pipe's surface.

THE TOILET COMPARTMENT

The vanitory basin water pump and drain pipe gate valve require the same attention as the galley fittings, as will the shower, shower tray, pump and thru' hull skin fitting. Incidentally, electric and or hand pumps should be removed for storage and if a shower tray mounted electric pump is not being taken off the boat then it must be 'blocked' off the sole of the shower tray to avoid possible frost damage (Illus. 30).

Composite chemical toilets need only be flushed out and stored off the boat. Where a craft is fitted with a sewage holding tank pump it out, flush and empty again. Then examine all the pipework along its length, as well as the pipe clips. Missing deck and vent filler caps can be ordered now (Illus. 31a).

Unfasten the inlet and outlet pipes of the sea-toilet, if only at the pump end, drain the pump and empty the toilet bowl (Illus. 31b). Open up the toilet seacocks and spray with inhibitor. If the tapered seatings of the seacocks have been giving trouble, un-clip the pipes, remove the seacocks and service them. Often the seats require re-bedding, for which use a grinding paste, and why not replace the gland packing at the same time? If the conical seatings have distorted there is little choice but to throw the offending items away and replace the whole unit (Illus. 31c). After the necessary attention refit them, bedding down on sealant, replace corrosion worn fastenings, spray with inhibiting oil and ensure that there is a substantial backing pad. Make sure the fittings are clear of squeezed out sealant and refit the hoses with new, double stainless steel pipe clips. (Repetitious I know, but please note that all pipe clips on thru' hull fittings should be doubled up where possible and replaced every year). Why not take this opportunity to ensure that the valves are marked 'on' and 'off'? Most damage to valves and toilet pump units happens when 'yellow wellied chaps' are unable to understand why the system is not working. They tend to give the offending item the benefit of their 'attention', which 'loving care' usually does not come to light when securely moored up, but later, whilst at sea in a Force 8 gale. The unsuspecting toilet user unfortunate enough to discover the damage may well feel sick and, if he doesn't, certainly will do so when the contents of the toilet bowl slop over the porcelain edge! So, label the valves.

Illustration 30 Shower trays

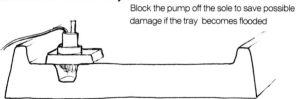

Block the pump off the sole to save possible damage if the tray becomes flooded

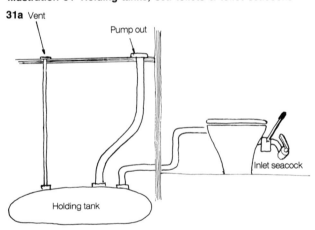

Thru' hull skin fitting & gate valve

One-way valve

In-hull pump

Shower tray

Illustration 31 Holding tanks, sea toilets & toilet seacocks

31a Vent

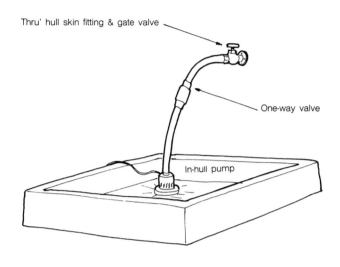

Pump out

Inlet seacock

Holding tank

Side elevation

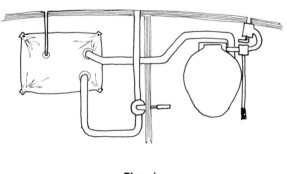

Plan view

31b A sea toilet *

Exploded view

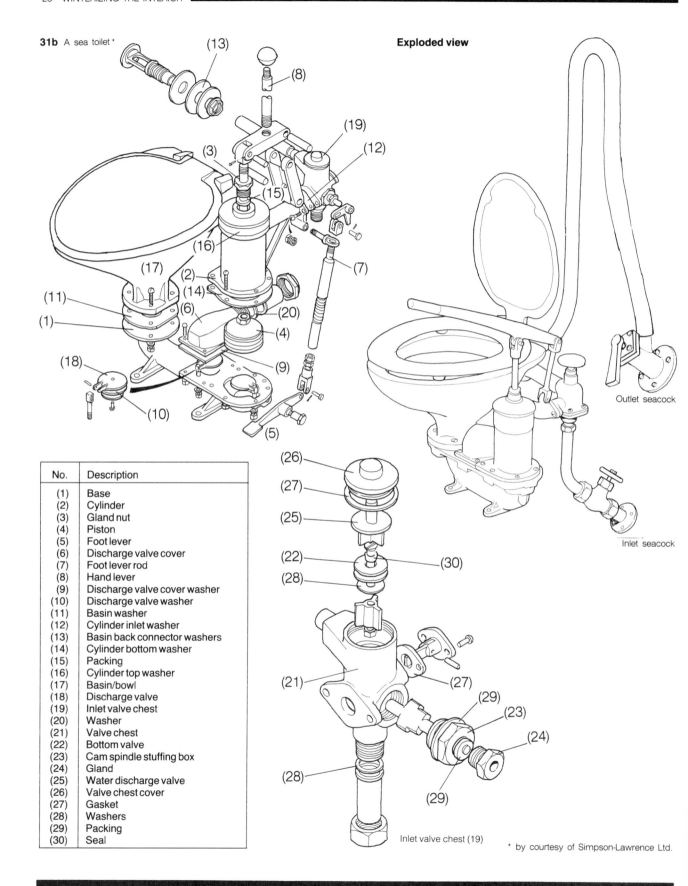

No.	Description
(1)	Base
(2)	Cylinder
(3)	Gland nut
(4)	Piston
(5)	Foot lever
(6)	Discharge valve cover
(7)	Foot lever rod
(8)	Hand lever
(9)	Discharge valve cover washer
(10)	Discharge valve washer
(11)	Basin washer
(12)	Cylinder inlet washer
(13)	Basin back connector washers
(14)	Cylinder bottom washer
(15)	Packing
(16)	Cylinder top washer
(17)	Basin/bowl
(18)	Discharge valve
(19)	Inlet valve chest
(20)	Washer
(21)	Valve chest
(22)	Bottom valve
(23)	Cam spindle stuffing box
(24)	Gland
(25)	Water discharge valve
(26)	Valve chest cover
(27)	Gasket
(28)	Washers
(29)	Packing
(30)	Seal

Outlet seacock

Inlet seacock

Inlet valve chest (19)

* by courtesy of Simpson-Lawrence Ltd.

SEACOCKS, THRU' HULL FITTINGS, GATE VALVES & PIPE CLIPS

Throughout the craft all these fittings and fastenings must be thoroughly checked for corrosion, that thru' hull skin fittings are adequately supported by backing pads and that gate valves and seacocks are working easily. Strip down any tight gate valves and seacocks, free off the action, grease and reassemble (*See* Illus. 31c). (Sounds like an evening out in a Unisex massage parlour. No! Oh well there you go). Inspect the run of the pipework for kinks and splits. Replace suspect fittings and or fastenings.

31c Seacocks & gate valves

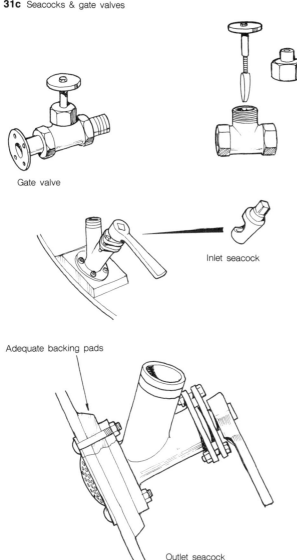

Gate valve

Inlet seacock

Adequate backing pads

Outlet seacock

See Illustration 16 for backing pad composition to suit various shell materials

BILGE PUMPING EQUIPMENT

Be they stirrup, plunger, diaphragm, electric, or a mix of the choices in action and activation, then it or they should be cleaned out, seals checked and the system inspected from the strum box all the way through to the hull fitting (Illus 32a & b). Change and double up pipe clips where necessary, ensuring they are stainless steel and properly fastened down on the reinforced pipe. Mention of the strum box reminds me to point out that all the 'gunge', fluff and debris should be cleaned from the 'tiny perforations'.

Although this is not an 'improvement' manual, one item that should be fitted, if not included in a manufacturers original specification, is either a gate valve on the thru' hull skin fitting or a one-way valve on the discharge side of the bilge pump. If the suction pipe is long and tortuous it is also worth inserting a one-way valve close to the suction end, thus ensuring the pipe is always primed. The requirement for a one-way valve is especially necessary where an in-hull mounted electric bilge pump is fitted as 'feed back' or siphoning can occur with interesting results!

Prior to draining the bilges, check the operation of any automatic bilge pump float switches, ensuring they are working and not rendered inoperative by, and or clogged, with oily bilge water.

VENTILATORS

Static or hand operated thru' deck ventilators require washing down and greasing where a spindle is fitted and electric vents should be sprayed with an inhibiting oil (Illus. 33b).

Before closing this chapter, and although in danger of irritating repetition, please ensure that all the deck fitting and thru' hull, skin fitting backing pads are sufficient in size. If not fit larger ones, bearing in mind that they can be of a variety of (compatible) materials as long as they adequately spread the load and are well bedded on sealant. Steel and alloy craft may well have doublers welded in the relevant positions which should require no attention (*See* Chapter Two & Illustration 16).

For the winterization of the domestic electrics, navigation equipment, engine, rudder and steering gear, please refer to Chapters Seven, Eight and Nine.

Let us hope nothing serious has come to light, but perhaps that is too much to expect!

Illustration 32 Bilge pumping systems & pumps

32a

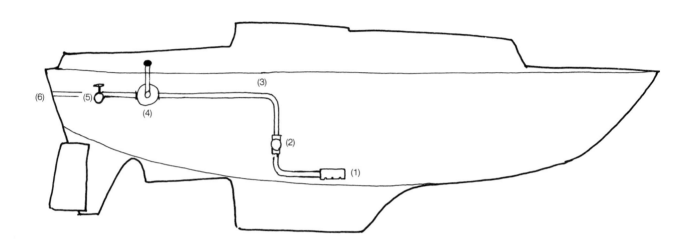

(1) Strum box   (2) One-way valve   (3) Reinforced hose

(4) Gusher thru' deck mounting   (5) Gate valve   (6) Thru' hull skin fitting

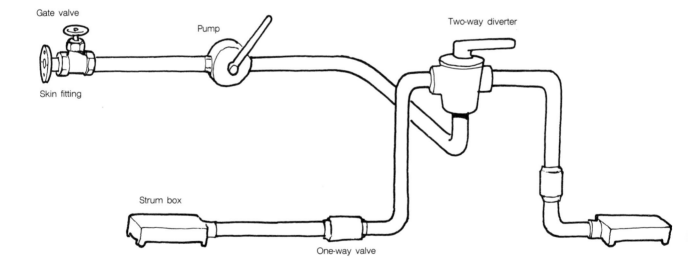

32b Bilge pumps*

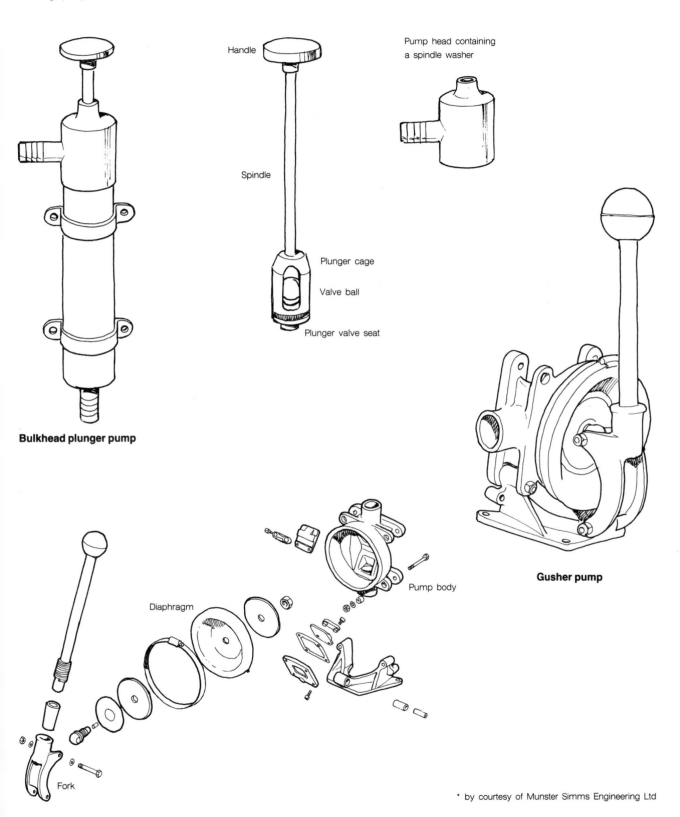

Bulkhead plunger pump

Handle

Spindle

Plunger cage

Valve ball

Plunger valve seat

Pump head containing
a spindle washer

Gusher pump

Diaphragm

Pump body

Fork

* by courtesy of Munster Simms Engineering Ltd

Illustration 33 Ventilation & deck vents

33a

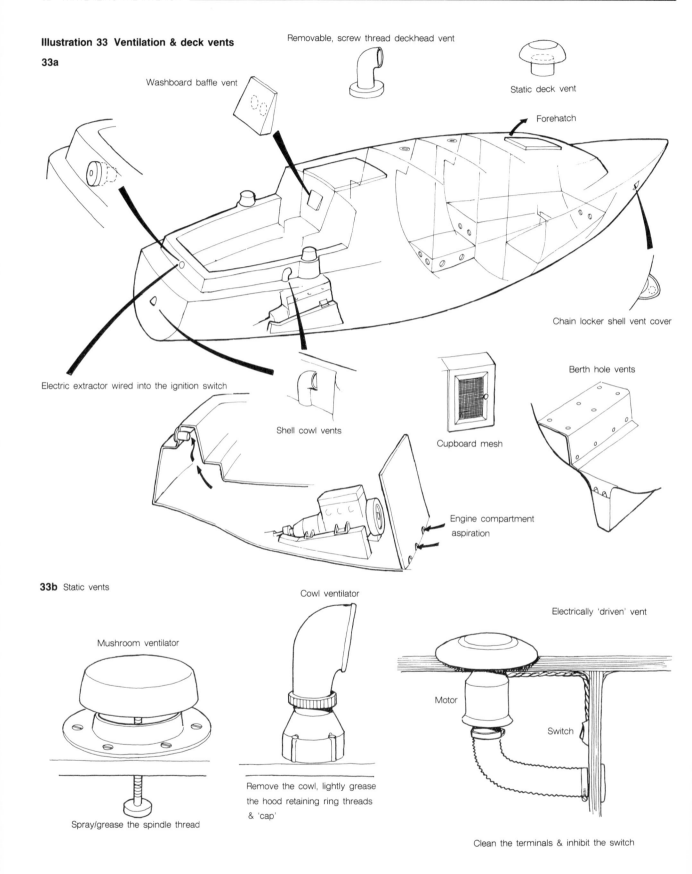

Removable, screw thread deckhead vent

Washboard baffle vent

Static deck vent

Forehatch

Chain locker shell vent cover

Electric extractor wired into the ignition switch

Shell cowl vents

Cupboard mesh

Berth hole vents

Engine compartment aspiration

33b Static vents

Mushroom ventilator

Spray/grease the spindle thread

Cowl ventilator

Remove the cowl, lightly grease the hood retaining ring threads & 'cap'

Electrically 'driven' vent

Motor

Switch

Clean the terminals & inhibit the switch

4

WINTERIZING — SAILING CRAFT

It will be necessary, prior to placing a sailing craft on hardstanding, to attend to the 'The Free Motive Power' arrangement.

SAILS

The sail wardrobe should be correctly bagged (Illus. 34a & b), not crushed and jammed in the forecabin and or the cockpit lockers. And before stowing them in a heap in the garage (to be forgotten until the spring) a number of simple disciplines will be beneficial for both the sails and an owner's pocket.

The majority of modern sails are manufactured of man-made materials, principally polyester and nylon, but much of that which follows is also relevant to canvas.

Firstly, why not give them a valet? A bath can cope with a sail area up to about 14-18 1/2sq m (150-200 sq ft), that is if the 'management committee' allows the immersion to take place (Illus. 35a)! The water, to which should be added a soapless detergent, must be no hotter than 'human' bath temperature. The process is akin to treading grapes. You know, wade up and down and leave for a few hours after which rinse the sail and tackle stubborn marks with a nail brush and bar soap. Safe grime, stain and dirt 'persuaders' include:-

Swarfega: oil, grease and tar.
Domestos (diluted): mildew and blood
Spirits (including methylated & white): oil, grease, tar and paint.
Trichloroethylene: The more stubborn stains and tar streaks.

Ensure that after treatment any cleaning agent used is thoroughly washed off.

Whilst dragging the sails downstairs, watch out for priceless ornaments on display in the hall as this sort of careless damage can cause so much family friction! The sail should not be put away wet but first hung out to dry in order to avoid mildew damage. Only suspend the sail from its luff, which is reinforced, and to stop the sail 'flogging' use the clew as a fastening point, perhaps to a convenient part of the house (Illus. 35b).

DO NOT iron sails or use conventional detergents. If the sails are coloured, badly stained, too big for the

Illustration 34 Bagging the sails

34a Mainsail

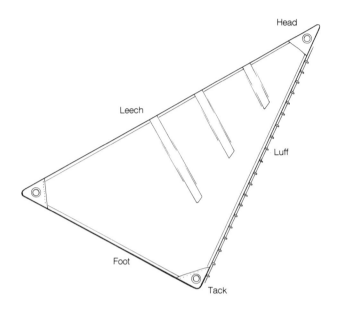

34b Headsail

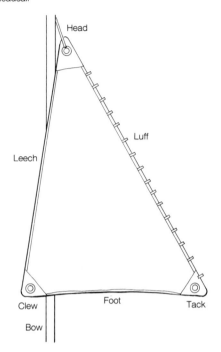

Remove the battens then fold
parallel to:- the luff or the foot

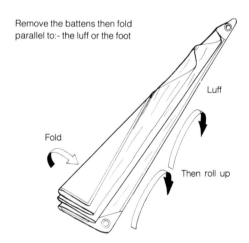

Roll up from the Head
parallel to
the Luff

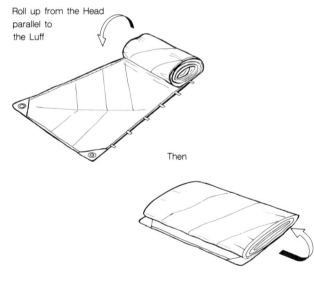

Then

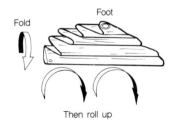

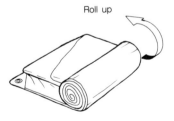

Roll up

bath, or the whole thing seems too much trouble, obtain quotations from 'your friendly' sailmaker to valet and quote for necessary repairs. Inspect the sails before shipping them off and make a note of the defects in the yacht's log (well okay, on the back of a cigarette packet) . Pay particular attention to stains, all the seam stitching and reinforcing patches. Depending on whether the sail is a main or foresail, inspect the:-

headboard, tack and clew stitching, rivets and brass rings; luff boltrope, slides, eyelets, hanks, snap hooks and reef cringles; leech; foot slides, eyelets; battens and batten pockets as well as mainsail cunningham eyes and slab reefing arrangements (Illus. 36a & b).

Illustration 35 Give them a bath & hang them out to dry

35a Valeting in the bath

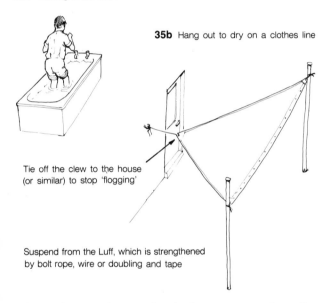

Tie off the clew to the house (or similar) to stop 'flogging'

35b Hang out to dry on a clothes line

Suspend from the Luff, which is strengthened by bolt rope, wire or doubling and tape

Sails also require scrutiny in those areas where the guard rails and stanchions, and the shrouds and or spreaders may have caused wear during the sailing season. This is more likely to have occurred if the sails have been allowed to flog from side to side, or care has not been taken when goose-winging. Inspection might for instance reveal that a low cut genoa has rubbed on the guard rails — sew on a leather patch; the mainsail or foresails have chafed on the spreader ends — fit a protector (to the spreaders); foresails have scraped against the rigging — fit parrel balls and nylon tubing or spiral electric cable wrap; the boom topping lift has sawn away at the leech of the mainsail — hold it off with shock cord to the aft backstay (Illus 37).

Check sail bags are fitted with bottom ties or a cord and snap shackle, if not ask the sailmaker to fit them (Illus 38). At the same time why not ask them to stamp Head, Clew and Tack on the appropriate corners? It

does make for easier foredeck handling, especially if an owner has a 'gash set of pointed end guerrillas'!

If sails are treated similarly to car chamois-leathers — you know rung out and chucked to one side until required again, then spars and rigging are usually treated in an even more cavalier fashion.

Illustration 36 Points of the Sails

36a Mainsail

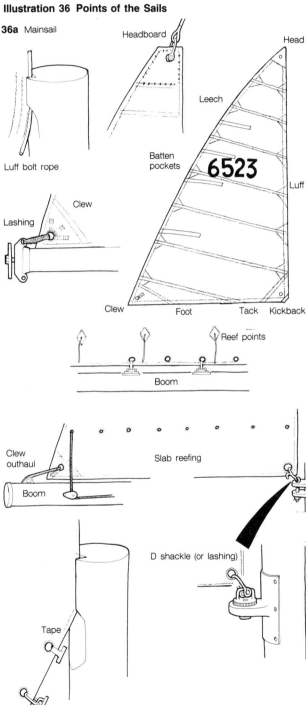

36b Foresail

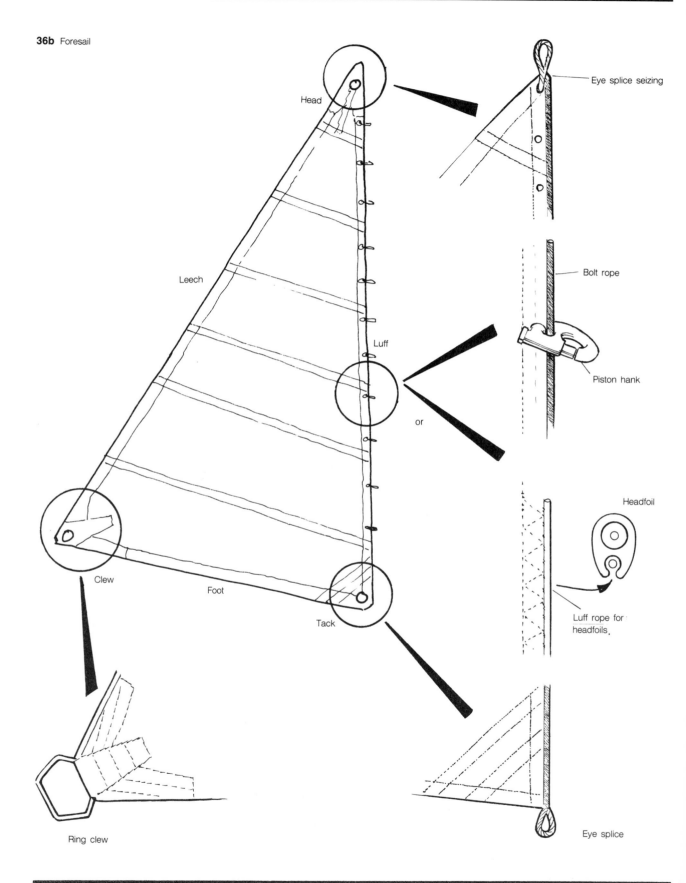

Head

Leech

Luff

or

Clew

Foot

Tack

Ring clew

Eye splice seizing

Bolt rope

Piston hank

Headfoil

Luff rope for headfoils.

Eye splice

Illustration 37 Sail wear points

Guard rail/stanchions wear low cut sails, especially genoas when close hauled

Parrel ball & tubing

or fit a proprietary rigging screw cover

Tape up having greased up

Rigging screw

Toggle

Sail surface rubbing against the Spreader end and or Cap shroud

Fit a boot & spiral wrap the rigging

Backstay

Topping lift

Shockcord tie

Mainsail

Illustration 38 Sail bags

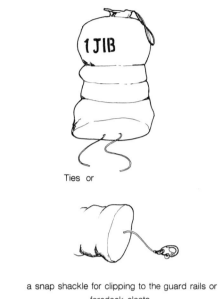

Ties or

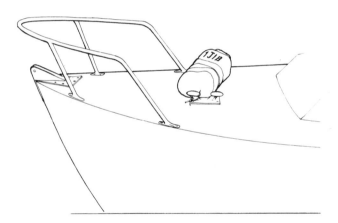

a snap shackle for clipping to the guard rails or foredeck cleats

MASTS

I get that 'ash shovel on tiles', teeth-grating sensation when I note some of the winter treatment of spars and their attachments, but there you go. The overwhelming majority of masts are of anodised aluminium tube fabrication and the following suggestions are primarily written with them in mind. On the other hand, most of the proposals are pertinent to timber spars and they have a section to themselves.

First the NO, NO's. Do not overwinter the main mast along the deck or cabin top, bearing only on the pulpit and pushpit. Have it stored and separately racked, properly supported along its full length, otherwise a permanent 'set' or bend may result. Do not store the spars with the standing rigging still attached and the whole wrapped together in a writhing mass. Aluminium, like any other metal, is subject to erosion by electrolysis, the chances of which are increased if the spars are left salt encrusted and then receive a soaking with the rigging still in contact. Furthermore, the very detachment of the standing rigging encourages a detailed inspection of the fastening point attachments, as well as the masthead box, sheaves, bushes, pins,

Illustration 39 A deck stepped mast

39a The mast

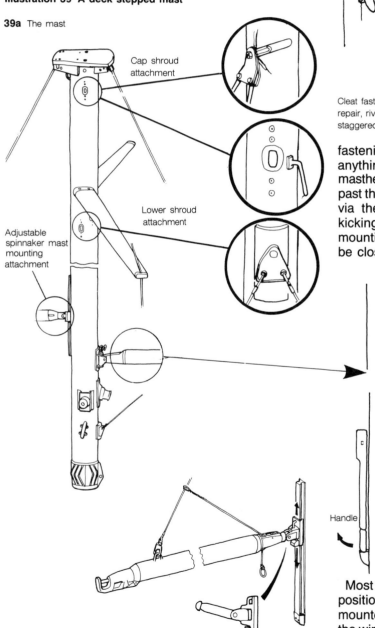

Cap shroud attachment

Lower shroud attachment

Adjustable spinnaker mast mounting attachment

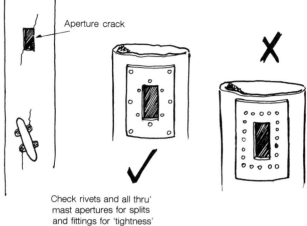

Aperture crack

Check rivets and all thru' mast apertures for splits and fittings for 'tightness'

Cleat fastened with rivets but mast tube cracked due to cleat 'working' To repair, rivet a plate to the mast tube. Ensure the rivets are well spaced and staggered, not in line and close together otherwise a long split may ensue

fastenings, clips, toggles, clevis and split pins (plus anything else I may have missed out). From the masthead, and its attendant box of tricks, working down past the spreaders, lower standing rigging attachments via the various mast mounted boom attachments, kicking strap (or boom vang) fitting, spinnaker mountings, cleats, plates and winches, each item must be closely scrutinised (Illus 39a & b).

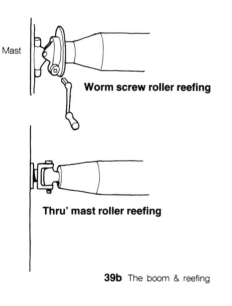

Mast

Worm screw roller reefing

Thru' mast roller reefing

Handle

39b The boom & reefing

Most mast fittings these days are pop riveted in position. Mast mounted winches are insulated, being mounted on tufnel pads (or a similar material) between the winch and the winch bracket. Where cleats, or any other fittings for that matter, are fastened with stainless steel, self-tapping screws, they require regular

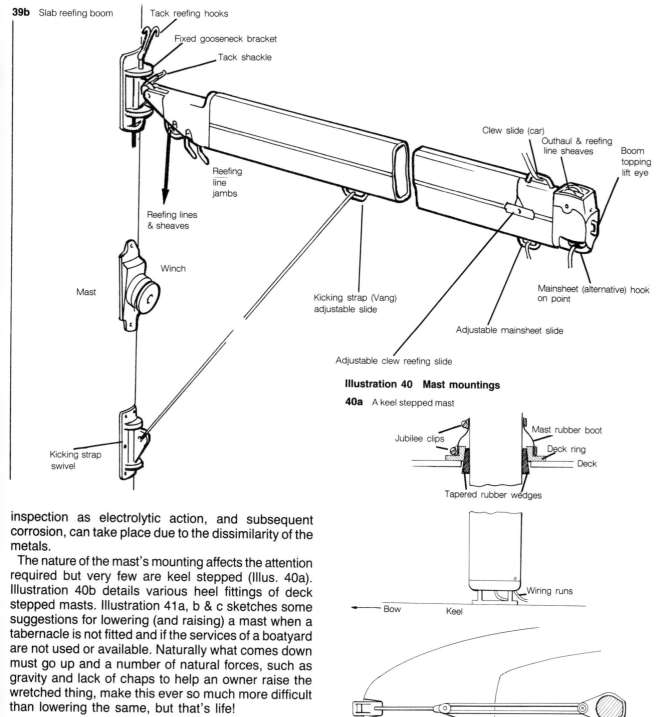

39b Slab reefing boom

Tack reefing hooks

Fixed gooseneck bracket

Tack shackle

Clew slide (car)

Outhaul & reefing line sheaves

Boom topping lift eye

Reefing line jambs

Reefing lines & sheaves

Winch

Mast

Kicking strap (Vang) adjustable slide

Mainsheet (alternative) hook on point

Adjustable mainsheet slide

Kicking strap swivel

Adjustable clew reefing slide

Illustration 40   Mast mountings

40a A keel stepped mast

Jubilee clips

Mast rubber boot

Deck ring

Deck

Tapered rubber wedges

Wiring runs

Bow   Keel

Use a block & tackle to position the aft taper wedge or chock after inserting the forward rubber. Alternatively fit the after rubber wedge and use the sheet winches to strain the mast back to slip in the forward chock.

inspection as electrolytic action, and subsequent corrosion, can take place due to the dissimilarity of the metals.

The nature of the mast's mounting affects the attention required but very few are keel stepped (Illus. 40a). Illustration 40b details various heel fittings of deck stepped masts. Illustration 41a, b & c sketches some suggestions for lowering (and raising) a mast when a tabernacle is not fitted and if the services of a boatyard are not used or available. Naturally what comes down must go up and a number of natural forces, such as gravity and lack of chaps to help an owner raise the wretched thing, make this ever so much more difficult than lowering the same, but that's life!

Remove the top navigation light early on after un-stepping the mast as it is prone to damage whilst the 'stick' is being moved about, and take the opportunity to check the mounting bracket. The light will, well should be tested before stepping the mast on launching, but in the meantime, wrap it in some polythene and take home for safe storage.

Where internal halyards are fitted, then the mast heel sheaves, bushes and pins must be inspected and any wear rectified by replacement. Why not label the halyard exits and cleats (and for that matter the mast electric cables)? It saves so much shouting, swearing, family dissension and long term loss of crew! (Illus. 42). Mainsail reefing is usually achieved by roller (*See* Illus. 39b) or slab reefing (Illus. 43) which systems determine the type of boom fastening to the mast and the

40b Deck stepped mast heel fittings

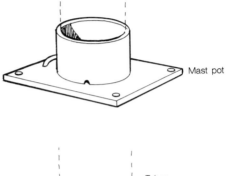

Mast pot

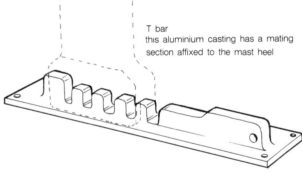

T bar
this aluminium casting has a mating section affixed to the mast heel

Tabernacle by removing the bottom locating bolt the mast can swivel on the top bolt

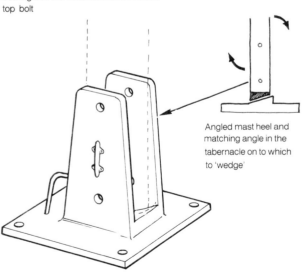

Angled mast heel and matching angle in the tabernacle on to which to 'wedge'

Illustration 41 Mast lowering (& raising)

41a

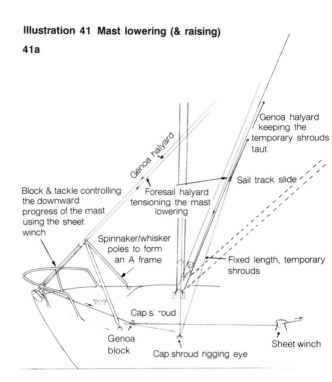

Genoa halyard keeping the temporary shrouds taut

Sail track slide

Block & tackle controlling the downward progress of the mast using the sheet winch

Foresail halyard tensioning the mast lowering

Spinnaker/whisker poles to form an A frame

Fixed length, temporary shrouds

Cap shroud

Genoa block

Cap shroud rigging eye

Sheet winch

The mast must be steadied from side to side. Unfortunately, unless the cap shroud rigging eye is directly in line with the mast pivot, an additional pair of temporary shrouds must be utilised (and tensioned).

41b

Hinged round the pivot bolt of the T bar fixing

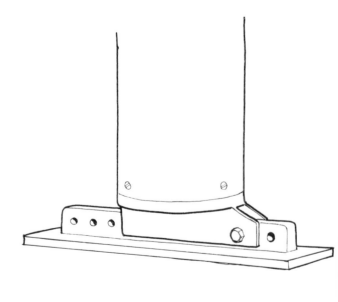

41c Pivoting

Pivots round the pivot

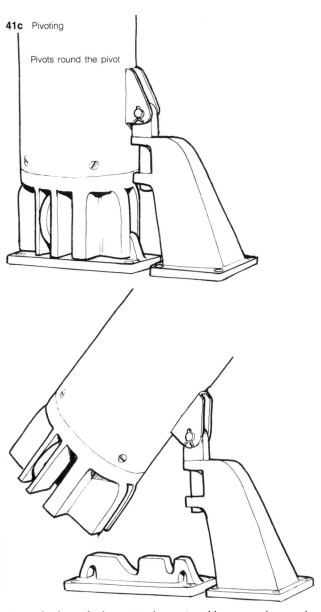

Illustration 42 Running rigging (and mast cable) identification*

Running rigging identification stickers makes sailing easier & makes for more effective sail handling even with an established crew.

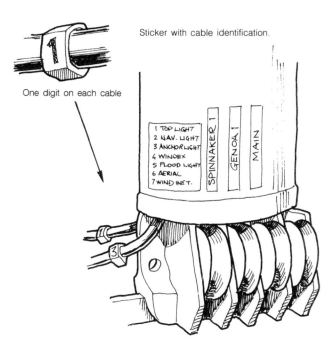

Sticker with cable identification.

One digit on each cable

1 TOP LIGHT
2 NAV. LIGHT
3 ANCHORLIGHT
4 WINDEX
5 FLOOD LIGHT
6 AERIAL
7 WIND INST.

SPINNAKER 1
GENOA 1
MAIN

MAIN
GENOA 1
GENOA 2
TOPPING LIFT
SPINNAKER 1
SPINNAKER 2
SPINNAKER LIFT 1
SPINNAKER LIFT 2
INBOARD LIFT
STAYSAIL
CUNNINGHAM
OUTHAUL
REEF 1
REEF 2
KICKING STRAP
SPINN. DOWN HAUL

complexity of the attachments. Here again each mechanical component requires inspection.

Allow the spars to dry after washing with warm, soapy water and rinsing. Rectify scratches or abrasions that have cut through the anodising, for which cellulose touch-up paint is excellent (*See* Chapter Ten). This is vital because unprotected aluminium corrodes unless treated. Pay especial attention to cleaning out the mast and boom tracks, as well as all the slides and grooves, for this is where salt encrustation causes serious problems in raising and lowering the sails during the season. Keep the mast and boom apart when stored with, say, a thin layer of foam padding, prior to which treat them to an application of wax polish which greatly lengthens their working life.

* by courtesy of Kemp Masts Ltd

Illustration 43 Mainsail slab reefing

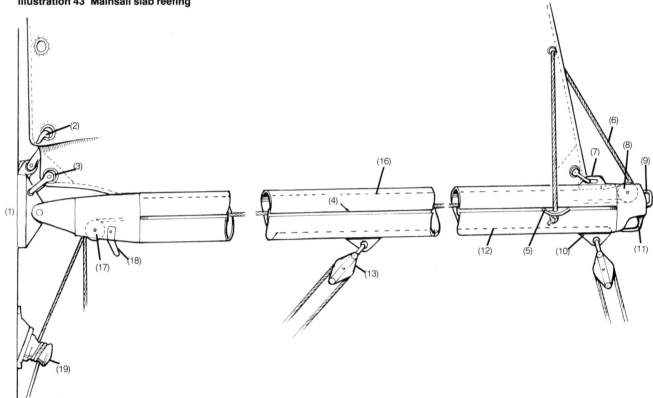

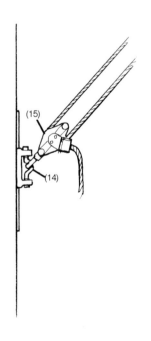

(1) Gooseneck — fixed   (2) Tack hook   (3) Tack shackle

(4) Clew reefing slides track   (5) Clew reefing slide — adjustable

(6) Clew reefing line   (7) Clew car — to tension mainsail leech

(8) Outhaul & reefing line sheaves   (9) Boom topping lift eye

(10) Main sheet slide — adjustable   (11) Alternative main sheet eye

(12) Main sheet and kicking strap (vang) slide track

(13) Kicking strap (vang) slide — adjustable

(14) Kicking strap swivel — fixed   (15) Kicking sheet jamming block

(16) Mainsail foot track & clew car slide   (17) Clew line sheaves

(18) Jam levers for clew lines

(19) Clew line winch — angled to 'dissuade' riding turns.

Illustration 44 A gaff rig with timber spars

44a

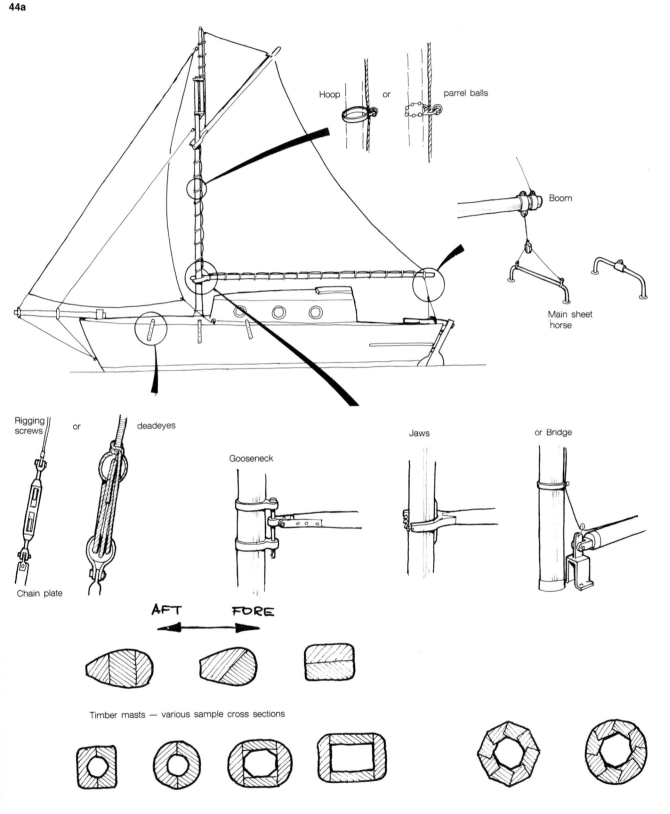

Hoop or parrel balls

Boom

Main sheet horse

Rigging screws or deadeyes

Chain plate

Gooseneck

Jaws or Bridge

AFT ← FORE →

Timber masts — various sample cross sections

Timber Masts Traditionally constructed, timber spars are delightful to observe but . . . . they require much more tender loving care than their modern-day counterparts. Perhaps that is as significant a reason for their demise as the lack of craftsmen to make and repair them and the shortage of suitably seasoned spruce or pine of a sufficient length. Whatever, if an aluminium spar needs careful attention then a wooden mast and its fittings must be treated almost as a 'terminal' case. They certainly must be overwintered carefully, ensuring that they are chocked so no 'set' is induced.

Most wooden spars are made up of glued sections and the glue lines must be carefully inspected and re-glued where necessary (*See* Illus. 44a). Inspect all fittings and attachments, especially the cleats and track fittings, for fit and secureness. Any movement and the fitting must be removed, re-bedded and fastened, or preferably glued and re-fastened. To ensure the snug fit of a wooden cleat to the mast, tightly hold an upturned section of sandpaper round the mast's periphery, where the cleat is to be fastened, and rub the fitting across the sandpaper's surface.

Rot and compression shake are the greatest enemy and the root (sorry) of these ills is more often than not poorly secured fastenings and mast bands. Compression shake, caused by mast whip, is rather difficult to spot in solid spars because the damage is internal. If found, the mast must be rebuilt to be able to cut out the damaged section.

As a varnish finish is the 'order of the day', in order that the state of the timber can be more easily ascertained, one of the most common and easily cured faults is weathering, evidenced by blackening of the wood. Chapter Ten gives details of the necessary treatment.

Once the surface has been returned to an acceptable state, and after sanding down, the first coat of oil-based varnish should be thinned by up to 30% with the addition of equal parts white spirit and linseed oil. Then build up a further three coats of varnish after which

44b   Possible wooden mast defects

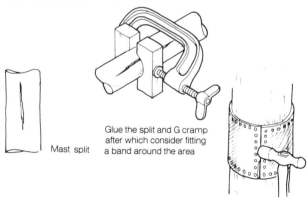

Mast split

Glue the split and G cramp after which consider fitting a band around the area

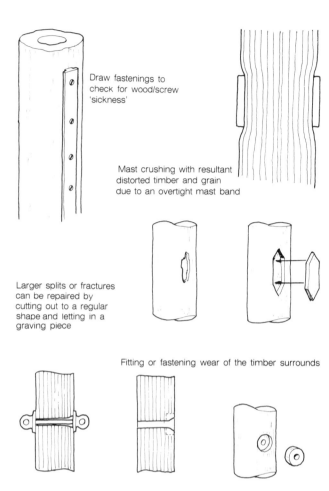

Draw fastenings to check for wood/screw 'sickness'

Mast crushing with resultant distorted timber and grain due to an overtight mast band

Larger splits or fractures can be repaired by cutting out to a regular shape and letting in a graving piece

Fitting or fastening wear of the timber surrounds

Repair by removing the fitting, cut out a section, plug and re-drill

wax working surfaces such as the luff groove. Illustration 44a details a 'typical' gaff rig and Illustration 44b some of the possible defects which may require overwinter care.

STANDING RIGGING

If there is the possibility of muddling up the various standing rigging wires in the spring, tape plastic garden labels to the appropriate wire, with the relevant nomenclature (forestay, lower backstay and etc., etc.,) written on the label with waterproof crayon.

On removal inspect each stay from top to bottom, from the mast terminal to the deck rigging toggle (Illus. 45). Most terminal endings are hydraulically swaged on to the wire and the joint is worthy of close scrutiny, as are the rigging screws and their split pins. Talurit spliced stays and proprietary end fittings, working on a compression cone to body basis, require exactly the same inspection but they should be treated in accordance with the manufacturer's recommendations,

Illustration 45   Standing rigging & possible defects

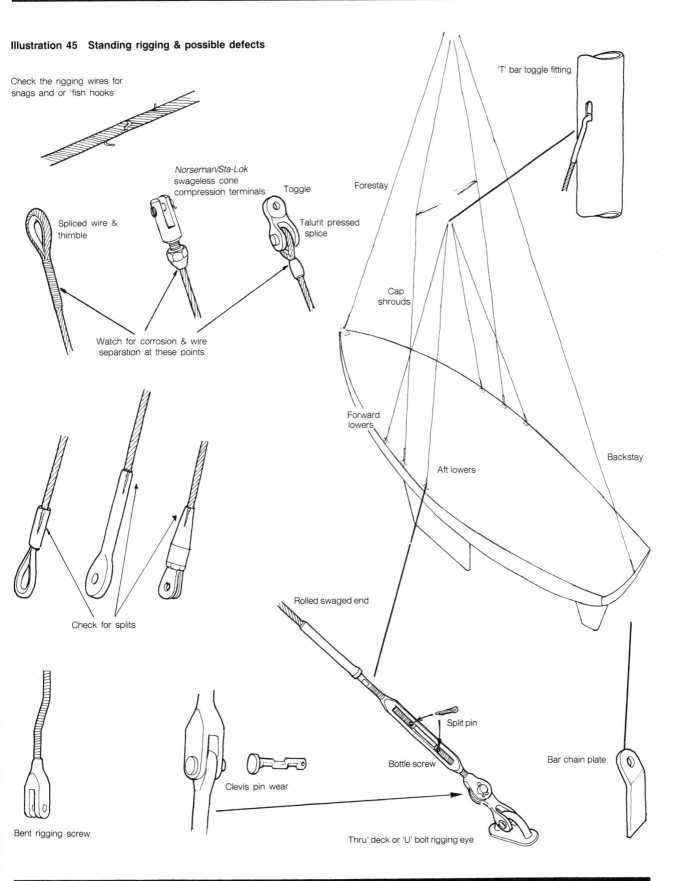

Check the rigging wires for snags and or 'fish hooks'

Norseman/Sta-Lok swageless cone compression terminals

Toggle

Spliced wire & thimble

Talurit pressed splice

Watch for corrosion & wire separation at these points

Check for splits

Bent rigging screw

Clevis pin wear

Rolled swaged end

Split pin

Bottle screw

Thru' deck or 'U' bolt rigging eye

Bar chain plate

'T' bar toggle fitting

Forestay

Cap shrouds

Forward lowers

Aft lowers

Backstay

Illustration 46 Running rigging

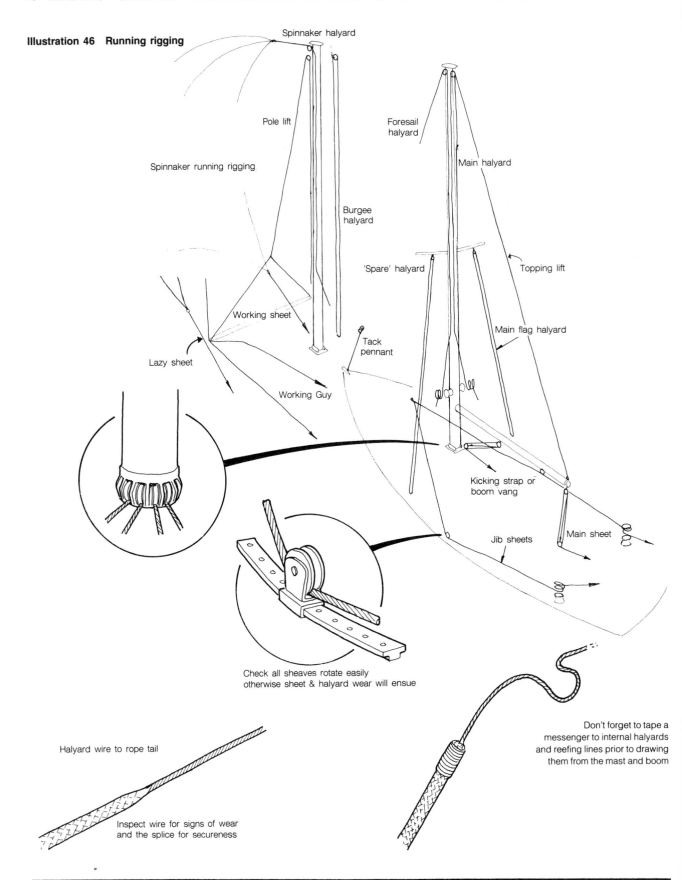

Spinnaker halyard

Pole lift

Spinnaker running rigging

Foresail halyard

Main halyard

Burgee halyard

'Spare' halyard

Topping lift

Working sheet

Tack pennant

Main flag halyard

Lazy sheet

Working Guy

Kicking strap or boom vang

Jib sheets

Main sheet

Check all sheaves rotate easily otherwise sheet & halyard wear will ensue

Halyard wire to rope tail

Inspect wire for signs of wear and the splice for secureness

Don't forget to tape a messenger to internal halyards and reefing lines prior to drawing them from the mast and boom if it varies from the above. Carefully check the wires themselves by running a hand gently up and down their length, feeling for any snags or frayed wires. (Do be careful as spiked fingers hurt.) If only one or two are found tape them up, more and the particular stay must be replaced in its entirety.

After the investigation, wash the rigging with warm, soapy water, dry and spray from top to bottom with an inhibiting oil. To store, wrap up individually in a large intertwined loop and hang off a suitable peg. Lastly, do not forget the tack pennant, if one is fitted.

RUNNING RIGGING

Remove the ropes and wires and inspect over their length for signs of wear, especially at chafe points, remembering that jammed sheaves cause very rapid deterioration. The splice on wire tailed halyards, as well as the wire itself, must be subject to eagle-eyed scrutiny. Prior to removing internal halyards, remember to attach a messenger (marlin or whipping twine) which should be left inside the spar to save problems when reinstalling. Do not forget that included in the running

rigging are the main sheet and kicking strap or boom vang tackle (Illus. 46).

Rod rigging deserves a mention although it is usually fitted where money is not a prime consideration and winter checks will probably be carried out by a boatyard to the manufacturer's recommendations.

RIGGING FIXINGS

These include thru' deck eyes and chain plates, in fact whatever method is used to secure the deck end of the standing rigging, and must be examined to check not only for wear in the fittings themselves but that their fastenings are secure (Illus. 47). Untoward movement, flexing or undue deterioration can, at the best (!), loosen a mounting, resulting in leaks or, at the worst, the total loss of the fixing, rigging and, ultimately the mast (Illus. 48a).

Nowadays, with the almost mandatory fitting of toggles to the lower, or deck end of standing rigging, not so much damage or wear occurs to the rigging fixings. None the less attention must be paid to them. Possibly more important is to inspect the craft's shell or skin

Illustration 47   Standing rigging fixings

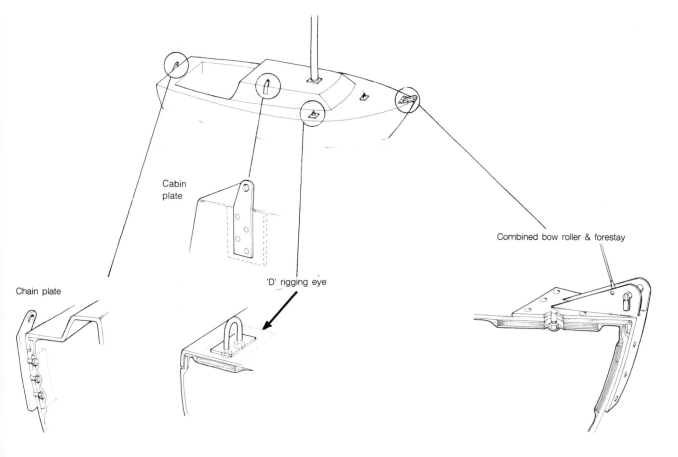

in the area where the rigging fixings are mounted. Any signs of cracking, distortion or flexing requires close and immediate investigation as to the cause and the action necessary to correct the same. This might include replacement of the rigging fixing, fitting larger backing pads and replacing worn fastenings. Excessive panting of a deck, brought about by movement induced by the standing rigging, may require a tie bar or sub bulkhead to be fitted (Illus. 48b).

DECK FITTINGS

Winches must be winterized. The usual treatment is to remove the cover, wash the gearing with fresh water, dry, grease and spray with an inhibiting oil before re-assembling. It pays to individually cover the winches with canvas covers or, more simply, modified ice-cream boxes (Illus. 49a).

Inspect for wear and secureness the foresail snatch block deck eyes (or blocks and tracks) and the genoa and spinnaker blocks and tracks as well as their fastenings. Loose or worn items and their fastenings must be attended to or replaced, after which lightly spray with an inhibiting oil. (Illus. 49b).

Illustration 48   Some standing rigging faults, built in defects & correction

48a

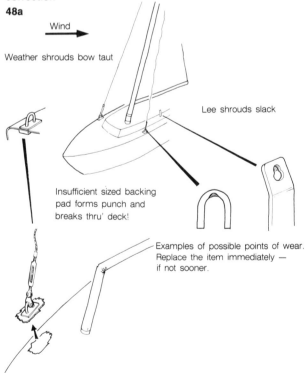

Wind

Weather shrouds bow taut

Lee shrouds slack

Insufficient sized backing pad forms punch and breaks thru' deck!

Examples of possible points of wear. Replace the item immediately — if not sooner.

The unexpected load on the remaining windward rigging fixings causes them to part and the mast buckles

48b Panting deck due to large, unsupported side decking

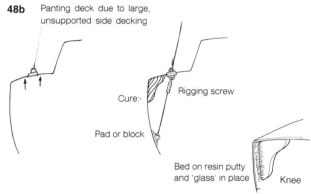

Cure:-

Rigging screw

Pad or block

Bed on resin putty and 'glass' in place   Knee

Fit internally mounted deck eyes, one to the hull and the other beneath the side deck rigging fixing. Connect with a wire or bar tensioner and or fit a sub bulkhead, or knee, ensuring the bearing surface is broad so as not to induce surface stresses

Illustration 49   Deck fittings

49a Winch winterization

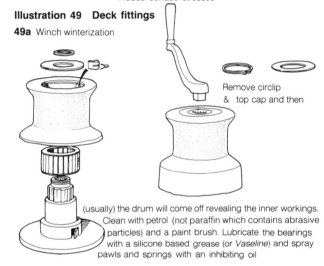

Remove circlip & top cap and then

(usually) the drum will come off revealing the inner workings. Clean with petrol (not paraffin which contains abrasive particles) and a paint brush. Lubricate the bearings with a silicone based grease (or *Vaseline*) and spray pawls and springs with an inhibiting oil

Only dissemble and reassemble with the relevant manufacturer's technical leaflet to hand

Upturned ice-cream container

Canvas 'diddy' cover with draw strings

49b

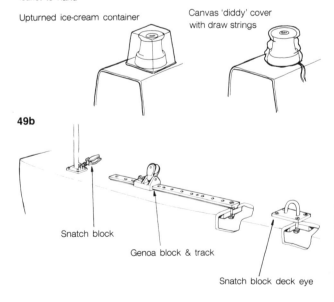

Snatch block

Genoa block & track

Snatch block deck eye

HINTS, TIPS & IDEAS FOR FASTENINGS, DRILLING, LIFTING & 'HANDRAULICS'

While carrying out an overhaul, maintenance and or repairs the matter of undoing 'insubordinate' fastenings, be they keel bolts or fashion piece fixing screws, causes more problems than should be the lot of an unfortunate boat owner.

General unfastening hints include the use of heat, tightening up (sic) and applying shock. Heat expands, thus helping to break the lock between the surrounding material and a fastening, as does tightening (Irish as it might sound) and lightly tapping. This last method is greatly assisted if the fastening is simultaneously being 'torqued'. Other general aids include applying a freeing agent, if the surroundings will not spoil. For instance, headlinings are not improved by a liberal dose of penetrating oil.

Spanners and the length of their arm are designed so that, using normal force, a nut or bolt cannot be over tightened. This must not be relied upon, especially in respect of smaller diameter fastenings and or where the material is not steel but, say, brass. Similarly screw

head slots are machined to take a certain size screwdriver blade.

It is possible to cheat a little and various dodges exist to increase the turning moment applied to a fastening. For instance, instead of using a conventional screwdriver, fit a brace with a screwdriver bit and when using a ring or open ended spanner slip another ring spanner or a tube over the other end (Illus. 50).

Working from the bottom up, in both size and sheer cussedness,

without doubt the most defiant fastenings encountered are the:-

Keel Bolts These may well require every method of persuasion known to mankind (well, nearly) including the use of:-

1. **Freeing Agents:** Penetrating oil which can be purchased in cans or aerosol sprays and is best applied over a number of days or weeks prior to the more drastic methods listed below. It may be

Illustration 50   Unfastening dodges

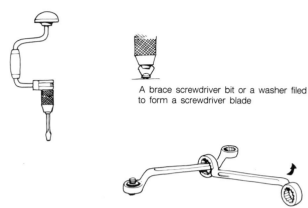

A brace screwdriver bit or a washer filed to form a screwdriver blade

'Ware the extra ring spanner does not move out of the plane of the ring spanner being persuaded!

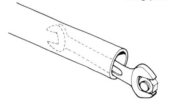

Beware the spanner does not slip over the flats of the nut

necessary to fashion a 'coffer dam' of plasticine to trap the fluid round the head of a fastening. (Illus 51a).

2. **Heat:** Be careful not to set fire to those parts of the boat surrounding the fastenings. It is worth packing the area with well soaked rags and using a gas cartridge appliance with a fine nozzle (Illus. 51b)

Illustration 51   Keel bolt persuaders

51a   Freeing agents

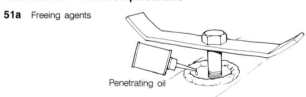

Penetrating oil

Plasticine coffer dam to contain a reservoir of penetrating oil around a recalcitrant keel boat

51b   Heat

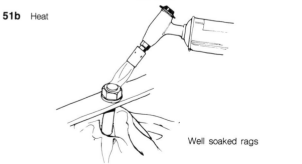

Well soaked rags

3. **Tightening:** Just a touch. Incidentally it may well be necessary to weld a long tube on to a socket head with provision for a hefty tommy bar (Illus. 51c).

4. **Shock:** Well, more realistically belting the top of the bolt head whilst somebody else is applying a turning moment to the wretched thing. Do not use the sledge-hammer you normally throw at the next door neighbour's cat. A copper headed hammer is ideal or, failing that, interpose a brass drift between the potentially damaging steel face of the hammer and the head of the fastening (Illus. 51d).

It is worth noting that some keel bolt nut heads are let into the keel, being accessed thru' a slot that is 'sealed off' with lead or another suitable stopper (*See* Illus. 26).

5. **Lock-nuts:** Where a keel bolt stud can be fitted with a second nut, try undoing the bottom nut against a top, lock-nut (Illus. 51e).

51c   Tightening or extra torque   **51d**   Shock or brute force

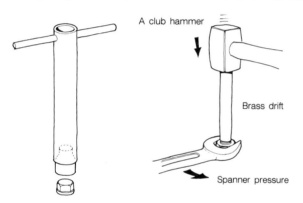

A club hammer

Brass drift

Spanner pressure

A tommy bar tube welded to a socket head. It may be necessary to have the tube long enough to clear adjacent berth fronts so as to be able to employ a really long tommy bar.

51e   Lock-nuts

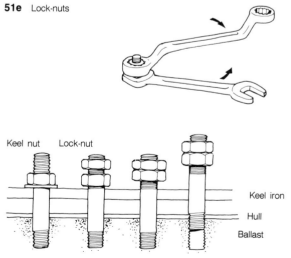

Keel nut   Lock-nut

Keel iron

Hull

Ballast

Keel nut tightened up to and together with the lock-nut

6. **Jacks:** Depending on the amount of room available one or three jacks may be able to be brought to bear, as it were (Illus. 51f).

Thru'Hull/Deck Fastenings: Other fastenings may well require a combination of some or all of the above methods, only the scale is different. In addition, if really necessary, a nut splitter can be used, as can a counter rotation thread tap, which requires a bore hole to be drilled (Illus. 52a) The problem here is that the drill tends to wander off line. Rather than engage in the brutality of drilling out 'reluctant' bolts and wooden hull spikes, they can be eased out by the use of threaded bar, some steel channel and a welder (Illus. 52b).

51f Jacks

To get two jacks *in situ* weld an extension bar or tube with a top plate on to the top of the keel bolt

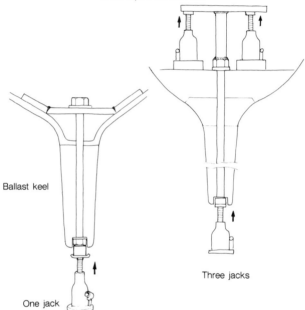

Ballast keel

One jack

Three jacks

Illustration 52 Other persuaders

52a A nut splitter

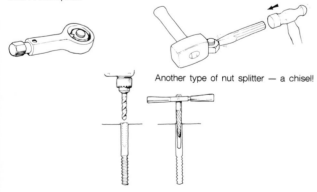

Another type of nut splitter — a chisel!

A counter rotation thread tap is useful where a bolt has broken off but care must be exercised to ensure the drill does not wander off line

52b Reluctant fastening

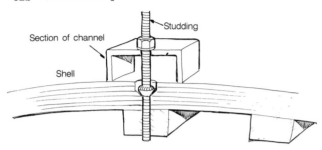

Studding

Section of channel

Shell

Weld a length of threaded studding to the fastening. Take a section of channel drilled with a hole just large enough to allow clearance and slide the channel down the length of the stud to ground on the shell. Then run a nut (with a fastener) down the thread and just keep on tightening.

Screw Fastenings: Supplementary procedures include the use of a pad saw behind panels, or drilling off the head part of the screw, then levering off the cover piece and using a mole wrench to undo the projecting part of the screw (Illus. 53).

Several types of specialised tools have been developed over recent years to help unfasten bolt and nut heads. These include the ratchet-spanner from which has been developed one or two patented gadgets which are even able to unfasten nuts and bolts where the flats have become rounded. Cruder methods include the use of a pin punch against the side of one of the flats of the nut or bolthead. These and various other good wheezes for loosening different and difficult fastenings are detailed in Illustration 54a. Illustration 54b sketches a few methods of re-introducing fastenings into awkward places.

Illustration 53 Screw movers

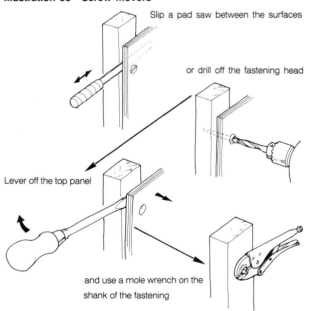

Slip a pad saw between the surfaces

or drill off the fastening head

Lever off the top panel

and use a mole wrench on the shank of the fastening

Illustration 54   . . . & more persuaders

54a A pin punch

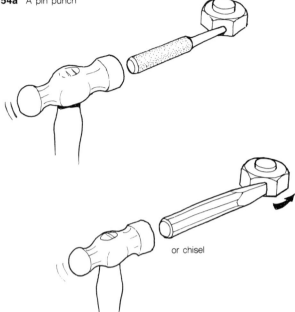

or chisel

but the chisel blade must not be too sharp

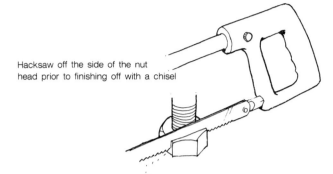

Hacksaw off the side of the nut
head prior to finishing off with a chisel

Awkwardly situated nuts, screws, machine screw heads & bolts modified for
the future ease of removal

Cut/file out flats for a spanner where a screwdriver
cannot get in

Cut screwdriver slot in nut heads

Screwdriver slot in screw thread end

Normally inaccessible bolt heads fastening say a starter motor or alternator
can be lengthened by welding on an extension bolt

Extension bolt

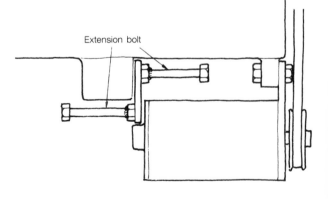

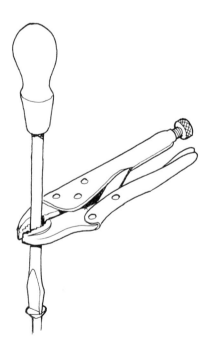

A mole wrench clamped to the shank of a heavy screwdriver to increase
the turning power

54b Getting a screw or nut & bolt into an area as confined as this sometimes requires some additional help . . .

Where a nut and washer have to be introduced back off the start of the nut's threads with an oversize drill to ease the introduction to a bolt

then

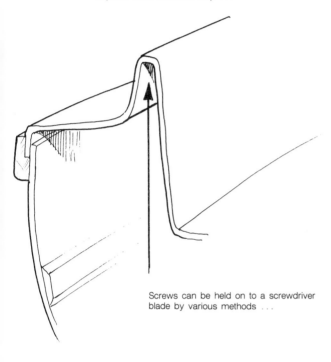

glue the nut to a large diameter washer with clearance to the nut's threads ensuring the backed off side of the nut is face on to the washer. Allow the glue to set off, checking the nut's threads are clear of glue. Apart from it being necessary to 'nut up' on a washer, the washer holds the nut in place when placed into a tube spanner or socket head

Screws can be held on to a screwdriver blade by various methods . . .

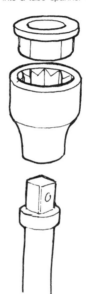

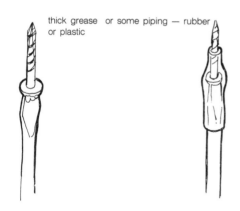

thick grease   or some piping — rubber or plastic

It may well be necessary to remove internal panelling and, or, headlinings to gain access to thru' deck fastening nuts and Illustration 55 sketches some of the methods used to fix panels in place (Also *See* Illustration 58).

Quite often when fitting additional items, it will be necessary to have three arms (one of which should be 17 feet long and treble-jointed), X-Ray sight and extra sensory perception. Illustration 56 sketches some of the alternative methods that can be employed, other than interfering with evolution!

Hose clips are extremely confusingly sized by the various manufacturers but the tables in Chapter Twelve should help sort out the jungle and ONLY use stainless steel clips. Due to standardisation over recent years, it is preferable to substitute metric sized machine screws for Imperial fastenings more especially, as use of the latter may well double the cost (*See* the tables in Chapter Twelve). It may well be useful to have the tables of metal and wire gauge equivalents and sizes for easy reference. There is nothing more infuriating than being unable to communicate with a supplier or to have gauge numbers with no way of converting them to really useful information such as thickness. This usually occurs at a weekend, according to Murphy's Law, so the tables, which may well only be used once or twice in a lifetime, are also listed in Chapter Twelve as are are other various tables, equivalents and formulae.

To close the Chapter, Illustration 57 gives some ideas for the art of 'handraulics', or managing the impossible!

Illustration 55   Headlinings

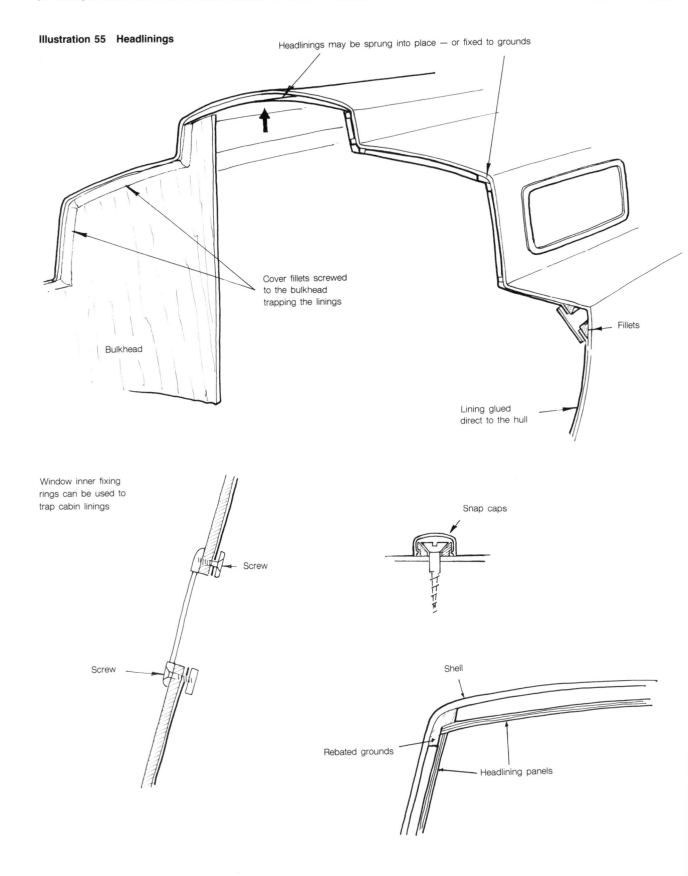

Headlinings may be sprung into place — or fixed to grounds

Cover fillets screwed
to the bulkhead
trapping the linings

Bulkhead

Fillets

Lining glued
direct to the hull

Window inner fixing
rings can be used to
trap cabin linings

Screw

Screw

Snap caps

Shell

Rebated grounds

Headlining panels

Illustration 56   Blind fastenings or interfering with evolution!

56a   To drill very large holes use a scrap piece of rectangular ply to make a drill jig. Drill two holes on the pitch center diameter, as close to each other as possible.

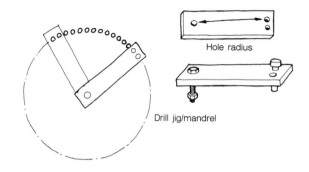

Hole radius

Drill jig/mandrel

Drill a hole at the centre of the planned circle, bolt the jig thru' this and drill the first outer hole. Plant the mandrel in this hole and drill the next hole and so on. When finished, pad saw away the remaining material and file out to a smooth finish

56b   If a hatch or companionway is handy . . . make an 'alligator' jaw drill mandrel

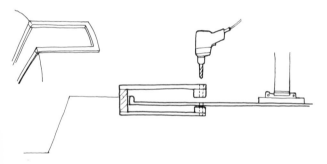

56c   Where there is insufficient room to drill out from the inside and the hull is GRP, try a strong light with a tube, shielding and concentrating the light source. The antifouling in the area will have to be scraped away.

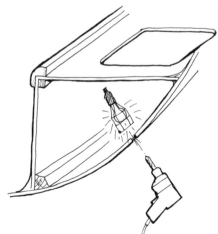

Illustration 57   'Handraulics'

57a   Apart from the ubiquitious block & tackle the main sheet or boom vang can be used . . .

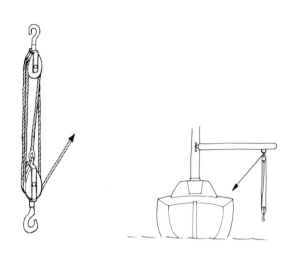

57b   As can the Spanish windlass

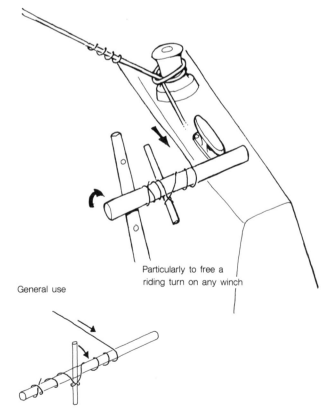

Particularly to free a riding turn on any winch

General use

57c   The tide rises and so does the block

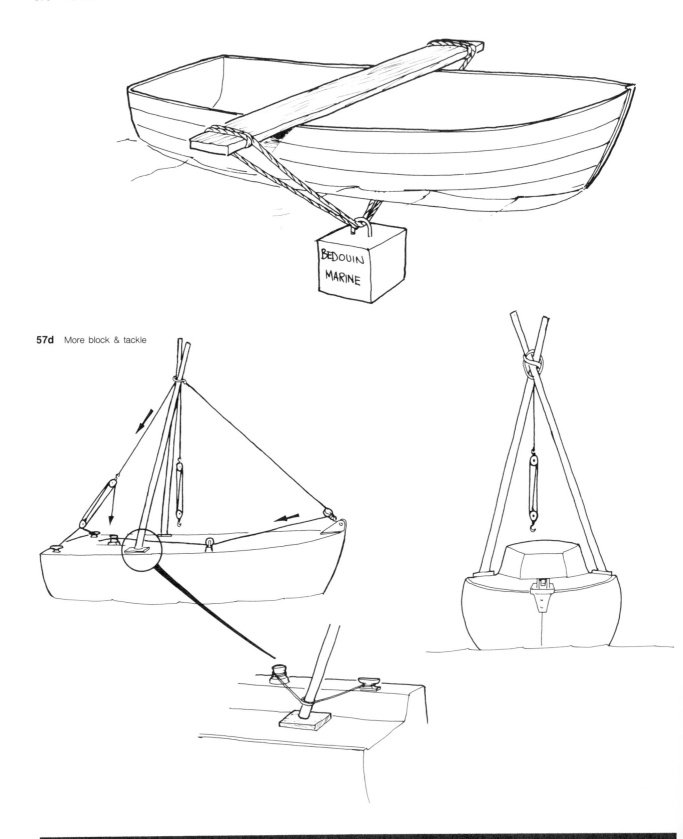

57d   More block & tackle

57e Halves the weight

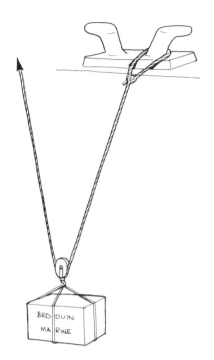

57f Ensure the plank is securely fastened!

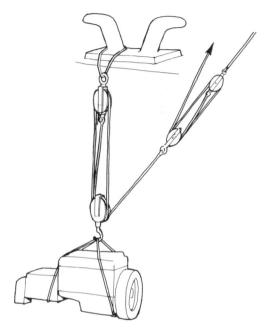

Removal of large tanks or an engine up the side of a quay wall

57g Wedges & levers to lift

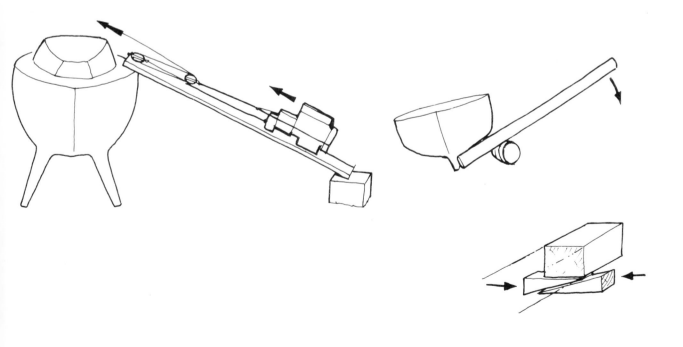

6

SPECIALIST REPAIRS

If Chapter Two represented the 3,000 mile service then this Chapter covers the 12,000 mile overhaul!

The material used to manufacture the craft's hull and deck determines the possible specialist repairs that may be necessary — well it would, wouldn't it?

LEAKS

All boats are subject to leaks, none more so than hard used, GRP constructed yachts, even those only a few years old. Whatever the craft's material of manufacture, it never ceases to amaze me that so many owners put up with drips, or even minor torrents, which will not go away, rather than face up to the fact that there is an ingress of water and get on with the job of solving the problem.

The most problematical boats are those fitted with internal linings, for Murphy's Law says that the actual place where the leak manifests itself may be a long way from the point of intake. With any luck the headlinings have been fitted in detachable panels (No, oh well there you go!). If so, they are usually sprung into place and held with fastenings and trims which,

when removed, free the relevant section, allowing it to pop out (*See* Illus. 55). The point of a leak's entry may now become apparent due to staining but, if not, the first fittings to bear inspection are the hatches and windows. Quite possibly the sealant that the frame or perspex was originally bedded down on was not applied correctly or has, over the years, dissolved. Certainly it does no harm to remove the windows, portholes and hatches at three to five year intervals, reseal and re-fasten them. The trick is to ascertain how the particular unit has been secured (Illus 58a). Inland Waterway craft may have hopper or louvred windows fitted. If so it is quite likely that drain holes are positioned to take away excess water and these should be cleaned out (Illus. 58b). If the windows are not the problem, then the bedding of the various deck fittings and the grabrails profit from inspection (*See* Illus 16 and Chapter Two). Unfortunately some boat manufacturers fail to concede that, sometime in the future, access might be required to the internal fastenings of a particular fitting. The solution may be to 'trepan' out the internal lining in the area of the relevant fitting. For this it will be necessary to take careful measurements to get as close to the

Illustration 58 Window fixings

58a Sample methods of fastening windows
Self tapper into a
channel section

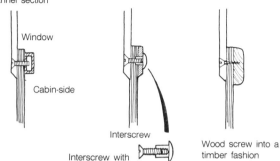

Window

Cabin-side

Interscrew

Interscrew with
inner aluminium trim

Wood screw into a
timber fashion
piece

58b Hopper windows

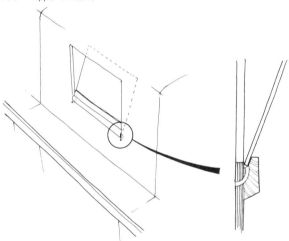

Drain holes let through the cabin sides and lined with a bell mouthed tube

Illustration 59 Access hole & cover

Drilling out the inner lining to gain access to the fastenings of a deck mounted
fitting

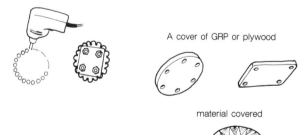

A cover of GRP or plywood

material covered

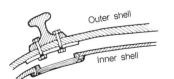

and screwed up on to the
inner lining

Outer shell

Inner shell

spot as possible. The easiest and neatest hole to cut
out is a circular one (*See* Illustration 56a) to which a
cover will have to be fitted, but this is not a difficult task
(Illus. 59).

One other area worthy of inspection when attempting
to track down a mysterious water intake is the deck
to hull joint. Let us hope not! This fault is most common
on GRP craft and the type of hull to deck join dictates
the necessary action to be taken. Illustration 60 details
a sample of commonly employed connections and the
necessary corrective action. Take courage, it only
requires assistance, time and remember 'Boating is
Fun'.

Illustration 60 GRP gunwales

It may be necessary to remove the
gunwale timber to seal the external join

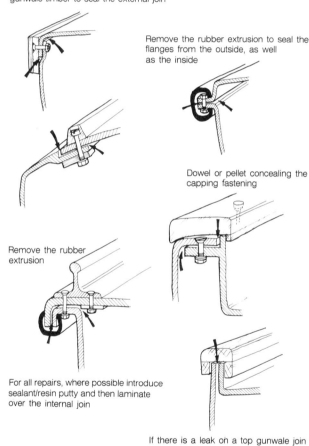

Remove the rubber extrusion to seal the
flanges from the outside, as well
as the inside

Dowel or pellet concealing the
capping fastening

Remove the rubber
extrusion

For all repairs, where possible introduce
sealant/resin putty and then laminate
over the internal join

If there is a leak on a top gunwale join
it will be necessary to remove the
capping to 'get at' the join.

GRP CRAFT

Prior to getting down to the 'nitty-gritty' of repairing
GRP, an expansion of the terms used may be of
assistance. Below is an extract from a companion book
in the series, '*The Boat Building Book*', which
(hopefully) says it all.

'Technical Terms

include:

Lay-up: Where used in connection with a Glass Reinforced Plastic (GRP) hull and superstructure, is expressed in terms of 'grammes' lay-up and indicates the weight per sq metre of the glassfibre mat, i.e. 450 grammes per sq metre (or g/m²) (1½ oz/ft²).

GRP: Glass reinforced plastic, often incorrectly called 'Fibreglass' (a registered trade name), is the term used to describe the finished product which is made up of the following basic materials:-

Polyester Resin: A thermo setting plastic material, popularly called resin for short, which has to be activated by a:-

Catalyst: An organic peroxide in paste, powder or liquid form which cures the resin or 'mix', exothermically (by heat). Throughout the book 'Resin Mix' or 'Mix' denotes a portion of catalysed resin.

N.B. Most resins for boat construction, or fitting out, are supplied pre-accelerated thereby doing away with the need for another constituent, i.e. the accelerator. Ensure any resin purchased is marine grade and pre-accelerated.

Glassfibre Mat (E Glass): This is exactly what it says — fibres of glass in mat form. By laying up the glassfibre in the resin solution, the relatively low strength resin and high strength glassfibres result in a material possessing an excellent strength to weight ratio, high impact strength, dimensional stability as well as good weathering and chemical resistance properties.

Glassfibre for boatwork is usually supplied as Chopped Strand Mat (CSM). Other types of mat include Woven Rovings, Cloth and Tissue.

Note: 300g/m² = 1oz/ft²; 450g/m² = 1½oz/ft²; 600g/m² = 2oz/ft²; 900g/m² = 3oz/ft².

Acetone: The usual and most easily available liquid for cleaning, wiping down surfaces prior to applying a laminate and for washing out brushes and other GRP applicators such as paddle rollers. 'Reclaimed' acetone is often sold as 'brush cleaner' and is significantly cheaper than refined acetone.

Resin Putty: Polyester resin in a putty or paste form which, when mixed with a paste hardener, 'sets off' fairly rapidly. This putty acts as an excellent filler and bedding compound.

Gelcoat:A resin formulated in such a way as to give a water impervious, hard, shiny surface up against the waxed mould and which becomes the exterior or outside surface. The internal or exposed side of the coating, which should be ideally about 0.4mm (1/64") thick, will be of a tacky, rubbery nature.

Bucket life: The period of time in which a (catalysed) resin mix can be used.

Cure time: The period of time taken for a lay-up (of resin and glassfibre) to cure and set off.

Laminate: Throughout the book 'To Laminate', 'Laminating' or 'Glassing In' means to apply a lay-up of 'Resin Mix' and glassfibre whilst 'A Laminate' refers to one layer of resin and glassfibre.

Useful fact: 450g/m² (1½ oz/ft²) CSM, with a resin to glass ratio of 2½ to 1, gives a thickness of about '40 thou' i.e. 6 layers equals about 6.35mm (1/4").

Tools of the Trade (Illus. 61)

include:

Cheap polythene buckets in which to mix the resin and catalyst and contain it for application.

Cheap paint or GRP brushes for stippling the resin.

Lambswool and paddle or washer rollers to consolidate the resin and glass laminate.

Illustration 61   GRP tools of the trade

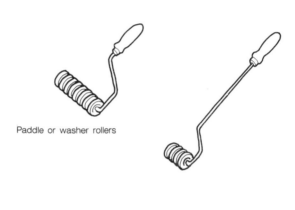

Paddle or washer rollers

Cheap polythene or plastic bucket

Laminating brush

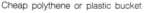

Lambswool roller

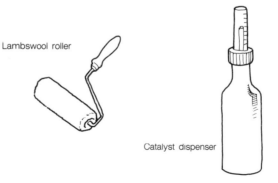

Catalyst dispenser

Trimming knife and spare blades.

Catalyst dispenser.

A large pair of scissors to pre-cut the mat to the approximate size.

A small set of hand scales to weigh the resin (in the bucket).

An electric fan heater.

A decorator's wallpaper type table on which to measure and cut mat to size.

For the application of small quantities of resin mix, plastic lemonade bottles and vinegar shakers with the tops cut off are very useful but do not use glass containers.

Hints on Application of GRP Laminate

The average ratio of resin to chopped strand mat is 2 to 2½ parts of resin to one part of mat. Usually resin is purchased pre-accelerated and only requires the addition of a carefully measured quantity of catalyst.

The amount of catalyst controls the cure time of the lay-up, but an average measure is 4cc to 0.45 kg (1lb) of resin. This gives an average bucket life of 20 minutes and the process cannot be held up or reversed. But note that the percentage of catalyst to be added is very dependent on prevailing weather conditions. The warmer the day the less catalyst is required and, conversely, the colder the day the more catalyst is needed. As the catalyst is an exothermic activator (that is it produces heat), the more catalyst used the 'hotter' the mix and the 'faster' the cure.

A further, often forgotten fact is that the humidity must not be too high and damp days are likely to result in humidity being an adverse condition. The only way of coping with this problem, outside of a factory controlled situation, is to heat up the surrounding air thus reducing the humidity and, incidentally, aiding the laminates to set off more quickly. An electric fan heater is ideal for the purpose. Make sure it's an old one as somehow it will end up covered with resin and mat — a fact not welcomed by the 'soulmate' when he or she wishes to warm up the guest bedroom!

It is a good idea to test a sample mix in order to check the ratio is correct. Enquire of the GRP supplier for further back up information, if required.

Points to Remember

1. Always rough up the area to which the laminate is to be applied with very coarse sandpaper, an old file, hand wire brush, rotary wire brush or grindette. Then clean with acetone, bearing in mind later strictures in respect of acetone in the last paragraph of this section. If in doubt apply a proprietary, recommended GRP Yacht Cleaner.

2. Employ polythene buckets to mix the resin, and have two or three available. Rotate them, as 'hot-bedding' a new mix into a recently used bucket can result in it being activated too quickly by the residue of the now fast curing left overs.

3. Do not mix more than 0.9-1.8 kg (2-4 lb) of resin. The bucket life must not be exceeded and once the solution goes rubbery it should be left to go off. An unused resin mix sets in a solid block and can be knocked out of the bucket and dustbinned.

4. To 'wet out' or impregnate the mat use a piece of hardboard (or similar), apply some catalysed resin to the board, lay the mat (cut to the approximate size) on the resin coat and apply more resin to the top of the mat, pulling it through by stippling with a hard brush. Then coat the surface to be laminated with some resin, apply the already wetted out mat and stipple again.

Apart from brushes to stipple out the wetted mat there are a variety of lambswool and paddle washer rollers. Lambswool rollers are used for initially applying resin, whilst brushes and washer rollers pull the resin through the layer of mat being applied and ensure an air free lay-up. Do not over-roll otherwise the laminate just spreads out further and further and further . . . .

5. Do not apply more than two layers of mat at a time as the heat developed can, for instance, ignite nearby woodwork and cause distortion of existing laminates.

6. Trim when the laminate is just going off.

7. Put some acetone in two containers, one in which to place dirty laminating tools after use and another with which to remove any excess resin mix, including drips or runs on existing laminates. When the 'duty' container becomes too 'gungy' throw the sludgy solution away and start a new pot.

8. Where bulkheads and interior mouldings are being laminated in position it is best to mask up the surrounding area, thus ensuring a clean edge as well as protection for the surfaces of the bulkheads or other woodwork. Brown packing paper held on and edged with masking tape is the usual method where laminating above a vertical surface or simply masking tape when laying up to a pre-determined edge.

9. Resin and CSM can cause severe skin irritation, if not dermatitis. Prior to going into action, apply barrier cream to the hands and lower arms and, whilst actually laminating, wear rubber 'washing up' gloves. When the job is completed clean up with acetone, which results in a sticky feeling, scrub with soap and finish off with plenty of handcream.

10. Be very, very careful when using or storing catalyst as it can cause severe injuries to the eyes if splashed around and is highly volatile. Even when carefully stoppered catalyst must be stored well away from other materials.

11. Whilst laminating large areas, styrene fumes are released which can, under certain circumstances such as lack of adequate ventilation, cause severe headaches or light-headedness.

12. Do not smoke when working with GRP and ask long suffering friends who have been cajoled into viewing one's handiwork to resist 'lighting up'.

Illustration 62   GRP repairs

62a   Cut back the damaged laminates to solid material

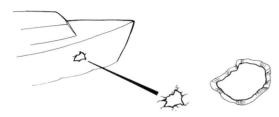

After jig-sawing the bulk use a grindette to finish off (not forgetting to wear eye protection), bevel the surround, clean and rough up the interior surface to enable the repair to make a good key

Do not bevel the gelcoat in an outward direction as the resultant repair will show up as a band of shade

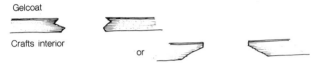

Gelcoat

Crafts interior

or

The external pad should be a smooth faced material such as formica or perspex both of which will bend to three dimensional curves.

Perspex may have to be 'encouraged' with gentle heat as for instance steam from a kettle, an infra-red electric heater (as fitted in bathrooms) or a fan assisted electric heater. The smooth aspect allows the gelcoat to have a satisfactory finish but do not forget to wax the surface of the pad to discourage 'stickability'. Apply two coats of gelcoat. If the repair is other than small, the pad cannot be held tight in place by tape and shoring is impossible then it will be necessary to fasten the pad with self tapping screws.

Build up the layers of wetted out mat so that they well overlap the edge of the repair and that the laminates are at least 25% thicker than the thickness of the GRP in the area of the repair.

62b   Working from the outside

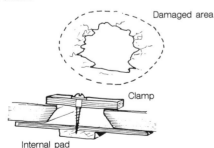

Damaged area

Clamp

Internal pad

Clean up, cut out the damage back to sound laminations, making the hole elongated so that the face clamp drops through the hole, prior to be turned round through 90°. Don't forget to bevel the edges of the surrounding GRP.

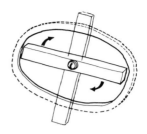

Prior to wriggling in the backing plate of, say, plywood, the outward face must be roughed up so the laminations will incorporate the pad into the repair after the job is finished. So as to make as good a job as possible, brush the face of the plywood with resin and apply two layers of wetted out mat introducing the board immediately the second coating has been applied. As soon as the two layers of mat have set off, the clamp can be unfastened and further laminations applied. When close to the level of the surrounding surface it will be necessary to smooth over the repair with a resin putty, after which two coats of gelcoat can be brushed in. The second, last gelcoat should be sufficiently 'proud' of the surrounds to allow it to be sanded back with wet and dry prior to polishing.

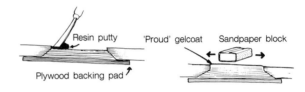

Resin putty   'Proud' gelcoat   Sandpaper block

Plywood backing pad

If the repair is on a sloping face it will be necessary to tightly stretch and tape down a sheet of waxed paper or polycarbonate sheet over the surface of the gelcoat to stop it drooping or 'dewdropping'.

Waxed paper or polycarbonate sheet

62c   Laminating in a cut-out

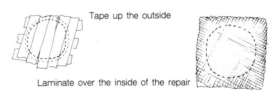

Tape up the outside

Laminate over the inside of the repair

'Back off' the cut-out as well as bevel the repair, tape the cut-out in position and then laminate the inside with 3 or 4 layers of 450g/m^2/600g/m^2 (1½/2oz) CSM, well overlapping the surrounds to the repair

Remove the external tape, float gelcoat into the crevice gap, leaving it proud of the surrounding surfaces. After which lightly sand the gelcoat back with wet and dry and then polish.

Damage Repair

There are a number of methods of repairing damage to the craft's shell, depending on the size. Large fractures or holes require the defaced material to be completely removed. It must be hoped that access can be gained from the inside as it is easier to achieve a satisfactory finish. This is because the gelcoat can be applied to an externally fixed, regular surfaced, glossy faced pad (Illus. 62a), thus producing a smooth, matching surface to the surrounds of the repair. Where the job must be effected from the outside it is necessary to introduce and hold steady an internal pad (Illus. 62b) against which to apply the wetted out mat.

To save a lot of work, where the repair is a flat area, it is worth considering letting in an already laminated cut-out, shaped to the hole, keeping the gelcoat face to the outside (obviously!). This is only possible as an option if access can be gained to the inside of the repair, when the job is comparatively easy (Illus. 62c).

Despite being outside the scope of this book's intention to be an owner's maintenance manual, where damage has resulted in a really big breach, and the craft is a current production boat, it is the practice to request the manufacturer to supply the relevant section of the moulding. It is then cut-in to fit, after which the procedures are as detailed above, taking care to ensure the section either side of the repair lines up accurately. But then it is to be hoped that this would be covered by insurance and thus executed by a professional firm.

Where the GRP shell has a balsa or sandwich core the basics remain the same (Illus. 63).

Illustration 63 GRP repairs to balsa core craft

63a The relatively thin outer skin relies on the sandwich core for support. Urgently attend to bruising or crazing in order to ascertain that the balsa has not been crushed. If the balsa is no longer supporting the outer GRP laminates 'panting' will occur followed by a breakthrough which will allow water to gain ingress and sabotage the very core of the craft.

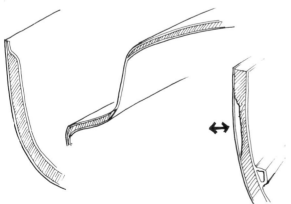

Differences to conventional repairs include:-
(1) the use of woven rovings in the place of chopped strand mat
(2) the necessity to cut away both the inner and outer skin and replace the balsa core, when in doubt

63b If the repair does not necessitate the total removal of the core, remove the balsa in the way of the outer skin & cut back so as to be able to tuck woven rovings in the undercut

63c Where both the balsa sandwich core and the inner GRP skin require attention:-
(1) Drill thru' the centre of the repair to locate the interior focal point

(2) Cut away the inner skin and hollow out the balsa core in such a way as to give a decent overlap on the outer skin — say a minimum of 4-5cm ($1\frac{9}{16}$ "-2"").
(3) Repair the outer skin as previously detailed but using woven rovings in the place of CSM. Replace the balsa core, bonding it to the inner face of the outer skin. If it is necessary to achieve a compound curve, the balsa can be built up in layers.

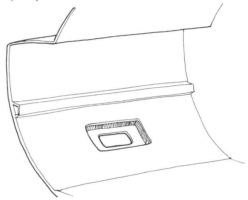

To obtain the necessary bond and compactness it is essential to apply pressure with weights or braces.

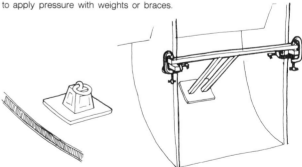

Osmosis

The treatment of this cancer of the glassfibre boatworld is a lengthy process but the following outlines some of the known problems, causes and corrections. An owner must make up his mind if it is a job he can undertake and see it through to the end. Certainly I have known one or three boat owners take on the job over a period of several years.

Osmosis, for which 'boat pox' is a slang expression, is a word borrowed from more scientific pastures to describe the phenomenon associated with GRP craft, wherein water is absorbed through the outer skin. Initially small pockets of vinegar smelling water form behind the gelcoat, as evidenced by blisters measuring some 1½ mm ($\frac{1}{16}$") to 3mm (⅛") in diameter. If left unchecked the pockets of water, and thus the blisters, expand in size to some 9mm (⅜") and at the same time the liquid diffuses into the surrounding laminate causing separation of the resin and the mat, the whole lay-up eventually going soggy.

Craft that have been bank stored every winter stand a very good chance of escaping the 'pox' and if antifouled with an epoxy based paint, the percentage chance of a damaged hull is reduced even further. It would appear that craft left afloat year in year out in warm, fresh waters are the most likely to suffer osmosis.

Incidentally it is important not to forget that water can also permeate from the inside so it is vital to completely mop out a boat every so often and, if not already in place, apply two coats of bilge paint or, preferably, epoxy resin.

It is suggested that the faults encouraging the malaise are often built in by the manufacturers. It would appear the reasons are as widespread as the use of dirty resins; undermixed pigment and or over pigmented gelcoat; resin to which too much catalyst has been added; damp mat and or emulsion bound mat; out-of-date catalyst and the application of only one (thin) gelcoat, instead of the two recommended. Tell-tale signs indicating poor manufacturing materials and, or techniques (other than craters, blisters or pinholes), include extensive star crazing, minute cracks and fibres poking through the gelcoat. This latter fault allows 'wicking' or the capillary ingress of water. Perhaps the oddest and most puzzling fact is that boatbuilders with a positive pedigree are not immune from producing craft that suffer the disease. Conversely some backstairs, railway-arch builders, making boats in technically unacceptable conditions, avoid the scourge — but that's life.

Treatment really rather depends upon the extent of the disintegration and the length to which an owner wishes to proceed. There are two main paths down which to go, namely the application of epoxy paints or the replacement of the gelcoat and affected laminates.

Undoubtedly it is best for new GRP yachts to be treated with a gelcoat protection system, prior to antifouling, such as that produced by the Yacht Division of International Paints but . . . . craft already in use should be hauled out and have the present antifouling removed. Assuming there are no signs of damage, apart from items covered in Chapter Two, allow the hull to dry out over a couple of months, abrade the surface with wet and dry paper (grade 180-220) followed by two coats of solvent free, 'two pot' epoxy resin, the second

being pigmented. After 12 hours (or so) apply a primer followed by a minimum of three coats of antifouling. If the first and third coats of antifouling are of a different colour, then the paint wear can easily be checked.

Illustration 64   Osmosis treatment

64a   Removing blistered gelcoat

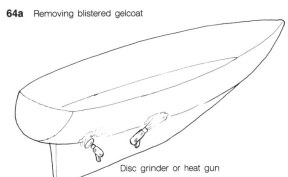

Disc grinder or heat gun

64b   Tenting up & drying out

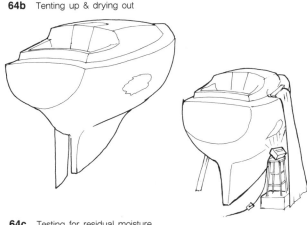

64c   Testing for residual moisture

64d   Trowelling on epoxy filler

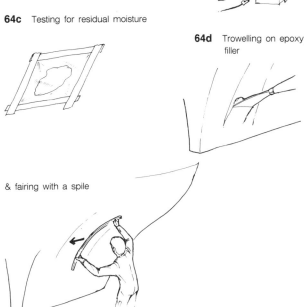

& fairing with a spile

'Minor' Osmosis

If osmosis is caught early on, treatment, although time consuming, is within the province of most owners but this presumes that only a small area is involved. The procedure includes grinding or heat gunning off the affected gelcoat (Illus. 64a). It is necessary to remove all the 'infected' gelcoat as well as any antifouling and then thoroughly wash with fresh water. After which allow the area to completely dry out, a process aided by surrounding the repair with a 'tent' of plastic and employing an electric, blown air fan heater rated at, say, 2kw (Illus. 64b). This treatment may help reduce the drying period of at least one, if not two months. Should a moisture meter not be to hand (and why should it be?), a practical method of testing for the presence of moisture is to tape a transparent square of plastic sheet to the area, leave for 48 hours (including two nights) and then inspect for evidence of condensation or fogging on the hull side of the patch (Illus. 64c). If none, then the area is dry, otherwise more time must elapse. When the drying period is at an end, brush on a solvent free, 'two pot' epoxy resin to a thickness of about 6 thou (150 microns). Not more than 24 hours after applying this first coat, trowel on a solventless epoxy filler up to about 2 cm ($\frac{3}{4}''$) thick and in a swathe up to 30 cm (11 $\frac{3}{16}''$) wide from keel to water-line. Initially fair in with a long, flexible spile or batten and, when cured, complete the process with a sander (Illus. 64d). Subsequently apply a second coat of epoxy resin with a roller to a depth of about 3 thou (75 microns) and, after a suitable interval, a final, pigmented coat of epoxy resin, again with a roller. Now the craft is ready to antifoul, as previously detailed.

Extensive Osmosis

Where osmosis damage is extensive, rectification may well be a job for a professional outfit as the gelcoat must be completely removed. The favoured method is wet grit or sand-blasting, the usual pressure required is 60-80 psi and the grit used is an aluminium oxide. An electric heat gun and scraper is the other popular process by which to remove the gelcoat.

After the gelcoat and any antifouling are completely removed, the procedure is much as that described above under *Minor Osmosis*, but more so and the drying out period may take up to 4 - 5 months. If the craft in question is in excess of some 7m (23ft) in length, and the job is to be carried out during an averagely hostile winter, it is desirable, if not mandatory, to keep the craft in a heat and humidity controlled atmosphere — that is under cover.

In carrying out the repairs above, acetones and etching paints are No, No's, — the possible chemical reactions of either causing more trouble than their use is worth. Please note that all paint and filler applications should be carried out in accordance with the guidelines set out in Chapter Ten but, more importantly, the particular manufacturer's instructions must be followed to the semicolon, more especially in respect of operating temperatures and humidity.

Illustration 65   Steel craft repairs

65a

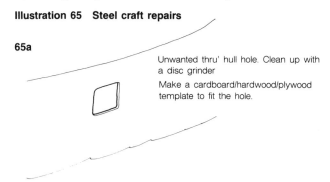

Unwanted thru' hull hole. Clean up with a disc grinder

Make a cardboard/hardwood/plywood template to fit the hole.

Cut the infill plate slightly smaller than the template to allow good weld penetration and bevel the edges with a grinder.

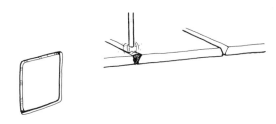

Tack weld round the plate's edge prior to completing the weld

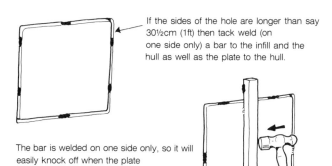

If the sides of the hole are longer than say 30½cm (1ft) then tack weld (on one side only) a bar to the infill and the hull as well as the plate to the hull.

The bar is welded on one side only, so it will easily knock off when the plate is completely welded in place.

65b   Corrosion points
Beware corrosion especially beneath seemingly sound paintwork

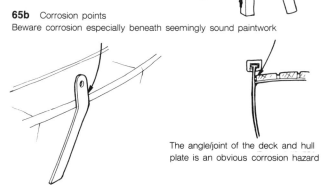

The angle/joint of the deck and hull plate is an obvious corrosion hazard

65c Persuaders

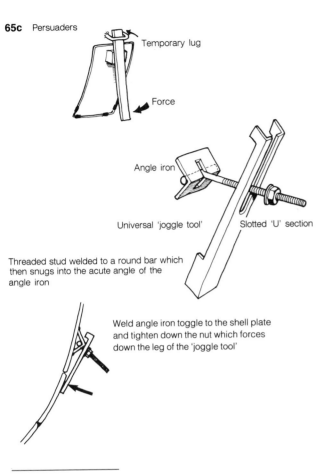

Temporary lug

Force

Angle iron

Universal 'joggle tool'

Slotted 'U' section

Threaded stud welded to a round bar which then snugs into the acute angle of the angle iron

Weld angle iron toggle to the shell plate and tighten down the nut which forces down the leg of the 'joggle tool'

STEEL CRAFT

Damage Repairs

Steel craft probably present less problems in this department than any other hull and deck material. Frankly, due to the large number of people who can use a welder competently and the comparative competitiveness of their service, it hardly seems worthwhile hiring or owning the equipment and becoming proficient in the art of welding. Even filling in unwanted holes is a relatively easy and inexpensive task (Illus. 65a).

There are various areas that require close inspection during an overhaul, more especially the crevices and crannies where hidden corrosion can take place (Illus. 65b). Internally it is important to ensure all limber holes are clear and that bilge-water cannot be trapped by one of the numerous frames and stringers that criss-cross the inside of a steel hull. It is usually quite easy enough to 'burn' extra drain passages wherever necessary.

When steel plates require to be bent round to fair in with the curve of the hull various dodges exist to avoid the necessity of using rollers (Illus. 65c).

One job that certainly pay's off is to insulate the craft's interior with two-pack expanding polyurethane foam.

I can do no better, once again, than repeat the relevant section from a companion edition to this book, '*The Boat Building Book*', a manual for home completion boat builders.

Illustration 66   Plywood graving pieces

Clean out the repair with a padsaw or jigsaw to an

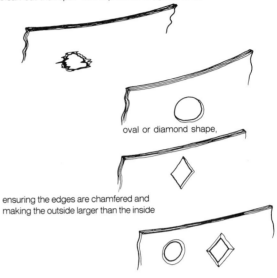

oval or diamond shape,

ensuring the edges are chamfered and making the outside larger than the inside

The patch should be similarly chamfered and the edges and inside face glued when fitted

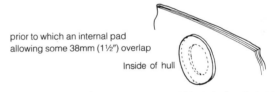

prior to which an internal pad allowing some 38mm (1½″) overlap

Inside of hull

While the glue is setting off, the patch should be tacked or stapled in position

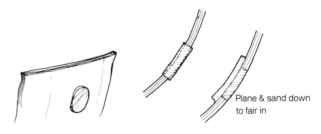

Plane & sand down to fair in

Where the repair is on a curve proceed as above but make the patch of a hardwood (rather than all the other complicated procedures necessary to get plywood to curve), plane and sand to the contour.

'Foaming Out

Once all the welding work is finished, shot blast and 'foam' out the inside of the hull with a two-pack polyurethane foam. Where applied to an unenclosed area it must be sprayed, for on the mixing of the two constituents a very fast chemical reaction takes place, the liquids foaming, expanding and forming multiple, closed plastic cells (which resemble the inside of 'Maltesers'). The resultant layer performs a number of functions for the price of one! It insulates in respect of both temperature and sound, provides buoyancy and acts as the perfect corrosion inhibiter. And don't worry, there is no way it will peel off for it sticks like . . . . . to a blanket.

Admittedly the buoyancy attribute is minimal, unless very large areas are treated, but the sound deadening property is an absolute bonus. Engine noise and deck clangs are greatly magnified in steel craft where no provision has been made to attend to the problem.

Incidentally, when foaming out an enclosed space, the two-pack liquids may be poured into the void and the resultant mixture 'left to get on with its own thing'. But beware, the rate and amount of expansion is phenomenal. I have seen the foredeck literally pushed off a plywood dinghy where foam was being introduced as a buoyancy aid. Little and often is the better way to apply the liquids, and a 'breather' hole other than the filler is advisable to allow for even expansion. Once set, the foam can be shaped and cut with a trimming knife.'

Illustration 67   A tingle

Fit a doubler inside, fill the crack with stopper and copper nail a tingle* over the outside of the crack.
Don't forget to mastic the hull face of the tingle

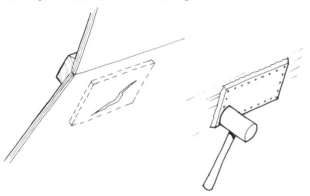

*A tingle is usually a sheet of copper with the edges bent over 'ever so slightly' so as to 'bite' into the surrounding material.

PLYWOOD CRAFT

One of the great disappointments to the boatbuilding industry has been the general failure of plywood to stand up to a number of years hard use, more especially where craft are allowed to experience severe winters without careful covering.

Cold and hot moulded hulls appear to enjoy greater longevity. Unfortunately, the topsides are usually constructed in the more conventional 'sheet' form thus suffering the usual shortcomings. These fall into the

Illustration 68   Panels, chines & frames

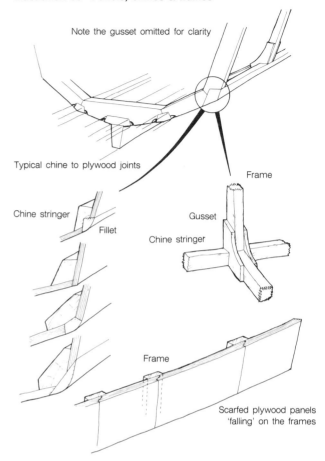

Note the gusset omitted for clarity

Typical chine to plywood joints

Chine stringer

Fillet

Frame

Gusset

Chine stringer

Frame

Scarfed plywood panels 'falling' on the frames

two categories of materials and manufacturing. Much plywood used is or has been of an inferior quality and, despite being stamped 'BS 1088', has not been of the same standard as the best British or Dutch marine plywoods. Manufacturing faults often centre around the failure to cap the end grain (See Illus. 22) and deck covering materials that have not been beaded in such a way as to completely stop the ingress of water around the deck to cabin join (See Illus. 15).

Once water has gained access to the end grain of plywood it soaks into the layers that make up the board. This delamination is greatly accelerated by frost expanding and freezing the moisture between the veneers. If this action takes place over a number of years, the plywood parts along the glue lines of the separate laminates and goes 'soft'. Sound plywood should 'ring', when tapped with a 'blunt' instrument while suspect portions of a panel have a 'soggy' sound and feel! With the above in mind, it will not need a Mensa intelligence to appreciate that it is very important to keep the bilges as dry as is possible. In addition to the preceding, general lack of owner maintenance often compounds the problems.

As part or complete sheets are used in the construction of plywood craft, repairs are easier to effect than might be thought, even substantial restoration.

Damage Repairs

It is permissible, where fairly small areas are involved, to simply grave or let in a replacement piece (Illus. 66). Alternatively, where the repair is nothing more than a split, it is just allowable to place a doubler inside, fill the crack or split and fit a copper tingle to the outside (Illus. 67). This latter method not only affects a craft's movement through the water, if the repair is beneath the water-line, but, perhaps more importantly, is not a particularly pretty sight.

Illustration 69   Plywood craft repairs

69a   The gripfast nail does just that! They usually require to be dug out

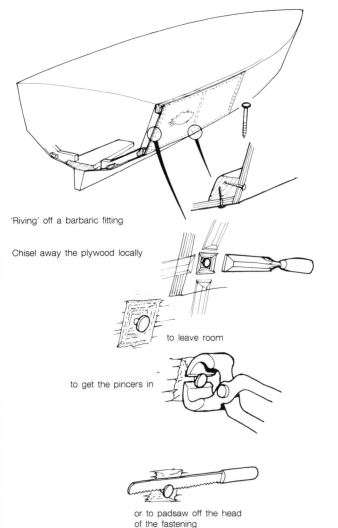

'Riving' off a barbaric fitting

Chisel away the plywood locally

to leave room

to get the pincers in

or to padsaw off the head of the fastening

69b   Cleaning up the frames & chines after removing a panel

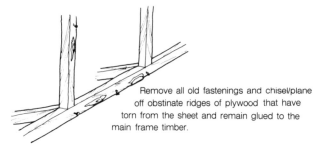

Remove all old fastenings and chisel/plane off obstinate ridges of plywood that have torn from the sheet and remain glued to the main frame timber.

69c   Conveniently positioned frames

Plywood panels butt jointed on a frame

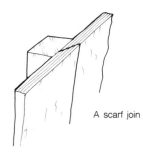

A scarf join

69d   Dummy frames or internal doublers

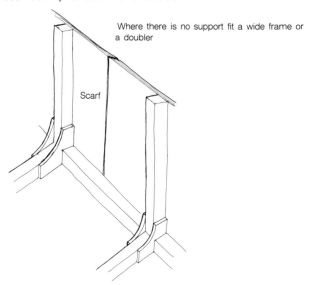

Where there is no support fit a wide frame or a doubler

Scarf

Make the doubler equal in thickness to the thickness of the plywood & bed on sealant

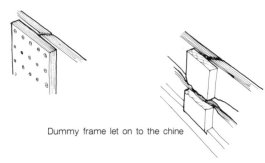

Dummy frame let on to the chine

69e Machine scarfed panel join

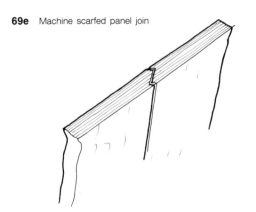

69f Making a scarfed joint

Finely honed chisel

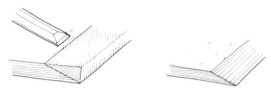

Move diagonally across the face & plane inwards from each edge of the plywood to stop the edges tearing

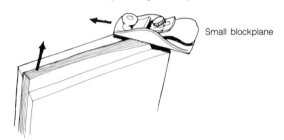

Small blockplane

Also clamp hardwood boards to each side of the plywood sheet, angling the hardwood to the scarf angle at the 'working face'.

More serious damage requires bold action, repairing panel by panel if necessary and Illustration 68 shows the general detail of a plywood constructed hull. Craft that have been glued and gripfast nailed in construction (but pray this is not so!) require (much as it should go against the grain, against the grain, oh dear!) a riving/ tearing method of removal (Illus. 69a). Where care (and luck) has been taken in removing a particular panel it can be used as the pattern for the replacement. The frames must be cleaned of plywood fragments and

fastenings (Illus. 69b). Hopefully, the portion removed reveals frames that are conveniently positioned to take the inset (Illus. 69c). If the join does not conveniently 'fall' on a frame, it will be necessary to fit a dummy frame and or an internal doubler (Illus. 69d). A problem that may well be encountered is that the boatbuilder used machine scarfed sheets (Illus. 69e) which requires an owner to decide whether to try and match the arrangement or to make a straightforward scarf joint. Whatever, if possible, resist the temptation to butt the joint. The correct method is to bevel the plywood, making a scarfed joint for which not only is patience required but a very sharp chisel and small block plane (Illus. 69f).

The conjunction of the hull to transom profits from being securely capped (*See* Illus. 22).

Decks

The following description is relevant to both plywood and timber craft. Where decking is suspect, it will be

Illustration 70 Canvas deck repairs

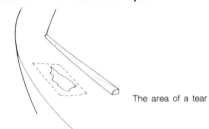

The area of a tear

Allow a 25mm (1″) overlap and tuck it beneath the surrounding area

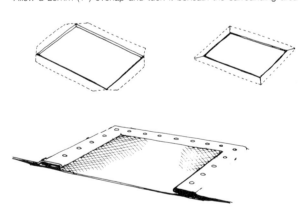

Slip in and beneath the overlapped edges a patch cut out some 38mm (1½″) larger all round than the area to be repaired.

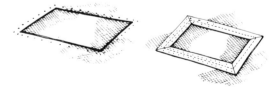

Then cut a patch to fill the outline of the repaired area thus 'flushing up' the surface

Illustration 71 Canvas deck replacement

71a Deck canvas trappings

71b Pattern up prior to cutting the canvas allowing plenty of overlap

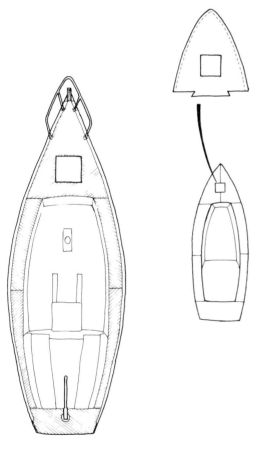

71c Tacked joins

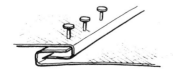

71d Stretch & fix fore & aft

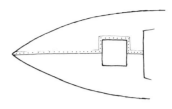

71e . . . and then side to side, wrapping the canvas around a batten with which to be able to pull it taut.

71f Gunwale trapping the canvas

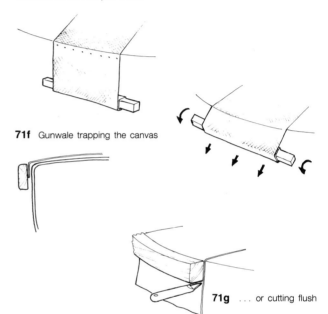

71g . . . or cutting flush

71h Capping the canvas joins

Brass convex capping
or
Copper weatherproofing extrusion

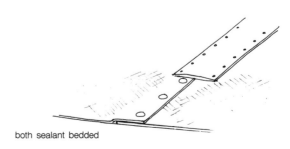

both sealant bedded

Illustration 72   Timber gunwale (& toe-rail) replacement

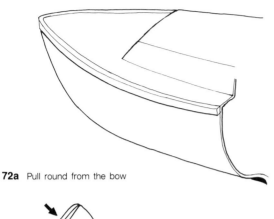

72a   Pull round from the bow

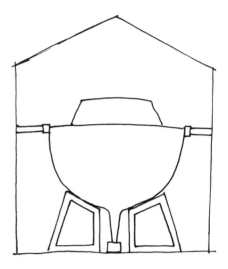

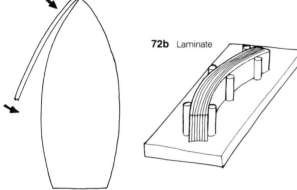

72b   Laminate

72c   Fabricate inner & outer strakes

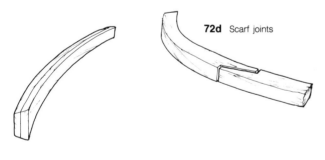

72d   Scarf joints

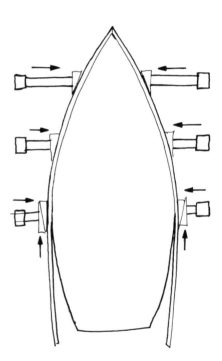

72e   No, no to coffin cutting

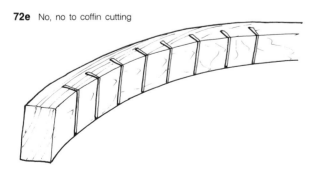

necessary to lift any canvas or composite covering, after removing the beading. When replacing deck covering this beading, that seals off the conjunction of deck to cabin, must be properly backed off with plenty of sealant run along the angle before final fastening. Ramin is the normal timber to use for the job and can be purchased in quadrant form, but as it tends to split, should be pre-drilled and countersunk prior to tightening down (*See* Illus. 15).

With any luck the craft will have a composition deck covering, simple repairs to which are detailed in Chapter Two. Canvas covered decks are another matter . . . . The problem with canvas is that years of paint applications may cover a multitude of leaks. Small repairs are similar to those applicable to composition deck covering, again as detailed in Chapter Two. On the other hand, when a piece has to be let in there are some differences, due to the fact that canvas is not usually stuck down with an impact adhesive. It is therefore necessary to modify the procedures as depicted in Illustration 70.

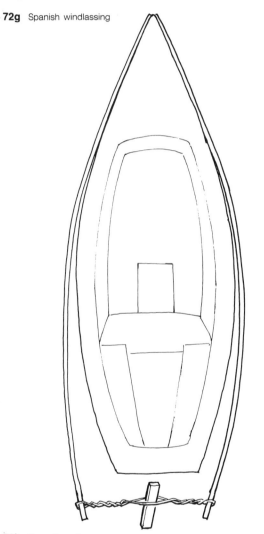

72g Spanish windlassing

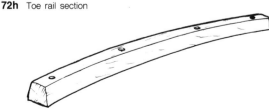

72h Toe rail section

At some stage the existing covering will have to be removed and replaced. The methods of sealing the edges of the canvas are similar to those used to trap composite deck coverings (Illus. 71a). Before hacking into the job of tearing off the canvas, take patterns and or measurements of the position of the various deck fittings — it is infinitely easier at this stage than to try and puzzle the matter out when the new canvas has been fixed down! Conversely, this is the time to reposition any inconveniently sited items. To completely remove the canvas it may be necessary to burn off those sections that remain stubbornly stuck down, after which allow the decks to dry out prior to smoothing them off. Any protrusion will, in the future, cause the canvas to wear whilst dips or hollows result in some of the surface not being completely stuck down, as well as stretching the canvas. After all the planing and stopping up, it will not go amiss to give the deck a coat of neutral preservative. Making patterns helps to determine the best method of cutting and laying the replacement canvas and do remember to leave plenty of overlap for the cabin sides, hatches and hull sides (Illus. 71b).

The unproofed canvas cloth weight should be between 227gms (8oz) and 312gm (11oz) with 283gm (10oz) representing a compromise between the weight required to maximise wear resistance and that allowing ease of handling and stretching.

It is possible to bed the canvas directly on to a deck overlaid with paint or one of the more traditional 'porridges', a version of which is a mix of varnish and white lead paste. Where the 'bedding' agent is to be paint, prime the deck first.

It is worth considering having some of the panels sewn together to reduce the number of tacked joins (Illus. 71c). The centre line and inboard ends should be tacked at 75mm (3″) centres using 12mm (½″), large head copper tacks, first stretching fore and aft and then stretching outboard and tacking around the gunwale edges (Illus. 71d). To fasten the outboard edges stretch the canvas out from the centre by wrapping the free ends around a timber batten (Illus. 71e) and pulling (and pulling) . . . . . Where the gunwale edge of the canvas is to be nipped by the rubbing band, trim now (Illus. 71f). Otherwise leave trimming until the rubbing band is back in position (Illus 71g).

Overlaps or tacking seams require a minimum of 50mm (2″) whilst a sewn seam needs a minimum of 75mm (3″) overlap. Long canvas joins should be capped by a brass section, although it is cheaper to utilise a proprietary, copper, door weatherproofing extrusion (Illus. 71h). Either must be bedded on sealant.

Do not apply gloss paints to finish off the job because they tend to promote cracking. Instead paint on some two or three undercoats, the first of which should be suitably thinned before finishing with a conventional deck paint.

Whilst re-canvassing the deck it is likely, if not an absolute probability, that removal of a timber rubbing band will result in so much damage as to make it necessary to replace sections, if not the whole strake (Illus. 72). There should be enough of the original left to act as a pattern but lacking access to a steam box requires the use of a few tricks to get the new timber to bend round the curve of the deck. One golden rule is to commence fastening at the bows (Illus. 72a), pulling the timber slowly round fastening by fastening. Other stratagems include laminating the bow section, where the sweep might be very severe (Illus. 72b); fabricating the strake from an inner and outer timber (Illus. 72c) and or constructing the replacement in short, shaped, scarfed pieces around the sharpest part of the curve (Illus 72d). To be deprecated is coffin cutting (Illus. 72e). Aids to help pull the timber round the gunwale include wedging off handy, shelter uprights (Illus. 72f) and Spanish windlassing at the stern of the craft. This reminds me to remind readers to cut the rubbing strake overlong leaving sufficient overhang to carry out the last manoeuvre (Illus. 72g).

Where applicable, the above rejoinders can be applied to the replacement of a wooden toe-rail (Illus. 72h) including lamination, fabrication and scarfed sections to help achieve the necessary shape.

Repairs to moulded plywood hulls draw on the techniques used for both plywood and timber craft.

TIMBER CRAFT

This is an extensive subject, and the possibility of an owner successfully carrying out repairs very much depends on the extent of the damage and the method used to build the hull. Craft are usually framed and the hull timbers attached to them by carvel or clinker methods of construction (*See* Illus. 23).

Most cruising boats, be they motor or sail powered, are carvel built so I have concentrated on this method of construction.

Repairs

Hull timbers or frames, are not outside the ability of an averagely 'gifted' owner. Frames (and ribs and futtocks for that matter) are easiest repaired by fitting a doubler to the suspect timber, which saves incurring the consequent and possibly extensive work in completely replacing the offending timber (Illus. 73). Some methods of 'taking shapes' are detailed in Illustration 74. If it is necessary to replace a frame read on.

Small splits in a plank can be patched with a tingle (*See* Illus. 67). Badly cracked, split or stoved planks may be repaired by 'letting' in replacement sections (Illus. 75a & b). When removing and replacing the odd plank, protect the faces of adjoining timbers with either

Illustration 73 Frames, ribs & futtocks

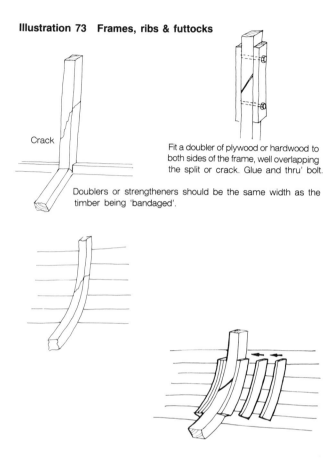

Crack

Fit a doubler of plywood or hardwood to both sides of the frame, well overlapping the split or crack. Glue and thru' bolt.

Doublers or strengtheners should be the same width as the timber being 'bandaged'.

Similarly for a cracked rib. Here plywood will probably be easier to fit to the required shape — even if it is necessary to build up or laminate a number of plywood sections together to achieve the necessary width.

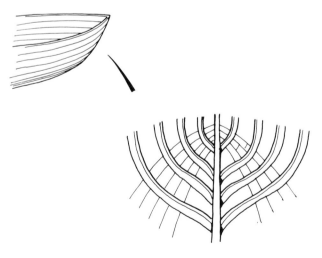

The difficulty is that due to the compound curves of a boat hull it can difficult to accurately bed a replacement timber to the shapes without 'achieving' a few high spots.

Illustration 74 Taking shapes . . .

To follow this curve lay a roughly shaped template close to the shape and using a block & pencil (a spiling block) transfer the undulations.

74a

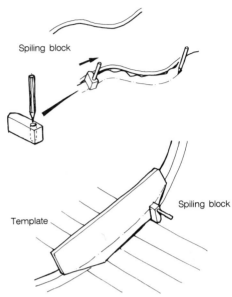

Spiling block

Template

Spiling block

74b Replacing a section in this area demonstrates the compound angle conundrum where not only is there the side to side curve to take into account but the fore & aft slope of the planks, which slope changes angle across the face of the timber to be replaced.

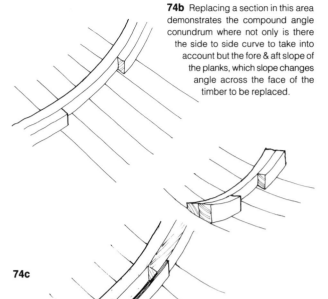

74c

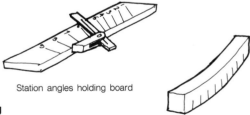

To overcome these difficulties place the shaped template (as determined in 74a) against the face of the section of the frame to be replaced and snuggled down on to the inside face of the planks.

74d

Then make a number of 'station' marks on both the hull and the template and number them.

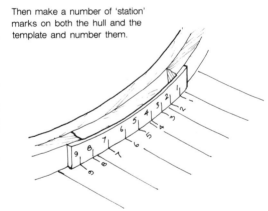

74f

Transfer these station angles to any clean, square edged 'holding' board — for future use.

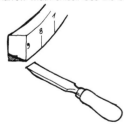

Station angles holding board

74g

Reverting to the template — mark off the side to side curve, on the replacement frame timber and cut to shape and length. Then mark on the stations. The hull face of the new frame now requires angling, taking the various angles off the 'holding' board, and chiselling the requisite angle at each station with a narrow width chisel. Use the bevel as a jig.

74e

Remove the template and replace with a straight edged piece of plywood clamped to the face of the frames and take the particular angle at each station mark.

Bevel

Join up the angled flats with a plane and spokeshave to achieve the smooth contoured hull face.

Illustration 75   Replacement planks

Where possible use the old plank as a pattern but . . .
simple replacements can be spiled as follows

75a   (1)

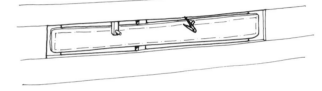

Frame

Butt block

Butt block

Spiling batten

Spiling batten temporarily nailed in position which saves offering up a heavy
plank and having 3 pairs of hands!

(2) Hardwood spiling block which can have a
number of 'pencil tight' holes drilled through
for ease of spiling different widths.

The spiling block and or dividers fixed setting must be wider than the largest
gap between the existing planks and the spiling batten. Once the spiling batten
is marked it is transferred to and placed on the replacement plank timber.

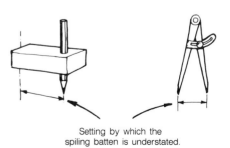

(3)   To the marked outline on the spiling batten must be added the fixed setting
width of the spiling block (or dividers) — because this is the amount by which
the outline marked on the spiling batten has been understated. Okay so far?

Setting by which the
spiling batten is understated.

To do this nail straight edged, narrow battens along the inside edge of the
spiling batten marks.

(4)   Narrow battens following the inside outline of the spiling batten

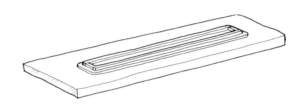

(5)   Then measure/mark out by the understated width of the spiling block
or dividers. This gives the actual profile of the outside edge of the plank.

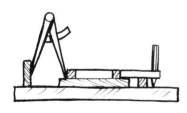

Beware not to tilt off the square otherwise the plank width will be reduced!

See below for details of how to fair the plank into the space (Illus. 75b) and
to the frame(s) (Illus. 75c).

75b

Where several planks have been removed an extension batten should follow the sweep of the existing plank from which it extends.

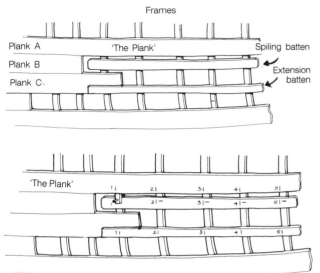

Mark off frame 'stations' on 'The Plank', the spiling batten and the extension batten.

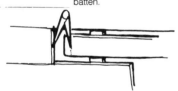

Using a spiling block or dividers, mark off a 'fixed measurement' (as in Illustration 75a) on the top of the spiling batten at the frame stations. The measurement chosen should be the maximum gap between 'The Plank' and the spiling batten, plus say 12mm (½").

Mark off the measured distance between the first frame station of the spiling batten and the adjacent plank end (Plank B), recording the measurement which determines the length of the plank in this (left-hand) direction.

Remove the spiling batten, transfer and fix to the timber to be used as the new plank, which should be somewhat thicker than the existing planks to allow for planing down to size and cutting in around the frames, if necessary.

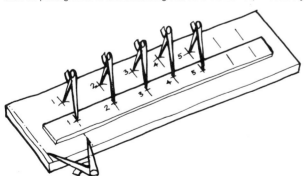

From the spiling batten mark off, on the new timber plank, the frame stations, the spiling batten outline plus the fixed measurement as detailed above (See Illus. 75a, (4) & (5)) and, using the recorded plank end measurement detailed above, mark off what is to be the plank end.

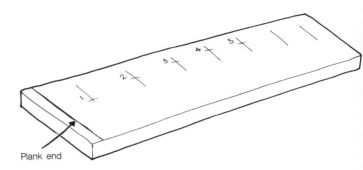

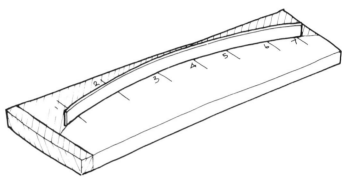

Remove the spiling batten, and using a flexible, straight edged batten, piece of perspex or thin piece of ply join up the various 'fixed measurement' marks at the frame stations and pencil in what is the top edge of the new plank.

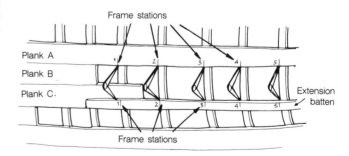

Now the top and near end of the new plank can be sawn, the plank turned over, the frame stations transferred to the back or inside face of the plank using a square (remembering to have marked TOP & STERN (or BOW) to the appropriate edges).

Remember the extension batten? Note this has been detailed as fixed to the lower edge of the adjacent plank (Plank C) to our new plank only because the 'eye-lining' in this case was easier.

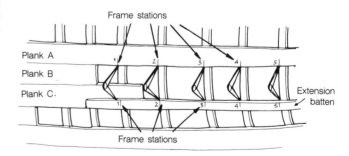

It could well have been fixed at the top edge of this particular plank. Whatever, this is now to have its hour and glory as it will determine the 'new plank's' width.

If the extension batten is adjacent to the new plank it will only require a straight measurement of the frame stations from Plank A to the top face of the extension batten.

If at the bottom the measurement should be made from Plank A to the bottom edge of the extension batten, deducting the width of Plank C at the various frame stations.

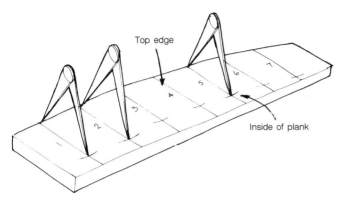

Top edge

Inside of plank

Transfer the width measurements to the inside of the 'new plank' at the frame stations and with a flexible batten join up the marks and cut the bottom edge, remembering to keep to the outside edge of the drawn line — it is always easier to take some more off, not so easy to put it back on!

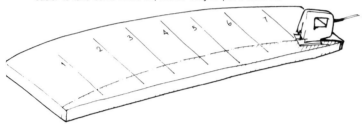

Now all that remains is to offer up the new plank and after finally fitting to the gap, mark off the frames width and position on the inside of the plank. Do not, I repeat do not, attack the face of the frame in order to snugly fit the plank but hatch out the inside of the plank with a chisel using small templates of the frame face outline to obtain the necessary curvature.

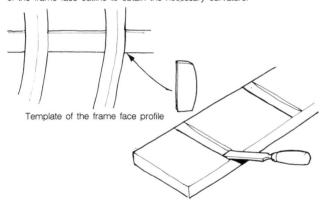

Template of the frame face profile

Prior to final fitting it will be necessary to plane off the caulking rebate. To achieve the correct dimensions measure off the existing planks. It is preferable to leave the top edge square and untouched so that wedges applied to this face, if necessary, will not tend to fall away. (*See* Illus 76, Plank persuaders)

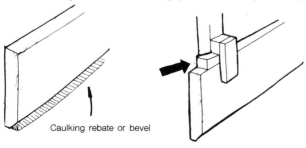

Caulking rebate or bevel

Where replacing a number of planks, DO NOT line up the plank ends, pretty I know but it weakens the structure!
Space the plank ends out by at least 2 frames and vertically make sure there are 2 planks in between ends that do approximate.

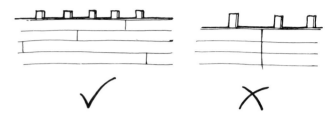

75c Butt Doublers (or block)

Where a plank join does not 'fall' conveniently on a frame it will be necessary to fit a butt doubler. Make sure the pad is angled so as not to trap moisture

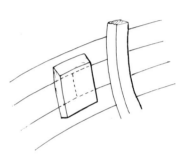

Fastenings should be spaced as above

The butt doubler must be a minimum of the same thickness as the planks, overlapping the planks above and below by some 380mm (1½"). Ensure the grain of the doubler runs vertical, that is the other way from the grain of the planks.

Illustration 76 Plank persuaders

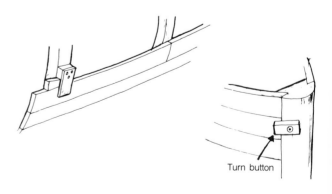

Turn button

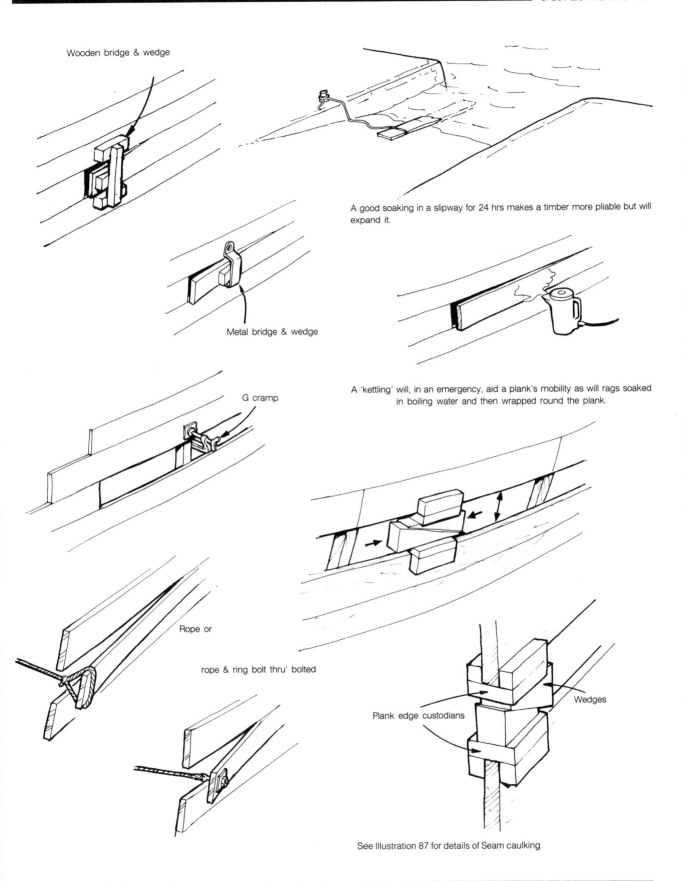

Wooden bridge & wedge

A good soaking in a slipway for 24 hrs makes a timber more pliable but will expand it.

Metal bridge & wedge

A 'kettling' will, in an emergency, aid a plank's mobility as will rags soaked in boiling water and then wrapped round the plank.

G cramp

Rope or

rope & ring bolt thru' bolted

Wedges

Plank edge custodians

See Illustration 87 for details of Seam caulking

thin pieces of plastic slid into the gap or, if space allows, slithers of hardwood. Where plank joins do not 'fall' conveniently on a frame it will be necessary to fit a butt block or a doubler (Illus. 75c). Assuming that a steambox is conspicuous by its absence, the pliability of a plank can be increased by wrapping it in hot rags or even soaking the timber. To help 'persuade' the plank into position there are a number of dodges apart from employing a couple of 'Minders' (Illus. 76).

Incidentally remember, if the original was fastened thru' the frames, to drill from the inside outwards. The plank should be treated with a wood preservative and the frame face to plank glued or compound bedded. After the final fitting of one or more planks, fair off the surface with a plane and sander using a flexible batten or spile to check the sweep (Illus. 77).

Illustration 77   Checking the fairing

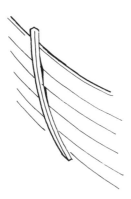

Plank ends at the transom often receive rough punishment on canal and river craft where lock walls are a constant 'aggressor' (Illus. 78). It may be possible to clean away the damaged bits and pieces and drive some copper nails in at various angles to provide a key for a paste of epoxy resin impregnated with sawdust. Personally, where at all possible, I prefer to both beautify the craft and sturdy up the construction by fitting 'sacrificial' cladding (See Illus. 22). Incidentally, I have heard this called 'quarter badging' but do not know the expression. Whatever, this solves the problem of crushed ends, at the same time as making a very attractive feature. I think it was the eye-catching Nelson workboats and launches that popularised the feature. Where unavoidable, new planking should be fitted but if it is necessary to carry out wholesale replacement of a number of plank ends it will be essential to renew complete lengths (Illus. 79). One or two 'shorts' may be fitted, without seriously affecting a craft's strength, but wholesale insertion might result in the stern end falling off!

Illustration 78   Transom damage

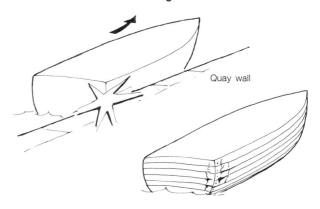

Quay wall

Crushed plank ends at the stern

Illustration 79   Transom & stern quarter plank ends

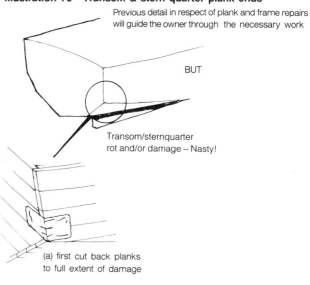

Previous detail in respect of plank and frame repairs will guide the owner through the necessary work

BUT

Transom/sternquarter
rot and/or damage – Nasty!

(a) first cut back planks
to full extent of damage

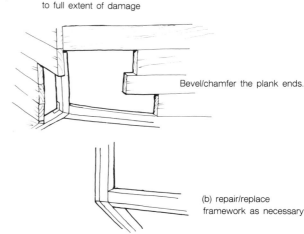

Bevel/chamfer the plank ends.

(b) repair/replace
framework as necessary

(c) then attack the planking. Doublers and butt blocks will be required.
Where circumstances allow it is best to fit doublers to fill the whole area exposed, rather than butt blocks.
Generally bed on sealant below the water-line — glue above

Replacement of, for instance, clinker planking, a garboard, stern post, keel, hog, forefoot, stem or stopwater are a more daunting prospect and outside the scope of this, a handyman's maintenance book. On the other hand, it is not beyond the skills of the average boat owner to 'dress up' the stempost and various deadwoods. (Illus. 80a & b).

Illustration 80   'Dressing up' a stempost or a deadwood

80a Repairs to the stempost

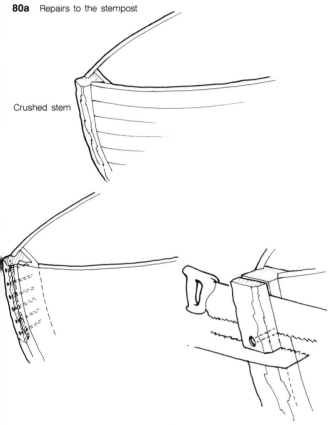

Crushed stem

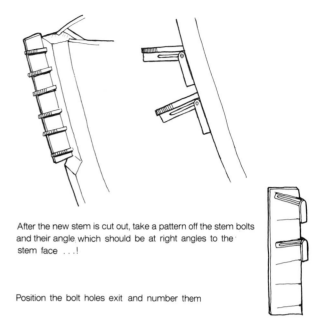

After the new stem is cut out, take a pattern off the stem bolts and their angle which should be at right angles to the stem face . . .!

Position the bolt holes exit and number them

Then record the actual angle, measured with a bezel, and mark them off on the pattern.

Withdraw the stem bolts and clean off the face of the stem with a plane.

Mark off the bolts position and drill thru' the replacement stem piece, at the individual measured angle, with a clearance drill to allow the bolts to easily slip through.

Remove stopping/dowels from the head of the stem bolts. Mark the timber to be removed. If the stem bolts will not easily drive inwards then saw down to the first bolt and across to a pre-set line just beneath the bolt. After which chisel out the unwanted timber and, if possible, now drive out the stem bolt

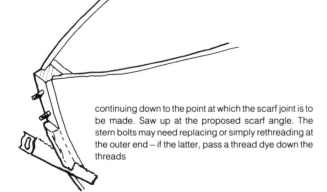

continuing down to the point at which the scarf joint is to be made. Saw up at the proposed scarf angle. The stern bolts may need replacing or simply rethreading at the outer end – if the latter, pass a thread dye down the threads

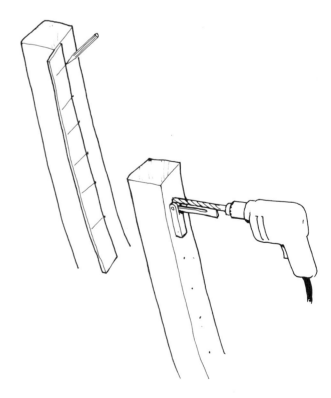

At the front of the replacement stem run a pre-set depth drill down to give clearance for the nut and washer.

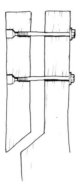

The two faces of the original stem and replacement capping piece can be glued or bedded on sealant. Prior to 'nutting down', place a twist of caulking cotton and daub of sealant beneath each nut washer.

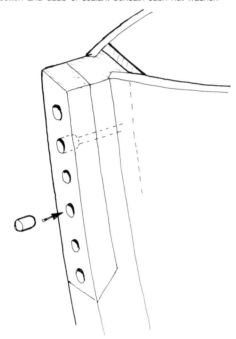

Bolt up, fair off the two with a plane and dowel the nut heads.

80b   Repairs to the deadwood   Stem

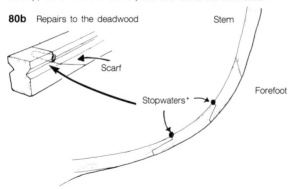

Scarf

Forefoot

Stopwaters*

* A softwood dowel to stop water progressing along the grain of a scarfed joint — a 'sort of' dampcourse

DO NOT, without expert advice, cut back beyond the plank line — the result can be similar to opening up a large, old spring wound clock working and prizing off the backplate . . .!

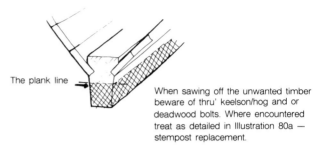

The plank line

When sawing off the unwanted timber beware of thru' keelson/hog and or deadwood bolts. Where encountered treat as detailed in Illustration 80a — stempost replacement.

Due to the possibly differing shapes at various points it may be considered desirable to laminate a replacement timber rather than cut one out of the solid — if so a jig will be required, after making a template.

To make a jig a sheet of shuttering plywood will suffice for the baseboard. In laminating the replacement timber err on the generous side to allow for cutting in & or bevels. It is easy enough to plane/sand some timber off if necessary — it is not so easy to put some back!

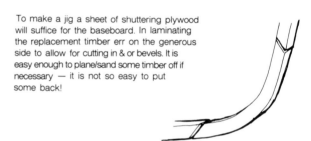

The fixed blocks on the outside of the curve should be fastened with cup screws set about 250mm (1″) off the template outline. The cup screws allow some swivel to accommodate tapered wedges to be hammered into the gap to tighten up the laminations whilst the glue is drying off.

A jig block or jaw

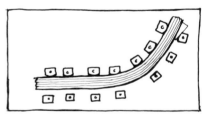

Laminations jig

Similarly, inside curve blocks should be fastened with screws and a cup washer so as to allow some swivel. Lightly round the face of the blocks so they do not dig into the inside face of the laminated frame.

A sheet of plastic should be laid on the face of the jig baseboard between the jig 'jaws' to stop the laminated section having to be prised off the baseboard when set. Build up the laminated sections of thin battens or slips of plywood with the inside faces well glued.

The template originally made to fashion the jig can be used to cut the lamination to shape, including any scarf joints, prior to offering up for final fitting. One other point to watch out for is that no thru' keel bolts encountered in the surgery are left unfastened!

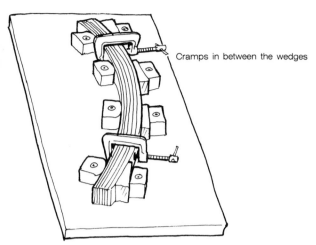

Cramps in between the wedges

Incidentally 'in-hull' frame laminations follow an almost similar pattern but . . . It would be nice to be able to attack the project without 'hindrance' but a multiplicity of chine and bilge stringers, and the sometimes acute bevel required either side of midships, often makes it impossible to 'cast' in one or even on the job — See Illustration 81.

Nor for that matter is the complete replacement of a frame (Illus. 81), although the job might be at the frontier of an owner's ability.

Illustration 81 Frame replacement

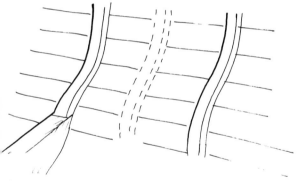

If possible, in the place of a removed frame, staple a sheet of waxed paper, plastic or aluminium foil over the area of the 'to be laminated' frame and drive a parallel row of nails either side of the frame outline.

Once the first two laminations have gone down the nails can be removed.

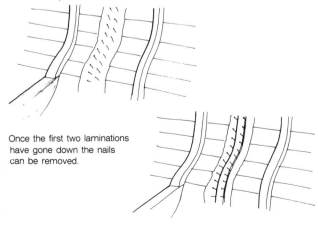

It may well be necessary to tighten up the first two or three laminations by screwing through them into the hull with a 'headed' and washered screw.

Wood/ply pad/washer & a 'headed' screw & washer

Ensure the laminations have the 'spare' glue wiped off as they are built up. Hard set glue does nasty things to the blade of a plane . . .

As soon as a few laminations have been built up it will be possible to clamp the embryonic frame with bridges or to work off the adjoining frames.

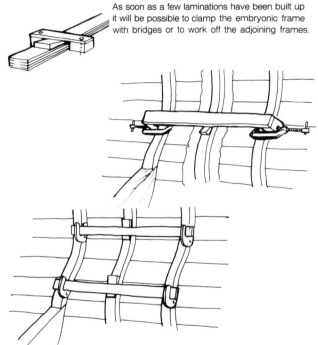

When the laminating of the frame is complete remove it, take away the 'underlay' and plane up, fair in, scarf where necessary, treat with wood preservative and finally fit.

Some situations may require the new frame to be scarfed and fitted with doublers.

Glue & screw the scarf joint & thru' bolt the doubler.

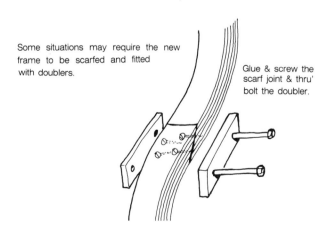

Repairs to cabin-sides that are made up of large planks is a matter of chopping out the damaged bits and graving in replacement pieces, with chiselled and regular, bevel edged shapes (Illus. 82a & b).

Illustration 82 Cabin-side repairs

82a Breaking thru'

Using a sheet of thick tracing paper, determine the most economic size to which to enlarge the hole to a regular 'graving size'.

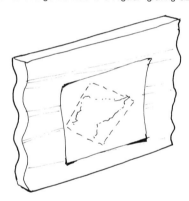

Jigsaw out undersize leaving sufficient surround to be able to chisel back a bevel, unless an angled jigsaw is to hand. If so it will only be necessary to use the chisel to clean up.

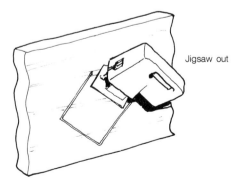

Jigsaw out

Make a template of the face of the hole, cut out the graving piece, offer up, bevel and trial fit, ensuring the repair is slightly proud, prior to gluing and forcing home.

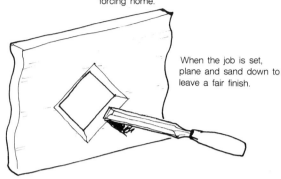

When the job is set, plane and sand down to leave a fair finish.

Repairs can be cut to various 'standard' shapes.

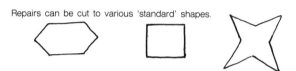

82b Graving a piece in

Where the timber is very thick or the repair small it may be preferable to let a graving piece into the surrounding timber without breaking through.

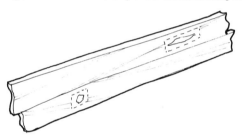

Brace & bit down, or use a router if available, to the minimum depth necessary and clean out with a chisel & bevel the hole edges.

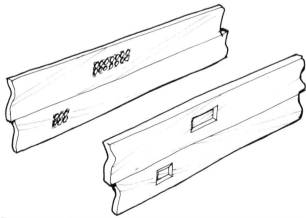

Template the surface of the repair to the surface dimensions and measure the depth required, cutting the graving piece so it will be just a little proud of the surrounding timber. Bevel the edges of the graving piece and make to fit prior to treating with preservative. Glue both recess and the graving piece and temporarily nail in position whilst the glue sets off. Then proceed as in 82a not forgetting to match the graining if the finish is varnish.

Attention might be needed to knees, (Illus. 83), side deck timbers, deckhead beams and or the deckhead king plank (Illus. 84a).

Illustration 84 . . . a deckhead kingplank & various timber joins

84a Side-decks, deckhead beams & king planks.

There are almost as many variations of cabin construction as there are positions in the Karma Sutra . . .!

Illustration 83   Knees to . . .

Rather than cut a replacement knee out of the solid, for which timber may be difficult to acquire, either:-
fashion from a suitable section of hardwood the necessary curve to allow a shaped set of laminations to be built up.

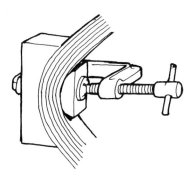

Glue the first laminate to the hardwood block so that the whole can be cut out

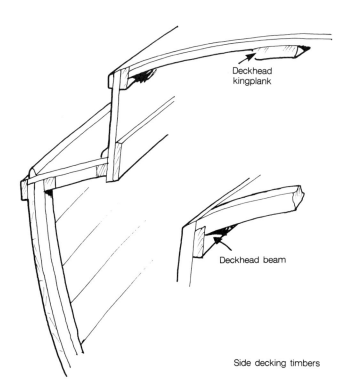

Deckhead
kingplank

Deckhead beam

Side decking timbers

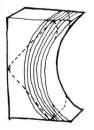

or:- laminate a large enough block to be able to cut out the required shape.

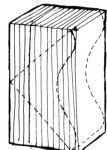

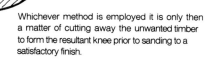

Whichever method is employed it is only then a matter of cutting away the unwanted timber to form the resultant knee prior to sanding to a satisfactory finish.

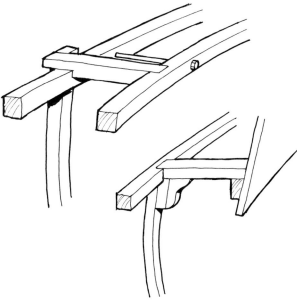

Similar techniques that applied to hull repairs are applicable to the topside and include bracing, doubling up and scarfing in replacement pieces. It is a great help to be aware of some of the possible timber joins employed —
See Illustration 84b.

Illustration 84b sketches timber joints that might be encountered in this jungle. Where possible, timbers should have their fastenings countersunk and dowelled (Illus. 85).

84b Joints in the 'jungle'

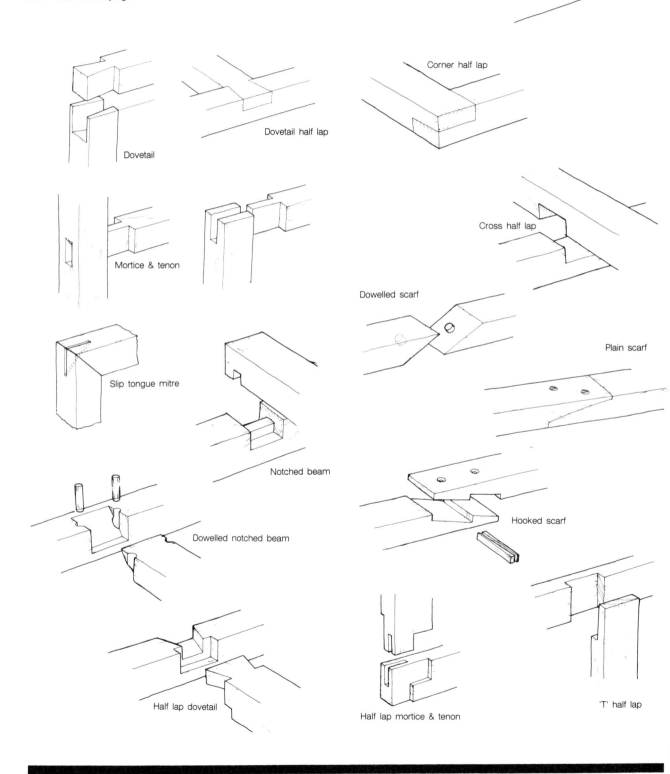

Straight half lap

Corner half lap

Dovetail half lap

Dovetail

Cross half lap

Mortice & tenon

Dowelled scarf

Plain scarf

Slip tongue mitre

Notched beam

Hooked scarf

Dowelled notched beam

Half lap dovetail

Half lap mortice & tenon

'T' half lap

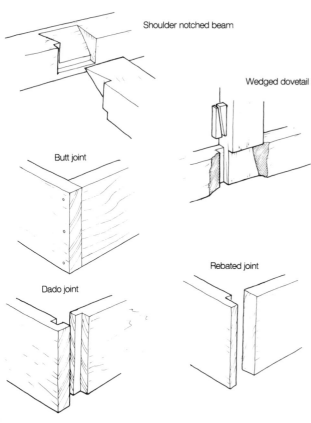

Shoulder notched beam

Wedged dovetail

Butt joint

Dado joint

Rebated joint

Illustration 85   Countersinking & dowelling

There are combination drill cutters to do the job in 'one hit' but otherwise three drills will b e required – root, shank & head clearance. If there is room, drill deep enough to allow sufficient depth to dowel or pellet

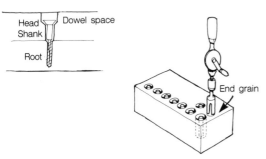

Head — Dowel space
Shank
Root

End grain

Dowel cutters can be purchased.

A very shallow dowel rather like a thick button.

The dowel must be 'backed off' at the bottom end and have a groove let into the length to allow excess glue to 'escape'.

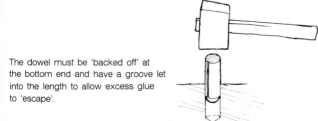

Double diagonal planking is usually only found on ex-services craft and more often than not requires professional attention. Due to the method of construction even the repair of a small fracture involves extensive re-timbering, the planks being laid diagonally with a calico or canvas interlining (Illus. 86). An exception to this sweeping statement is where the damage is restricted to the external planks but, as the timbers are more often than not of a thin cross section, this is rarely the case.

Illustration 86   Double diagonal planking

Where repairs are necessary to the outside planks it is mandatory not to damage the calico interlining or membrane. Once the fastenings have been located and the outer plank/planks cut through, slip a slither of ply between the outer planks and the calico. If the interlining is broken or torn soak some calico in boiled linseed oil and insert it over and around the repair.

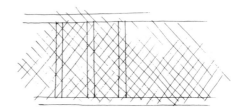

Generally the only way for an amateur to effect repairs to the inner planks is to remove enough outer planks to allow clear access to the area involved, cut out the damaged area with a jigsaw to a 'graving' shape, fit an internal backing place, let in a plywood graving, overlay a patch of calico and replace the external planking. Yes well, previously described repairs cover the various methods and skills required.

Just take a gander at this fastening pattern.

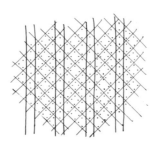

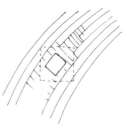

Seams, Fastenings & Caulking

Seams require attention if a number have 'started'. Fastenings need inspection if external paintwork shows signs of 'distress', staining and or weeping. It may well be necessary to strip the paint or varnish off to the bare wood and 'draw' or remove the fixing, be it a screw, bolt, nail or roving. A number of fastenings may have to be removed to check for signs of 'nail sickness' or galvanic action. The latter evidences itself as a 'wasting' and corrosive look — sounds like a Far East disease! If all is well, super, if not replacement is the order of the day and the crafts anodic protection must be closely inspected (*See* Chapter Seven). Chapter Five details various methods of removing fastenings.

Illustration 87   Caulking timber hull seams

87a   Rive out old caulking* with a tool similar to a horse's hoof pick. Old hands modify the handle end of a file by softening the tang with a burner flame, bending it round in the shape of a hook and putting it to the grinding wheel to sharpen up the trailing edge and form a point. The file portion can be bound with tape to protect the hands.

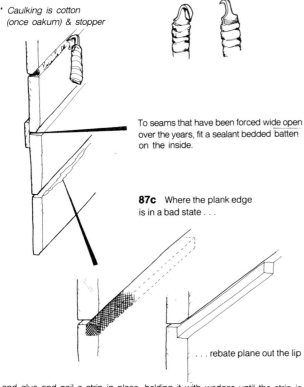

* *Caulking is cotton (once oakum) & stopper*

To seams that have been forced wide open over the years, fit a sealant bedded batten on the inside.

87c   Where the plank edge is in a bad state . . .

. . . rebate plane out the lip

and glue and nail a strip in place, holding it with wedges until the strip is firmly glued in place. Pin punch the nail heads beneath the surface to be able to clean up with a plane and scraper.

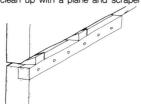

87d   A badly mauled plank edge can be saved by rebate planing out (with imagination).
After which proceed as in 87b but screw fasten or heavy nail the rebated strip in place.
Recess the screwheads or pin punch the nails beneath the surface.

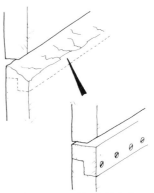

Prior to caulking, stipple some old paint into the seam.

87b   'Ironing-in' the caulking cotton

The caulking cotton is unravelled into say 3 strands and rolled or spun into a rope of cotton which is then lightly hammered in with a pointed edge iron, leaving even loops between the tucks. Every metre or so make the second 'attack' with a blunt edged iron when the loops are hammered in and then repeat the 'ironing' with a grooved tipped iron.

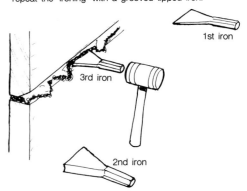

1st iron

3rd iron

2nd iron

The blows should ring on this third run through.
A tip is to rock the iron's whilst hammering which should, but probably won't, stop jamming. Don't attempt more than 6 metres at a go, overlapping the lengths.
Prior to applying sealing compound, stipple in some more old paint and then 'gun in' the mastic.

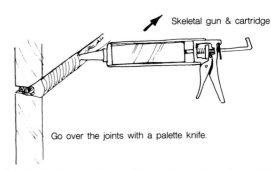

Skeletal gun & cartridge

Go over the joints with a palette knife.

Incidentally older hands swear by a caulking sealant made up in a mulch of linseed oil putty mixed with red lead powder and or paint, to which can be added some grease!

Hull seams might not require re-caulking every year but .... after raking out the stopping it may not be necessary to disturb the cotton caulking but here again Murphy says . .! When the seams between the planks have been thoroughly cleaned out (Illus. 87a), paint prime, then feed the cotton into the gap, tamping it down with wedge shaped bolsters, a chisel-type tool (Illus. 87b). Caulking 'rings' when it is correctly hammered home. If the gap is rather wide, twist the cotton round itself and bunch it up prior to 'paying' into the seam. If too much force is used to drive the cotton home, the planks will be pushed apart. On the other hand, not enough hammering and the cotton might come loose at a later date, added to which there may well not be enough room to introduce the sealant. If the gap between the timbers is too wide it is possible to batten the seam (Illus. 87a). Where the gap is not only too wide but the plank edges are scuffed, torn or split, it will be necessary to fit a replacement lip to the seams (Illus. 87c & d).

The great advance in modern day sealants and stoppers has resulted in greatly enhanced 'stickability' compared to materials available in days of yore, which were prone to dry out, detach from the seams and fall out — but don't tell that to the Old-Timers.

Timber Laid Decks
The timber usually used is teak and this type of decking looks marvellous but requires attention every so often (Illus. 88a).

Illustration 88   Timber laid decks

88a   Styles of timber laid decks

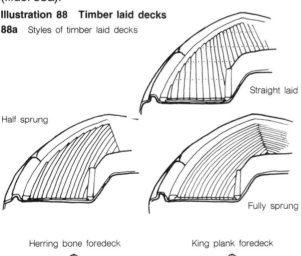

Straight laid

Half sprung

Fully sprung

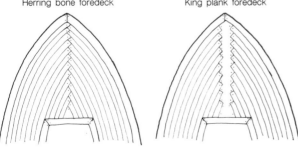

Herring bone foredeck   King plank foredeck

The method of 'manufacture' used on older boats was, for all intents and purposes, the same as for hull planking — deck planks being substituted for hull planks and deck beams for hull frames (Illus. 88b). The traditional stopping was pitch (Illus. 88c) but nowadays there are some excellent synthetic gun mastics

88b   Construction

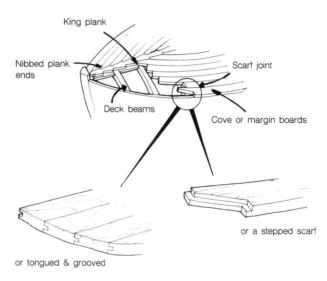

King plank

Nibbed plank ends

Scarf joint

Deck beams

Cove or margin boards

or a stepped scarf

or tongued & grooved

88c   Traditional stopping — pitch

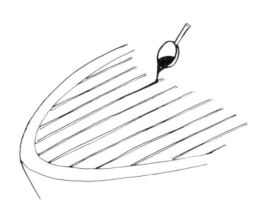

88d   Laid deck fastenings

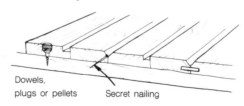

Dowels, plugs or pellets   Secret nailing

Note the sealant grooves or rebates will be constant, not a mix of, for instance, rectangular and V cut-outs but for the purposes of the illustration it has been necessary ...

88e Butt joints require a doubler & a stopwater
It is probably best to drill the two planks for the stopwater off the boat, in a jig.

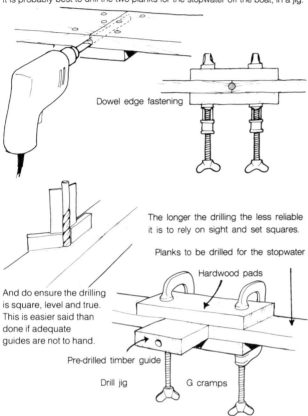

Dowel edge fastening

The longer the drilling the less reliable it is to rely on sight and set squares.

Planks to be drilled for the stopwater

Hardwood pads

And do ensure the drilling is square, level and true. This is easier said than done if adequate guides are not to hand.

Pre-drilled timber guide

Drill jig   G cramps

If the job is squared up with a level, then set squares and a level can be used with good results especially if a pre-drilled timber is fixed to the leading edge of the planks to start the drill true.

88f Plank persuaders

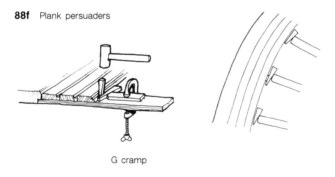

G cramp

'Upstanding guides' to enable a single plank to be let in

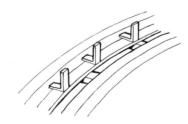

available. The problem with repairing traditional decks lies in the method used to fasten the decking. It is to be hoped that the fastenings are dowelled screws and not secret nailing as it is also to be hoped that the plank edges are not dowelled (Illus. 88d) nor that tongue and groove planking has been fitted (Illus. 88b). These latter require a certain amount of brute force, riving and tearing. Replacement planks are best machined from air dried and quarter sawn timber. The caulking seam cut-outs must be matched to those already in use, be they rectangular or V shaped. Plank joins are preferably placed over the deck beams and a stepped scarf with a caulked seam is probably the favoured joint (Illus. 88b). Where a butt joint is contemplated a doubler must be fitted and a stopwater drilled into the facing butt ends (Illus. 88e). 'Persuaders' may be required to curve the plank or planks into position and might include upstanding guides where a single replacement plank is being set into surrounding planking (Illus. 88f). On completion the deck should be sanded so the surface is fair.

Fortunately most modern day timber laid decks are placed over and fixed to a plywood underlay so fitting replacement timbers is a less exacting task, if for no other reason than that the sections used are much thinner and the assembly less critical.

To caulk the seams rake them out, sweep clean, wire brushing out any recalcitrant bits then firmly mask up either side of the seam to keep the surrounding deck planking as clean as possible. Skilled application of the sealant does away with the need for time-consuming scraping and sanding down. Before the sealant completely hardens up, but not before it has partially set off, carefully remove the masking tape leaving a neat and workmanlike job — we hope!

FERROCEMENT CRAFT

Damage Repairs

Where an impact has exposed the reinforcing mesh, allowing it to rust or causing it to be ruptured, then chip the ferrocement back until sound reinforcing is unmasked. The affected material is then cut out to leave at least a 5cm (2″) band of undamaged mesh, after which replacement reinforcing must be fitted, each end individually wired up to the surrounding mesh so reforming a composite shape. After which fix a pad or former to the external hull so as to describe the hull contour in the way of the repair. When the 'shuttering' is in place trowel a cement mix through the reinforcing from the inside of the hull — in much the same manner as the hull was originally manufactured (*See* Chapter Two for the cement mix 'recipe'). After about two days, when the cement has set, remove the external pad, sand down the surface and fill any depressions and join marks with trowel cement. During the curing time it may be necessary to cover the repair with wet cloths to stop cracking (Illus. 89a). Follow the painting instructions as set out in Chapter Ten.

To fix additional internal fittings it is only necessary to drill out the ferrocement. Use a masonry bit large enough to sink the whole bolthead and a washer into the shell, as far down as the reinforcing. Place the bolt in position and secure with an epoxy resin filler (Illus. 89b)

Illustration 89 Ferro repairs

89a Chipping back

89b Extra fittings & fastenings
To mount extra fastenings, drill out down to the reinforcing mesh to allow a bolt and washer head to be sunk into the recess

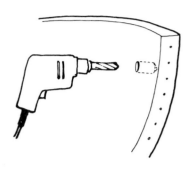

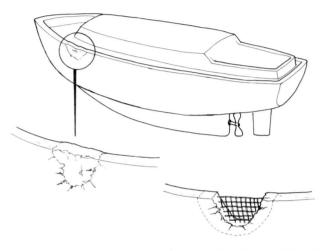

Chip out the cracked ferrocement to leave about 5cm (2″) of undamaged reinforcing mesh

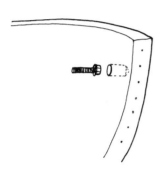

Wire in replacement mesh

Fit a pad to the external contour and trowel a cement mix thru' the mesh. Smooth off internally

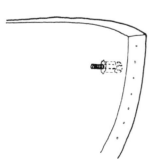

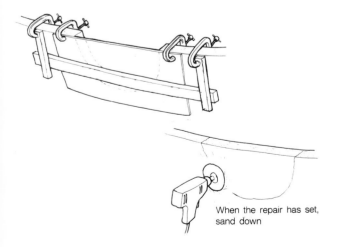

When the repair has set, sand down

Then secure the bolt with epoxy resin filler

ALUMINIUM CRAFT

Aluminium is very prone to electrolytic corrosion and great care must be taken in the selection of metals when carrying out repairs — even the use of different grade alloys of aluminium causes corrosion. Attention to insulation and anodic protection is absolutely vital. For example, it is absolutely necessary where a gunmetal thru' hull skin fitting has to be fitted instead of a plastic unit, that the following precautions are followed:-

1. Insulate the fitting and fastenings from the aluminium hull with backing pads, gaskets and sleeves (Illus. 90a). Suitable insulating materials include delrin, neoprene and tufnol. Nylon itself has the unfortunate physical property of taking up and retaining moisture, especially salt water! This is known as being hygroscopic and is not to be encouraged below the water-line when attempting to insulate two dissimilar metals.

2. Use sealants to which has been added some zinc chromate paste and or zinc chromate paints.

3. Fit zinc sacrificial anodes alongside each thru' hull fitting.

4. Use aluminium fastenings where practical and

5. sealant and paint as bedding and covering materials.

Loose rivets should be carefully drilled out and the next larger size fitted (Illus. 90b). In a long, riveted seam, it may well be that the plates were originally bedded on a sealant. If so it will be necessary to re-bed the seam, initially using a number of bolts to squeeze together the two plates. When almost fully tightened down, remove one bolt at a time and rivet (Illus. 90c).

Naturally, welding a crack is the best solution but, due to the difficulties of welding aluminium and the cost of the equipment, it is outside the scope of the average boat owner and should be left to the professional. Cracks not being welded require the ends drilled through, and a backing plate fitted. This should be bedded on sealant, after being shaped to and curved in the way of the hull or deck, and drilled out around the periphery at evenly spaced intervals. Initially bolt up the backing pad, thus squeezing down on the sealant, and finally replace, one by one, the bolts with rivets. After which fill the crack or cracks with a suitable trowelling cement and smooth off (Illus. 90d).

To correct large dents, drill a small hole in the centre of the depression to allow the stretched metal to retake its original shape (Illus. 90e).

Illustration 90   Aluminium craft thru' hull fittings & repairs

90a   New or replacement thru' hull fittings

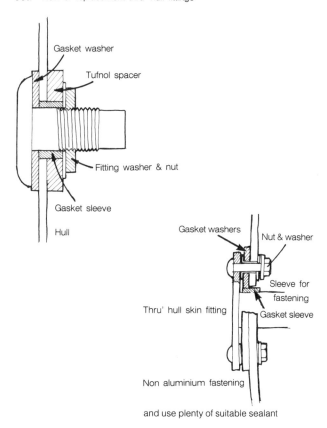

and use plenty of suitable sealant

90b   Loose rivets

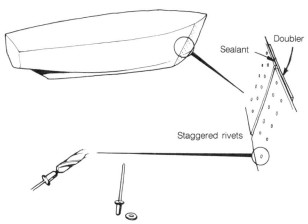

Drill out to next size up & fit a new pop rivet

90c Sealant bedded joints

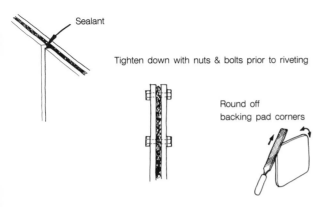

Sealant

Tighten down with nuts & bolts prior to riveting

Round off backing pad corners

90d Cracks

Weld cracks

If not, drill holes of a minimum of 1½ mm (¹⁄₁₆″), but not less than twice the crack's width, either end of the crack and pop-rivet a backing pad in place

90e Dents

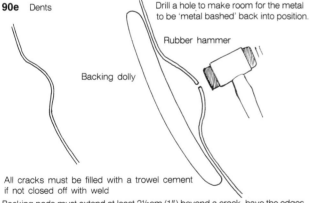

Drill a hole to make room for the metal to be 'metal bashed' back into position.

Rubber hammer

Backing dolly

All cracks must be filled with a trowel cement if not closed off with weld

Backing pads must extend at least 2½cm (1″) beyond a crack, have the edges rounded, be of the same grade material as the craft's aluminium and be bedded on sealant.

ENCAPSULATED BALLAST KEELS

This section pertains to craft fitted with internal ballast made up of other than cast-iron. Due to so many home completed GRP vessels coming on to the market with a sometimes horrifying jumble of alternatives to cast iron, the situation requires careful monitoring. The following may appear to be a rather lengthy treatment of the subject, but it is a very serious matter if left untreated.

Voids beneath the shell of a GRP hull can be checked for by tapping the external skin in the way of the ballast. They are revealed by a hollow sound and must be attended to urgently. Initially it is necessary to hand drill a pilot hole. Note that a hand drill is specified in case the craft's ballast has been poorly laminated over internally and bilge water has found its way into the ballast space. There is nothing worse than the possibility of finding oneself with a live, electric drill in hand and a fountain of water spraying all over the same (Illus. 91)! If water does emerge, drill a number of widely spaced holes, more especially at the lowest point of the keel and allow the liquid to completely drain off. Initially refrain from cutting out large holes, but slowly increase the size of the pilot drillings, in case loose internal ballast starts cascading out.

If the breakthrough of a pilot hole drilling results in water leakage, or be accompanied by a whoosh of air, then it is probable that the resin mix originally used to fix the internal ballast in place, failed to set off and is still 'working'. Apart from the fact that the ballast could break loose, any bilge water seeping down into the area can set off damaging chemical reactions in 'home completion' ballast of metal chunks and shot.

But before tackling that horror story, cut away large voids to a sufficient size to be able to squeeze in a 'porridge' of resin mix and finely 'diced' CSM. A cake icing nozzle is ideal for this task!

Test the laminations over the top of internal ballast by tapping and pressing them. Should there be any indication of hollowness, panting or 'give' then the lay-up must come off as it is quite possible that there never was a satisfactory bond with the ballast material. After completely removing the offending laminates place a fan heater in the hull in order to completely dry out the surfaces. After which, apply a thick overlay of resin putty to the ballast surface and, when set off, follow by at least six layers of laminate and then two coatings of gelcoat. To satisfactorily finish the job off, paint the surface with a suitable bilge paint (*See* Chapter Ten). If the ballasting material has decomposed, been eroded by rusting or appears to be unsatisfactory in any way, remove and replace it with a cold castable resin/iron ballast.

Illustration 91 Encapsulated ballast faults and a no, no!

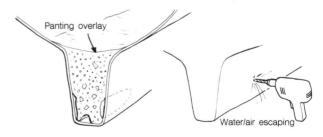

Panting overlay

Water/air escaping

7

STEERING, RUDDERS, STERNGEAR, ANODES & LIFTING KEELS

The 'engineering' and mechanical systems not only take a fair hammering during a season's use but are rather vital to a craft's movement through the water. They therefore require close attention during any refit.

STEERING

The simplest form is a transom hung rudder and tiller. Inspect the gudgeon and pintles for any untoward wear and absence of retaining split pins must be remedied. Although most applicable to timber boats, it is important on all craft to draw one of the gudgeon/pintle thru' transom fastenings to ensure that no wasting has taken place. Naturally the frequency depends on a vessel's age and construction. For a sea based wooden boat, the periodicity might be about every 3 years whilst the owner of a GRP yacht could stretch the task to, say, 5 years. Packing with washers can take some of the rattle out of a system, but do not mix metals (Illus. 92a).

The rudder blade, if plywood, should have been made of shatter-proof ply. Check no delamination has taken

place and fill any gouges. Pay particular attention to the leading edge of the rudder blade, be the construction of ply or GRP (Illus. 92b).

One other form of transom hung rudder, often employed on traditional, river motor cruisers, was actuated by wheel steering connected to the rudder by chain, wire and a quadrant or worm and rod (*See* Illus. 93a). This once popular method finally died away with the introduction of the spiral wound inner and outer or push-pull steering cable, known by various trade names, which include *Morse* and *Teleflex* (Illus. 93b).

Over the years the rudder stock has moved inside the boat to rotate within a hull mounted rudder gland. Where the rudder stock terminates close to the water-line, an inboard gland and stuffing box is usually fitted (Illus. 94a), rather in the style of a truncated sterntube installation. Where the rudder stock continues up to the top of the stern deck, the thru' hull fitting remains as above whilst the deck is fitted with a flanged, top mounted, screwed bush which firmly locates the arrangement. On GRP and ferro craft, as the top

Illustration 92   Transom hung rudders

92a   Gudgeon & pintles

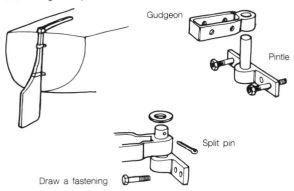

Gudgeon

Pintle

Split pin

Draw a fastening

92b   Leading edges

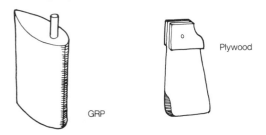

Plywood

GRP

Illustration 93   ..other forms of transom hung rudders & their actuation

93a

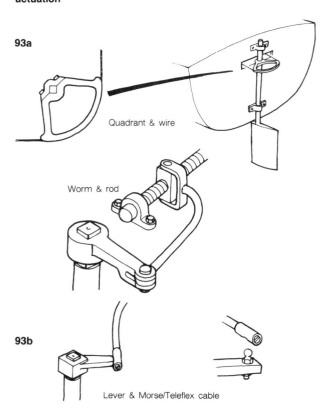

Quadrant & wire

Worm & rod

93b

Lever & Morse/Teleflex cable

bearing emerges sufficiently high above the water-line, it is only necessary that the rudder tube is 'laminated in' position, top and bottom, with perhaps a nylon bush at the hull end and a simple gland bearing on the deck (Illus. 94b). This latter make-up requires a high pressure wash out annually and a thorough greasing. Due to the inconvenience of getting to the bottom end of the tube, it is more often than not totally ignored (you know — out of sight, out of mind) thus it is worth considering fitting a remote greaser in order to deliver a 'life saving' dollop of lubrication every so often (Illus. 94c).

Smaller, lightly stressed spade rudders are not supported at their bottom end (Illus. 94d) but other, heavier craft will be fitted with a skeg and bearing (Illus. 94e). Naturally the skeg, and rudder to rudder stock fixings must be inspected, as must the rudder stock skeg bush, the bearing and packing at the inboard bearing and why not repack the greaser with new grease? The amount of wear and tolerances are more flexible than for sterngear and some slop can be tolerated before re-bushing becomes necessary.

Mild steel rudder gear must be wire brushed, the state of the anode inspected, the steelwork re-primed and painted (*See* Illus. 94). And do not paint over the anode.

Illustration 94   Inboard rudder mountings

94a   Inboard rubber gland

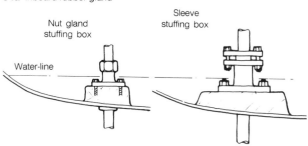

Nut gland
stuffing box

Sleeve
stuffing box

Water-line

94b   Deck mounted rudder gland

Hinged tiller fitting

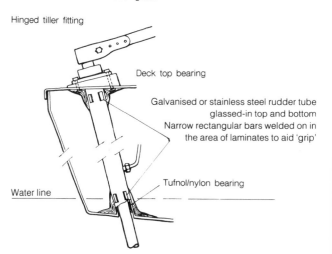

Deck top bearing

Galvanised or stainless steel rudder tube
glassed-in top and bottom
Narrow rectangular bars welded on in
the area of laminates to aid 'grip'

Tufnol/nylon bearing

Water line

94c Remote rudder tube greaser

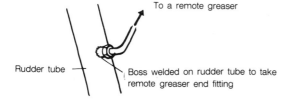

To a remote greaser

Rudder tube

Boss welded on rudder tube to take remote greaser end fitting

94d Spade rudder

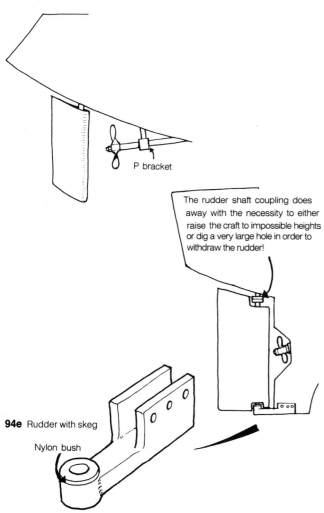

P bracket

The rudder shaft coupling does away with the necessity to either raise the craft to impossible heights or dig a very large hole in order to withdraw the rudder!

94e Rudder with skeg

Nylon bush

94f Mild steel motor sailer rudder & skeg

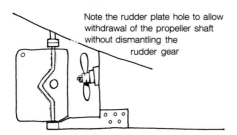

Note the rudder plate hole to allow withdrawal of the propeller shaft without dismantling the rudder gear

GRP moulded aerofoil rudders, with encapsulated rudder stocks, are usually two-pack, foam filled and it is essential to check that the rudder stock has not jarred loose and or that water has made an ingress. One of the problems associated with split moulded GRP rudder blades is that whenever a craft experiences a dead stop, the rudder stock's mass, being so much denser than the rudder blade, tends to try to go on (as it were). This results in a disposition for the stock to break out of the encapsulated surround. All this waffle is leading up to the fact that it is important to look over the rudder's join and if signs of cracking are present, chip out and re-gel the area (Illus. 95).

Illustration 95   Foam filled rudders

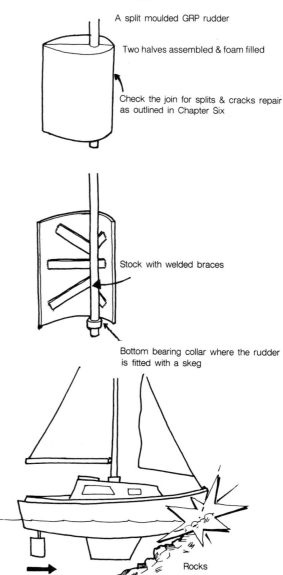

A split moulded GRP rudder

Two halves assembled & foam filled

Check the join for splits & cracks repair as outlined in Chapter Six

Stock with welded braces

Bottom bearing collar where the rudder is fitted with a skeg

Rocks

Craft mass pushes on as does dense stainless rudder stock while the rudder 'dallies

Generally speaking a rudder should not be able to traverse through more than 70°, as a reverse steering effect sets in, which results in the craft continuing in the direction that the helmsman is trying not to steer. Embarrassing! One of a number of methods of negating this effect may have been used and rudder stops, chains and or retainers should be examined (Illus. 96a, b, c, d & e).

Illustration 96   Rudder stops

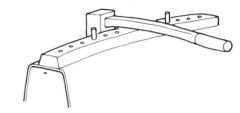

96a   Tiller stops

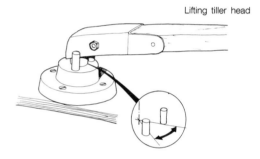

Lifting tiller head

96b   Quadrant stops

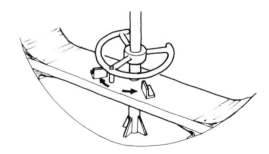

96c   Rudder lever stops

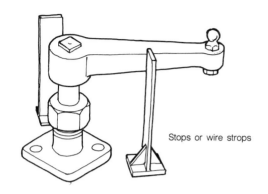

Stops or wire strops

96d   Skeg stops

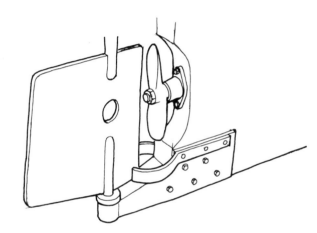

96e   Rudder chains

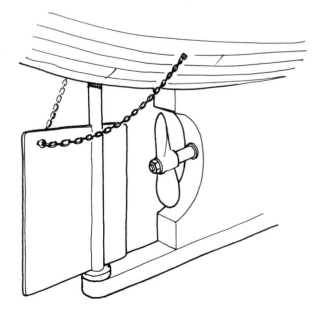

Wheel Steering

This option, fleetingly referred to above, may be operated via wire, chain and wire, proprietary inner and outer spiral wound cable, rod or hydraulics. (Illus. 97a, b, c, d, e & 99). Below are notes regarding each alternative.

Wires (Illus. 97a)

Wire, or chain and wire, and the attendant pulleys are probably the system that gives most trouble. First check the wheel to drum fixing, then the wire run around each pulley, as that is generally the point of wear. Are the pulleys moving or have they become immobile, leaving the wire to rub away on a static surface? Free off pulleys that have stuck and replace those that are seized. Consider fitting self-aligning pulleys as these compensate for the slight out-of-alignment that occurs as the wire lengthens and shortens on the drum.

Outboard motor installations require spring tensioners to compensate for the differing cable tensions as the wheel is turned from side to side (Illus. 98). Spray the pulleys and associated gear with inhibiting oil.

Illustration 97   Wheel steering alternatives

97a Wire

97b Chain & wire

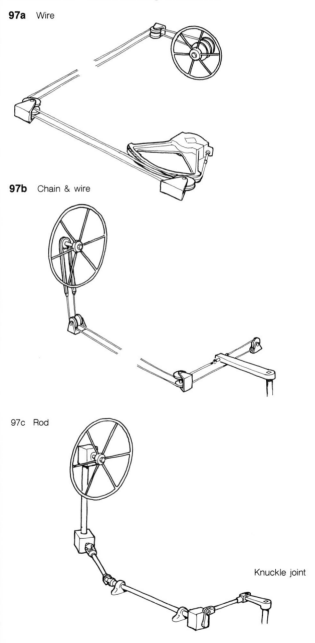

97c Rod

97d Proprietary inner & outer cable — Morse & Teleflex type

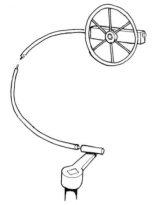

97e Hydraulic steering

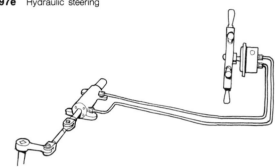

Push-Pull (Illus. 97d)

The condition of inner and outer cable systems, such as *Morse* and *Teleflex*, is very difficult to verify as most of the workings are hidden from view. Eliminate tight bends and check the ease of movement of the inner cable by disconnecting at both ends, thus doing away with the mechanical advantage of the wheel and the drag of the rudder. Any hint of snagging or stiffness and it is advisable to renew the cable, expensive as it may appear at the time.

Illustration 98   Outboard motor steering layout

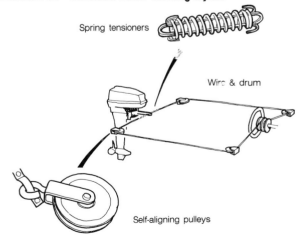

Spring tensioners

Wire & drum

Knuckle joint

Self-aligning pulleys

Rod (Illus 97c)

This type of steering depends on the connections being in mechanically good condition as any wear will be magnified by the mechanical advantage of the wheel. Change worn drag links, gears, steering and bevel boxes, universal joints and bearing assemblies.

Hydraulics (Illus. 97e)

They require the steering ram, helm pump and the pressure pipe or hoses to be in good condition. Leaking seals must be changed.

Pedestal

Another wheel steering alternative which may well be an amalgam of chain, wire, sheaves and inner and outer cables. Examine as detailed above (Illus. 99).

STERNGEAR

The components that go to make up the sterngear must be closely scrutinised from the propeller nut and split pin via the propeller, propeller shaft, outboard and inboard glands, flexible coupling right through to the propeller shaft coupling (Illus. 100a).

Illustration 99   Pedestal steering

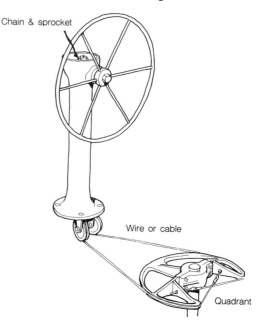

Chain & sprocket

Wire or cable

Quadrant

Illustration 100   Sterngear

100a   Conventional sterngear

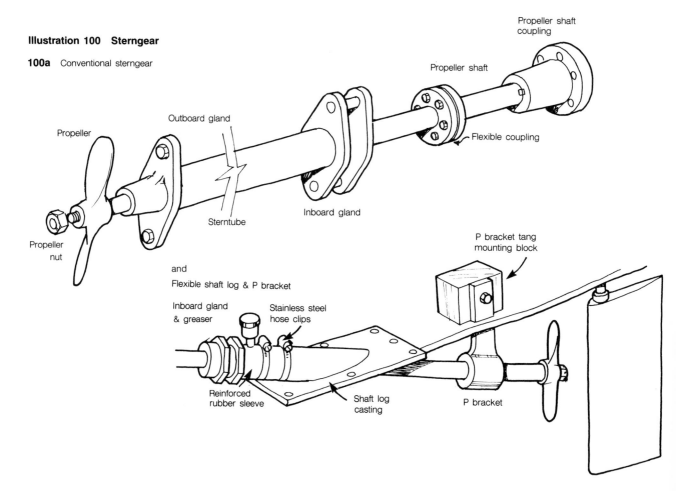

Propeller shaft coupling

Propeller shaft

Flexible coupling

Outboard gland

Propeller

Inboard gland

Sterntube

Propeller nut

and

Flexible shaft log & P bracket

P bracket tang mounting block

Inboard gland & greaser

Stainless steel hose clips

Reinforced rubber sleeve

Shaft log casting

P bracket

The overall state of conventional sterngear can be ascertained by disconnecting the propeller shaft coupling and checking the amount of side to side and up and down movement of the shaft in the inboard and outboard glands (Illus. 100b). Drop the shaft back and inspect in the way of the outboard gland, where most wear takes place. Undue slop in either or both glands and they must be repaired or replaced, as must the propeller shaft if worn.

The outboard gland bearing may be of non-ferrous material or a rubber cutlass whilst the inboard gland

100c Boring out an outboard gland for re-sleeving

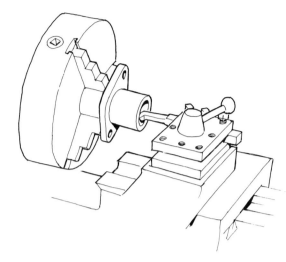

100b Checking the amount of propeller shaft movement in the bearings

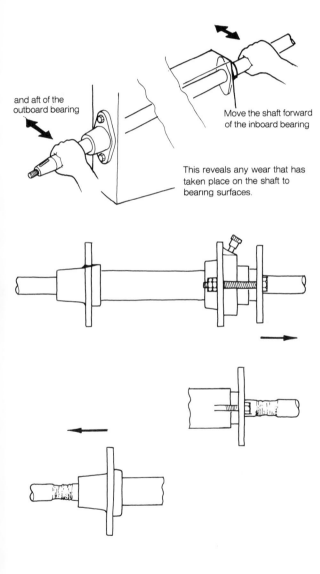

and aft of the outboard bearing

Move the shaft forward of the inboard bearing

This reveals any wear that has taken place on the shaft to bearing surfaces.

100d

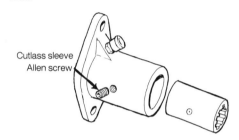

Cutlass sleeve
Allen screw

Cutlass rubber bearing sleeve withdrawn

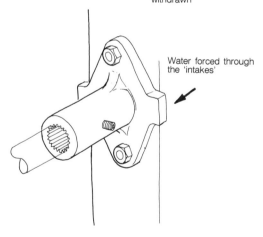

Water forced through the 'intakes'

is usually non-ferrous. Worn non-ferrous glands require boring out and re-sleeving (Illus. 100c). Cutlass bearings, which are grooved rubber sleeves bonded to an outer shell, are simply discarded and replaced as they are self-contained items held into the inboard, outboard or P bracket casting by a grub or allen screw (Illus. 100d).

Reference to a P bracket reminds me of the necessity to draw attention to this form of outboard bearing which, in common with the A bracket, lacks a conventional sterntube (Illus. 100e). It is very important to check the mounting of the strut and the thru' hull fixing, more especially when fitted to GRP and ferrocement craft where the inboard end is laminated in position (Illus. 100e). Any movement due to misalignment or looseness will result in the ingress of water!

100e A & P brackets

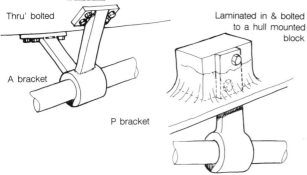

Thru' bolted

A bracket

P bracket

Laminated in & bolted to a hull mounted block

In order to remove an outboard or inboard bearing, the propeller shaft has to be withdrawn so let's hope the rudder, if in the way of the propeller shaft, has a hole or has been engineered so as to allow it to be withdrawn easily (Illus. 100f). Necessary repairs not carried out now may well interfere with the launching, as sterngear manufacturers, in general, tend to be very, very slow in executing orders.

100f Shaft withdrawal

Hole for a line to be attached
if there is any chance of losing the rudder!

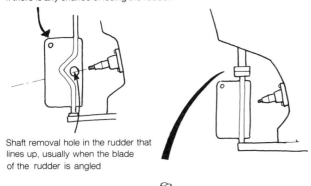

Shaft removal hole in the rudder that
lines up, usually when the blade
of the rudder is angled

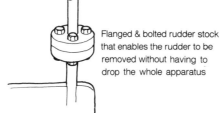

Flanged & bolted rudder stock
that enables the rudder to be
removed without having to
drop the whole apparatus

File the propeller blades to a clean edge where they have been bruised. If they are badly damaged, the propeller may require rebuilding by a professional or even replacing. To remove the propeller from the shaft, once the nut is detached, will, hopefully, only require a number of sharp taps with a brass drift in order to break the lock of the shaft taper and key. Take this opportunity to inspect the key for signs of deterioration. For instance, any slop between the key and keyway and it will be necessary to fit a new key, but they do not always easily give up their slot! Applying some 'freeing' liquid, and using a drift may aid the release but . . . a sharp edged chisel might have to be used to 'persuade' the projecting part of the key in order to give a drift a projection into which to bite (Illus. 101a).

Illustration 101   Propeller shaft keys

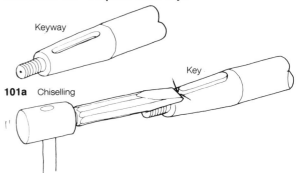

Keyway

Key

101a Chiselling

If the key is 'welded' in position it will be necessary to drill and thread tap through the key from the top, stopping when the drill bites into the shaft. (Note that key and propshaft's of a similar metal make it more difficult to know when the drill has broken through into the base of the keyway). Tighten a bolt down through the key on to the bottom of the slot, which should force out the key (Illus. 101b). To save all the above it may

101b Drilling & tapping to 'bolt'
a 'reluctant' key out of its slot

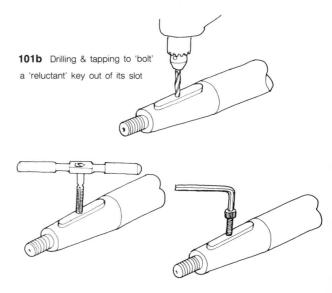

be possible to simply 'waste' the key with a series of drillings and then chip out what is left. On the other hand, where the result is a mangled mess it is no big problem, once the shaft is drawn, to toddle along to a local engineering works that possess a vertical milling machine and have them clean the slot out. Also take the propeller along so, if it is necessary to mill a new keyway, the width can be matched to the groove in the propeller (Illus. 101c). Corrective action in respect of a sloppy key fit includes fitting a stepped key (Illus. 101d).

101c   Drilling/milling away a key

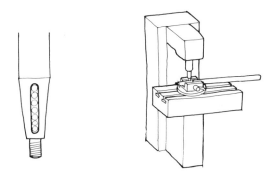

101d   Stepped keys & keyways

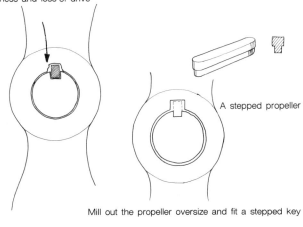

Wear & thus slop which probably will result in a mangled mess and loss of drive

A stepped propeller

Mill out the propeller oversize and fit a stepped key

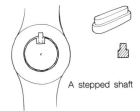

A stepped shaft

If the slop is in the shaft, mill out the shaft oversize

Most modern day shafts are stainless steel on seagoing craft and plain mild steel on Inland Waterways boats. Naturally this generalisation depends upon a number of factors including the engine's horsepower and a variety of other materials are used including monel and brass. It is possible to build up worn shafts, rather than go to the expense of replacement, but I can never see that the saving is really worth the candle on the diameter of shaft we are considering.

Both the inboard and outboard glands should be properly fastened. Not that a fastening can be 'improperly' fastened, it is just that many boatbuilders are not engineers and do not apply as much expertise to sterngear 'mechanics' as they should. The fastening nuts and bolts must be checked for corrosion and replaced where necessary. Trouble may well have occurred in the fastening of the outboard gland to the skeg due to the strains imposed by, variously, stray warps, nylon fishing lines, plastic bags, the odd tyre or supermarket trolley becoming wrapped around the shaft and the propeller. It is quite unbelievable that a fishing line caught between a shaft and cutlass bearing can wear a substantial groove, even in a shaft made of stainless steel. An outboard gland that becomes loose and has thrashed about is likely to have shed the fastenings, added to which the sternpost into which they were fixed may well have suffered so much damage that some rebuilding is necessary. (Illus 102a).

Illustration 102   Outboard & inboard bearing fastenings & deadwoods

102a   Outboard gland fixings

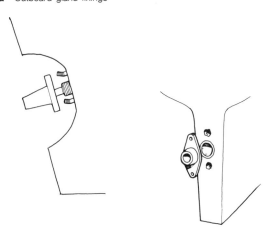

One of the problems encountered with a GRP hull is that the inside of the originally hollow skeg may have been (correctly) filled to counteract the crushing effects of skeg plate fastenings. Unfortunately this leaves a

Steel & aluminium sternposts require either a new section of plate welded in position or, having cut away or 'flamed out' the sterntube hole, a U section slipped over the face and welded in place

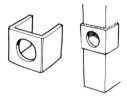

To repair the sternpost in the way of the outboard bearing:-
A plywood or wooden hull requires all the suspect timber grouting out & tacks driving in at any angle.

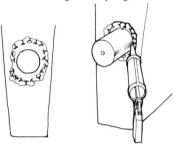

Then push the sterntube or a bar of similar diameter, well waxed, up the sterntube hole and 'gun' in a suitable epoxy filler.
When the filler is set corkscrew out the bar and face off the filler with a very sharp chisel, finally sanding down. More serious damage of the sternpost may require a new piece to be graved in. *See* Chapter Six & Illustration 80
To repair GRP and Ferrocement sternposts use a resin putty & mat mulch *See* Chapters Two & Six for further details

blind fixing at the internal end of the original fastenings (Illus. 102b). But bear in mind boating is fun, which doesn't help! For more constructive instructions read on.

102b A GRP sternpost blind fixing

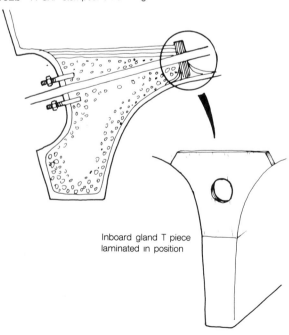

Inboard gland T piece laminated in position

Incidentally, damage incurred at the outboard end may well have caused problems at the inboard gland and the shaft log housing (Illus. 102c). Well it would, wouldn't it! A good wheeze (that can also be used for securing engine holding down bolts), is to have machined some round bar, preferably of the same material as the inboard and outboard gland fastenings,

102c Inboard gland & the shaft log
Repairs to the shaft log are as outlined for the sternpost. Also *See* Illus. 102e & f

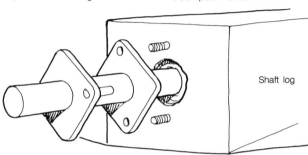

Shaft log

Studs/holding bolts bent/snapped resulting in the sterntube rotating and 'belling' the mouth of the sterntube shaft log, breaking up the sealant with resultant leaks

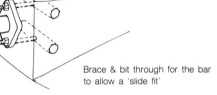

Brace & bit through for the bar to allow a 'slide fit'

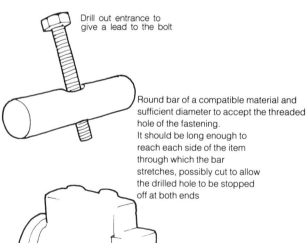

Drill out entrance to give a lead to the bolt

Round bar of a compatible material and sufficient diameter to accept the threaded hole of the fastening.
It should be long enough to reach each side of the item through which the bar stretches, possibly cut to allow the drilled hole to be stopped off at both ends

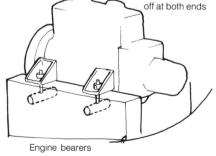

Engine bearers

102d Round bar blind fixings

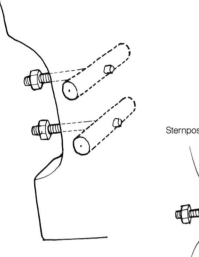

Sternpost & view from above

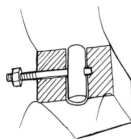

102f Shaft log leaks
A wooden craft

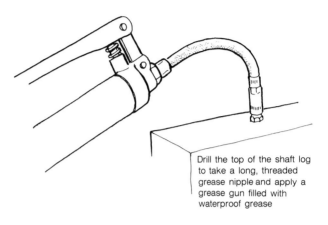

Drill the top of the shaft log to take a long, threaded grease nipple and apply a grease gun filled with waterproof grease

with a drilled and tapped thread through the diameter into which fastenings can be screwed (Illus. 102d). Illustration 102e also sketches another alternative to this problem and Illustration 102f possible shaft log repairs.

102e Affix a tapped & screwed angle bracket each side of shaft log to take bolts from a plate fixed over the inboard gland.

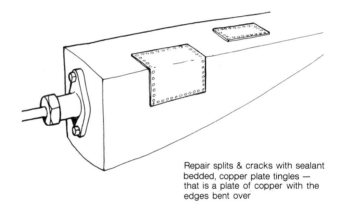

Repair splits & cracks with sealant bedded, copper plate tingles — that is a plate of copper with the edges bent over

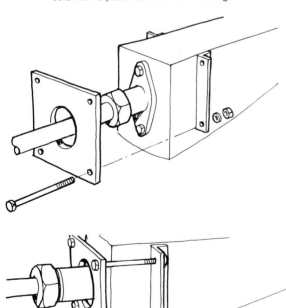

A GRP or ferro hull

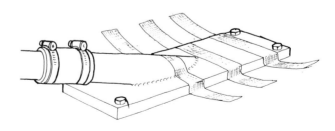

It may well be necessary to completely cut away the overlaying layers of mat and the 'bandages' of CSM that laminate the shaft log into position, re-bed on a resin putty and re-laminate in position

At the inboard end of the propeller shaft is the most oft ill-fitted, but vital piece of engineering — the propeller shaft coupling. It is simply not good enough to use only one method of fastening the coupling to the shaft. The minimum should be a lock bolt and a key or a tapered drive pin (Illus. 103a). Engines delivering horsepower in excess of 25hp require that the lock bolt is replaced by the shaft and coupling being tapered and fitted with a lock-nut as well as a key (Illus. 103b).

Illustration 103   Propeller shaft couplings

103a   A lock bolt & key or tapered pin

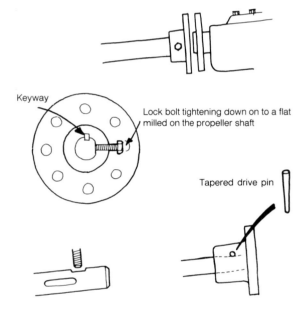

Keyway

Lock bolt tightening down on to a flat milled on the propeller shaft

Tapered drive pin

103b   Taper shaft & lock-nut

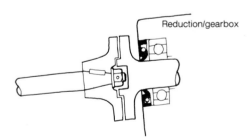

Reduction/gearbox

On reassembling the sterngear repack the inboard packing gland with separate rings of packing material which should be 'staggered' (Illus. 104a). Should the packing seem too thick to slide between the shaft and the inner recess of the bearing, gently hammer the packing flatter until it does fit. When tightening down an inboard gland packing sleeve, use feeler gauges to ensure the sleeve is not pitched and thus biting into the shaft. (Illus. 104b).

Illustration 104   Inboard gland packing

104a   'Staggering' the packing

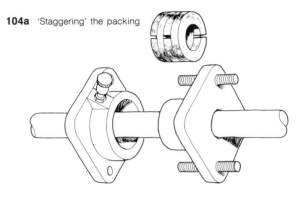

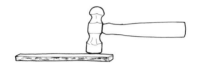

Flattening the packing

104b

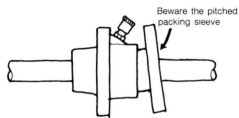

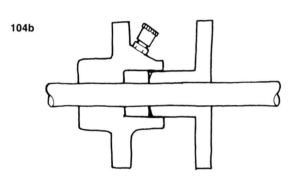

Beware the pitched packing sleeve

Insert feeler gauges to check that the gland packing sleeve does not pitch when pulled down on the two bolts and bite into the shaft

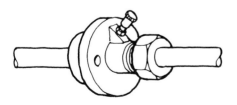

Hope that the inboard stuffing gland sleeve is a nut which can only tighten down square on the threads

Before finally 'nutting' up the propeller make sure it is not 'riding' on the key. This occurs where the key is too deep and does not allow the tapered bore of the propeller to tighten up neatly on the matching taper of the shaft. This state of affairs must be remedied (Illus. 105a). If not it is probable that the key will shear off, mangling the keyway slot in the process.

Illustration 105 Fitting the propeller

105a Riding keys

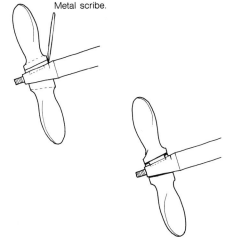

Metal scribe.

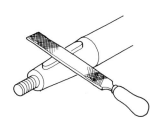

To test for 'riding' push the propeller on the shaft without the key in position, scribe a line at the back end of the propeller boss on the shaft
Then, with the key in position, push the propeller back on the shaft and rescribe
If the scribe lines do not line up the propeller is riding on the key

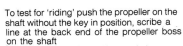

File off the top of the key until the scribe lines coincide. Don't forget to remove any burrs

One other point to watch at this end of the shaft is where the split pin slots of a castellated propeller nut and their shaft drilling do not line up on reassembly. Do not redrill, just file off the back of the nut, or the washer, until they do (Illus. 105b).

105b Propeller nut & split pin drilling

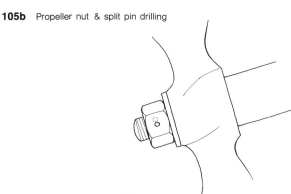

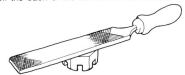

If the castellations/split pin drilling does not line up with the drilling in the propellor shaft, then file some off the back of the nut or the nut washer.

If the inboard gland is only fitted with a small grease cap, necessitating constant refilling involving removing cockpit sole boards, accessing over the engine, or down through a quarter berth, why not fit a remote greaser (Illus. 106)?

Illustration 106   A remote greaser
A conventional, inadequate grease cup

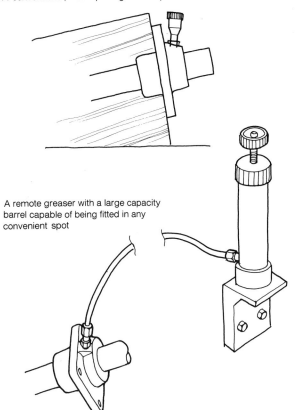

A remote greaser with a large capacity barrel capable of being fitted in any convenient spot

To check the reassembled propeller shaft alignment with the engine, do not start the engine and engage gear whilst bank stored where a cutlass bearing is fitted. That is unless cooling water can be forcibly fed down the outboard gland water intakes. A cutlass bearing is water lubricated (*See* Illus. 100d) and without an adequate supply of the necessary coolant things get very hot and seize up. In any case to check alignment it is necessary to use a clock gauge on the outer diameter faces of the propeller shaft and the engine couplings (Illus. 107a). If a clock gauge is not available a set of feeler gauges will suffice. First place a straight-edge on the outer diameter faces of the two couplings to obtain an initially acceptable line up (Illus. 107b). If this is correct the location shoulder of the propeller shaft coupling should slide easily into the recess of the gearbox coupling. When the two flange faces of the couplings are within 'feeler gauge distance', there should be no more than 0.05mm (0.002″) difference between feeler gauge clearance readings at various, opposite points around the couplings (Illus. 107c). To effect the correct line up it may be required to lower or raise the engine by the removal or addition of engine mounting packing shims. On the other hand it might be necessary to move the unit to one or other side or to shift the axis of the engine or to carry out any combination of the above (Illus. 107d). Where unacceptable and unrectifiable misalignment cannot be eradicated there is available a coupling that

Illustration 107   Alignment
107a   A clock gauge

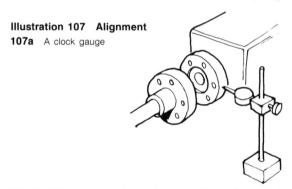

After the initial 'manoeuvres' place the pointer of the engineers clock gauge on one and then the other coupling diameter. The maximum permitted difference in readings is 0.05mm (0.002″)

107b   The preliminaries

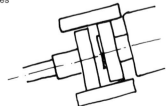

Place a straight edge on the outside diameter of the couplings to obtain the 1st line up. Then slide the location shoulder of the propeller half coupling into the recess of the gearbox coupling. They should easily & 'sweetly' mate.

107c   Feeler gauging the flanges

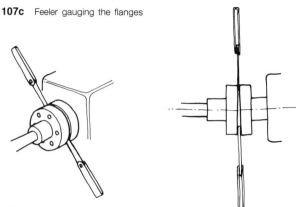

107d   Lining up the engine

It may be necessary to lift or drop the engine parallel to the engine beds, by the addition or removal of non-adjustable packing shims, or to lift or lower one end only. Where flexible mountings are fitted to lower may require chopping out the engine beds in the way of the mounting.

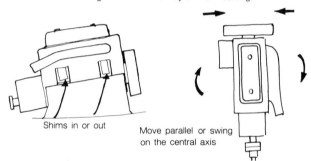

Shims in or out   Move parallel or swing
                       on the central axis

overcomes the problem, at a cost, forever negating the problem and generally making for a quieter and smoother installation.

Many Inland Waterway craft built of steel incorporate an inspection or weed hatch into the hull (Illus. 108a). This enables the external sterngear and rudder to be inspected and repairs to be carried out through the trunking.

Illustration 108   Inspection or weed hatches & outboard motor trunking & plug

108a   An inspection or weed hatch at least gives 'hand & arm' access to the 'externals'

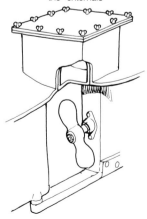

108b 'Top hat' lid.

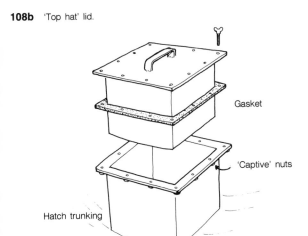

Gasket

'Captive' nuts

Hatch trunking

The trunking infill is to stop cavitation & turbulence that could occur where the trunking is not 'filled'.

The gasket and holding down nuts & bolts must be in good condition.

Illustration 109   Sacrificial anodes

109a   Mild steel rudder/fittings

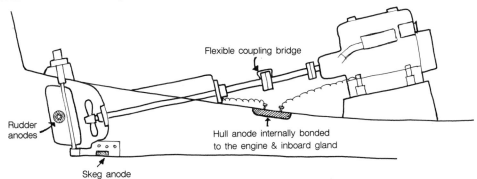

Flexible coupling bridge

Rudder anodes

Hull anode internally bonded to the engine & inboard gland

Skeg anode

inspect the gasket and holding down bolts as propeller thrust will seek out any lack of water tightness (Illus. 108b). Some smaller performance sailing yachts have a similar feature incorporated in the hull down which an outboard motor is fitted when required (Illus. 108c).

108c   Outboard motor trunking & plug

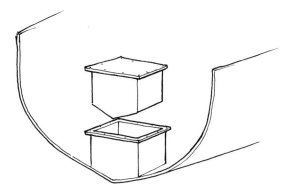

On a performance yacht the top hat section of the plug conforms to the exact shape of the hull in order to present as fair an underwater surface as possible.

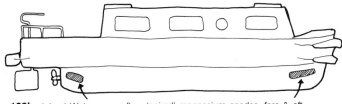

109b   Inland Waterway craft — 'paired' magnesium anodes, fore & aft

109c   Bronze/stainless steel rudder fittings

Rudder bar

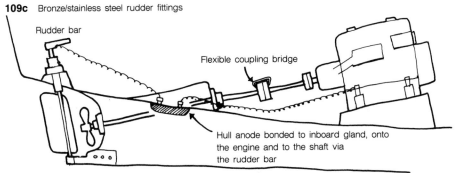

Flexible coupling bridge

Hull anode bonded to inboard gland, onto the engine and to the shaft via the rudder bar

SACRIFICIAL ANODES

If the boat is kept in salt water and the anodes have not experienced wastage, congratulations may well not be in order as some other fitting might be suffering electrolytic action — let's hope its nothing really important!!

Electrolytic action is where two dissimilar metals are immersed in water and are connected above water, as by a hull, and thus can form a 'couple'. An electric current flows, especially in salt water, resulting in the metal of the lowest 'nobility', the anode, being eroded, the 'nobler' metal becoming the cathode. The less noble, baser metals include aluminium and ordinary steels whilst the most noble materials include (passive) stainless steel and monel. Note that stainless steel fastenings are, perhaps surprisingly, not advocated for below water fittings. Just take my word for it. Certainly thru' hull brass and bronze fittings are best fastened with brass or bronze fastenings.

The table of nobility in Chapter Twelve lists various metals commonly found on boats. The overall problem is as nearly as not solved by fitting zinc alloy anodes in strategic positions.

Anodes must be replaced when erosion or severe pitting has reduced their effectiveness. The anodes may well include those connected and or fitted to the engine, skeg shoe, rudder stock, rudder blade (if made of metal or not) and rudder inboard gland, as well as the sterngear anodic fittings (Illus. 109a, b & c).

LIFTING KEEL

When bank storing a craft with a ballasted centreboard or lifting dagger keel, it is necessary to lower the keel so that it is supported by the hardstanding, thus keeping the weight off the hull. Also block up the hull in the way of the keel. Failure to carry out the above may well result in the hull distorting (Illus. 110a).

Lifting keels being movable and pivoting in an internal casing, are subject to much heavy abuse, sorry use. The types vary from dagger boards, made of shatterproof ply, to heavy, cast-iron drop keels set in a ballasted heel surround (Illus. 110b). The method of raising and lowering encompasses 'handraulics' to the 'flip of hydraulics'. Regularly inspect the pivot of the mechanism and the device used to lower and raise the keel, be it rope on a sheet winch, wire on a trailer type winch, a screw or a full blown hydraulic system.

110b Various lifting & drop keels

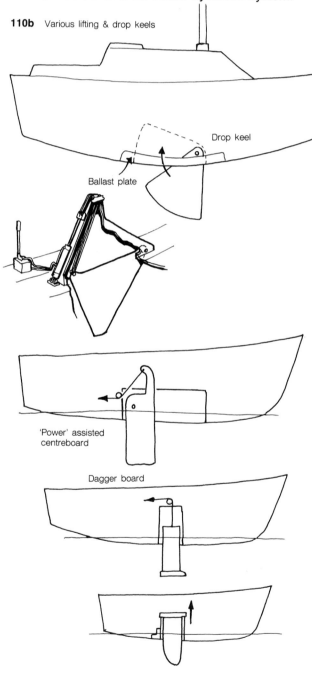

Drop keel

Ballast plate

'Power' assisted centreboard

Dagger board

Illustration 110 Lifting keels

110a Avoid distortion, block the keel

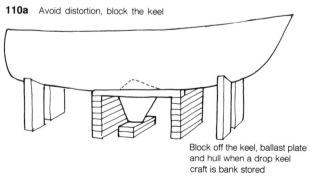

Block off the keel, ballast plate and hull when a drop keel craft is bank stored

110c Centreboard trunking

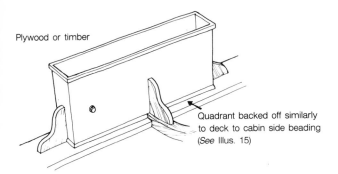

Plywood or timber

Quadrant backed off similarly
to deck to cabin side beading
(*See* Illus. 15)

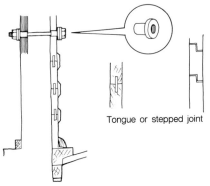

Tongue or stepped joint

It is necessary to high pressure wash out the keel trunk ensuring that all fouling and crustaceans are removed. Damaged ply needs replacing, unless the repair is a small one, and the centreboard trunking must be checked for leaks (Illus. 110c). Fabricated plates require freeing off if wedged in the trunking or straightening if stuck in the down position. Overall treatment obviously depends on the keel's construction, be it plywood, steel plate or cast iron, and should be carried out in line with the general descriptions elsewhere in the book.

8

'SPARKS' or DOMESTIC & NAVIGATION WIRING, REPLACEMENT, REPAIRS & ENGINE ELECTRICS

Boat electrics are usually neglected until the time when a particular unit does not work. Prior to the onset of winter all visible connections should be lightly sprayed with a water absorbing protection aerosol spray, such as WD40.

GENERAL

Wires that have been simply wrapped around terminals must be fitted with spade fittings (Illus 111a). Bare wire ends may have suffered corrosion, which is apparent as the ends discolour and eventually become hard. If 'contamination' has taken place cut back, say, 6mm (1/4″), strip off sufficient cable covering and re-connect. If there is not enough wire to make up the extra length required, fit a cable connector (Illus. 111b). Connections that have been made by wrapping wire ends together and encasing in a sheath of insulating tape, must be replaced with crimped connectors encased in nylon sleeves (Illus. 111c).

Avoid dry joints (which can occur when the connection is applied with, say, a pair of pliers) by using the correct crimping tool and 'running in' some multi-core solder with a soldering iron. Ensure the surfaces are 'fluxed' first and only apply just enough solder to form a good joint between the wire and the connector. Do not apply so much that it runs up the wires of the cable making them rigid and thus liable to fracture (Illus. 111d).

Suspect wiring runs can be replaced wire by wire using the old wire as a messenger or trace. Replacement of particular wires is made easier, in these days of multiple production of a particular boat model, as manufacturers often buy in and fit pre-made, colour coded looms. Similarly, marine engine units, almost without exception, come complete with a plug-in loom ensuring the various engine services and supplies are correctly connected.

Illustration 111   Wiring Do's and Don'ts

111a   Spade fittings

111e   Track the cable

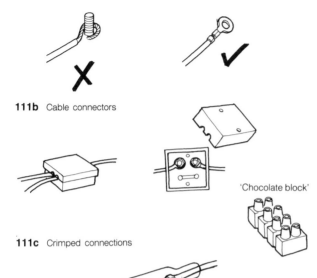

111b   Cable connectors

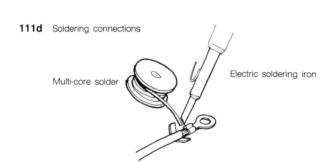

'Chocolate block'

111c   Crimped connections

111d   Soldering connections

Multi-core solder   Electric soldering iron

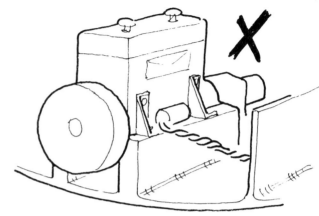

Unsupported wires draped from the engine to a bulkhead

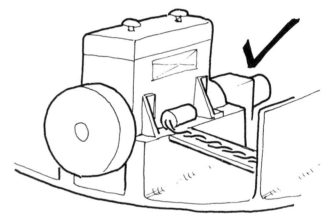

Wiring clipped to a timber track bridging the gap

DOMESTIC ELECTRICS

Lightly inhibit the domestic fuse box and panel, removing the covers and spraying the contacts. If any service has not been operating correctly, this is the time to employ an auto-electrician to use a meter and test the connections in case the actual feed is faulty and requires replacing. Remove and store cabin lamps for the duration of the lay-up and inhibit the holders. Should there be wires or services draped about the engine compartment, or elsewhere for that matter, then for goodness sake, make a track to which to fix them (Illus. 111e).

All the above ought to take place during the overhaul rather than leaving matters until the launching approaches, which may necessitate having to remove headlining and other panels, yet again!

NAVIGATION EQUIPMENT

Before storing equipment that is fitted with internal batteries, REMOVE the batteries and throw them away. Even leakproof batteries cause damage if forever left in position. Shore stow detachable items including the Echo Sounder, Log and VHF radio. This not only helps preserve them, but removes the temptation from light fingered gentlemen who may wish to appropriate the goodies! You have been warned.

THE ENGINE

As stated above, the engine is probably fitted with a wiring loom which reduces the problems associated with older installations where innumerable, widely disparate wires snaked hither and thither. Illustration

112a sketches a 'typical' engine wiring diagram and Illustration 112b a schematic, 'handraulic' battery switching arrangement.

The starter motor, dynamo/alternator/magnet, engine fuse box and electrics panel must be sprayed with an inhibiting oil.

THE BATTERY

The main battery, or batteries, which should be boxed and strapped in a vented box (Illus. 113), must be removed from the boat for charging prior to storage in a dry, cool situation. Check the state of the battery charge using a hydrometer and ascertain if the addition of an acid solution is required. If 'your friendly' boatyard can be trusted, allow them to place the battery on slow charge prior to storage. Before doing so crayon the vessels name on the sides. Do not leave batteries lying about on a concrete floor, which tend to be 'cold' and

Illustration 112   Engine wiring & battery switching

112a   Engine wiring

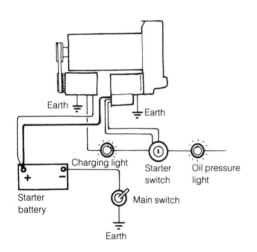

112b   Battery switching

Don't forget to switch off the engine ignition prior to turning the battery switch to 'Off' so as not to 'open circuit' the alternator and irretrievably damage the same

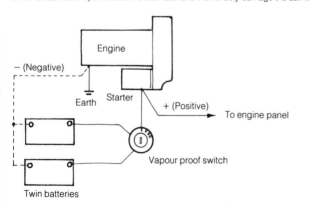

Illustration 113   A Battery Box

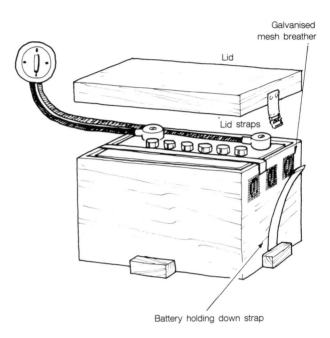

encourage frost damage. After cleaning the battery terminal posts, grease them and the battery cable terminals with petroleum jelly. A small amount of post and terminal corrosion (evidenced by a white deposit), can be removed with near boiling water followed by scraping, wire brushing and filing to 'show' a clean, good surface. On the other hand severely corroded cable terminals should be thrown away and replaced.

HINTS

Prior to leaving the domestic and navigation electrics, a number of pointers may not go amiss.

Thru' deck wiring to navigation lights must have deck plugs fitted, rather than being poked through the deck material and 'puttied' up (Illus. 114a); wires entering a fuse, connection box or fitting should have a drip loop (Illus. 114b); cables must be securely clipped over their length; where routed through a bulkhead fit a gland, or at least round off the bulkhead, and clip the cable either side (Illus. 114c). In respect of this latter item, to save expensive glands, why not fit a small, sink drain or nylon skin fitting with the threaded end filed off (Illus. 114d)? Unsupported cable looped across sole bearers or a gaping bilge must be fitted on a cable track of timber battening, or, if one must, the correct, big ship tracking (Illus. 114e). Where bearers or track are out of the question or the run borders the bilges, route the cables in a semi-rigid plastic tube. Where a number of electric wires are grouped together ensure that the wiring of navigation aids are not included in the bunch,

Illustration 114   Wiring hints

114a Thru' the shell deck plugs

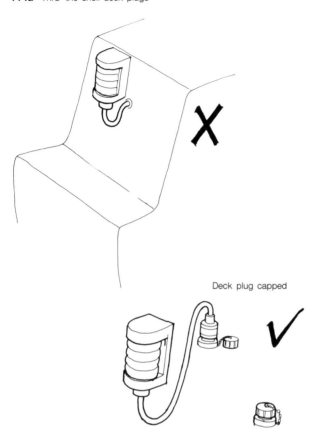

Deck plug capped

114b Drip loops

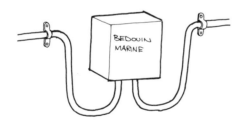

114c Securely clipped cables

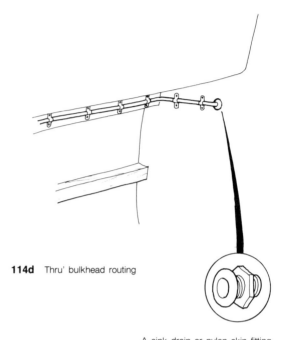

114d Thru' bulkhead routing

A sink drain or nylon skin fitting

114e Electrics track

114f Spiral wound cable wrapping

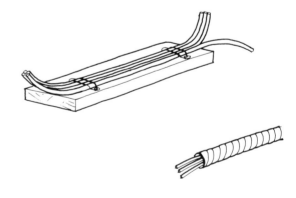

or are even adjacent; that cables are held together in clusters with long tailed, nylon cable straps or a proprietary, spiral wound nylon cable wrapping (Illus. 114f). A fuse box or 'chocolate block' connector mounted to metal, must be insulated from the grounds. Replace any non-marine electrical hardware — it will probably suffer from undue electrolytic action and an amazing ability to absorb water, with the consequent results.

If odd bits and pieces have been added to the system it may be necessary to ensure the particular wiring circuit is 'man enough' for the increased requirements and that overloading is not occurring. A table in Chapter Twelve details various equipment requirements and cable specifications and Illustration 115 details a possible, schematic domestic wiring layout.

Illustration 115   Schematic domestics wiring diagram

N.B. The negative return wires are not shown for the sake of clarity

Neon lamp

Filament lamp

Wires are not connected unless shown thus

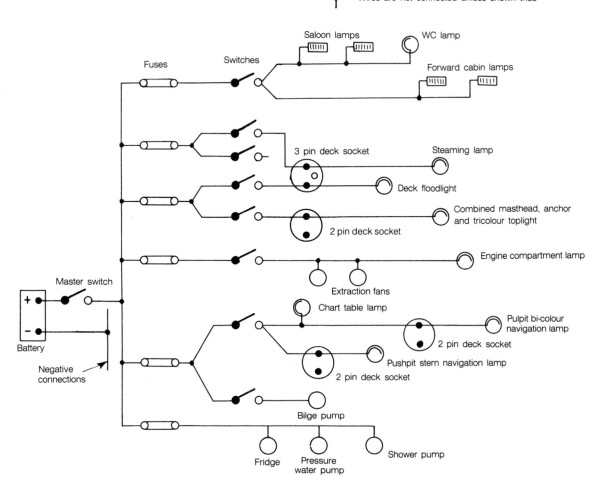

ENGINE WINTERIZING

Routine and annual maintenance procedures are set out in the tables detailed in Illustrations 129a & b. Note the differences in the treatment of outboard and inboard engines and then again between petrol and diesel units. For instance, during a long lay-up, petrol engine fuel tanks should be drained off completely, whilst, due to condensation problems, diesel tanks are generally topped up.

Carrying out routine and annual scheduled maintenance saves a lot of money in the long run, as well as unexpected bills at the commencement of the boating season for the repair or replacement of, for instance, the starter motor, dynamo/alternator or fuel pump.

Where the guidelines in this Chapter differ from the manufacturer's recommendations, then the manufacturer's instructions MUST be followed to the letter. And do heed the sequence of servicing, otherwise several jobs will have to be carried out all over again. For instance, if treatment of a diesel engine's fuel system is carried out prior to dealing with the engine oil lubricants, then fuel will probably have to be re-introduced Well it will have to be if it is deemed necessary to start up the unit in order to warm up the oils before draining off and filling with winter inhibiting lubricants . . . . .

Internal combustion engines must not be run without adequate water being supplied to the cooling water intake, that is except for air cooled units!

OUTBOARD ENGINES

Outboard motors, due to their comparatively low installation cost, might well be the main power unit for craft up to, say, 7m (23ft) housed in an outboard well (Illus. 116a), a tailored trunking (Illus. 116b), an emergency power-pack clamped to a bracket mounted on the transom (Illus. 116c) or the rudder (Illus. 116d).

During the cruising season keep to a regular schedule of oiling, greasing and lubrication, noting that craft kept in fresh water can halve the periodicity of servicing. Following the annual lay-up schedule will ensure a long operational life for the engine and do not leave an outboard clamped in position during the winter. Not only

Illustration 116   Outboard motor mountings

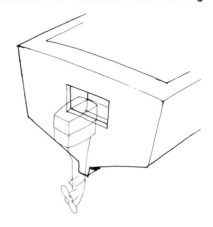

116a   Outboard motor wells

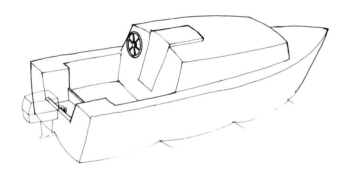

116b   A tailored trunking

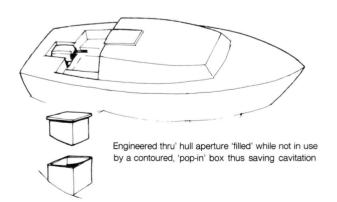

Engineered thru' hull aperture 'filled' while not in use by a contoured, 'pop-in' box thus saving cavitation

116c   Transom mounted bracket

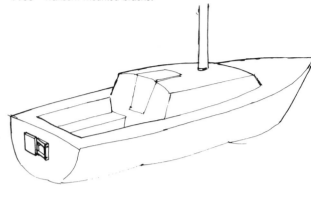

Some brackets are adjustable

Up & Down

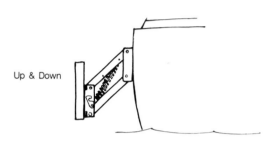

116d   Rudder mounted brackets

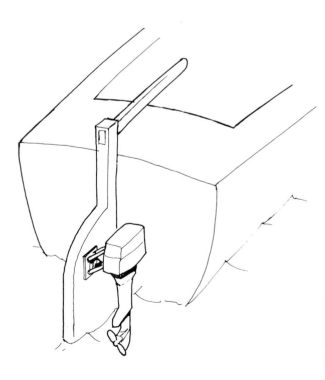

Illustration 117 Outboard motor care

117a A murky pond

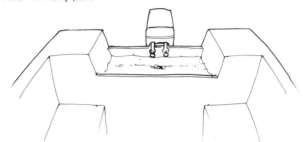

is the unit an easy target for the 'bolt crop equipped' thief, but it will unnecessarily deteriorate. Unattended outboard wells tend to fill with rubbish, slush and wet leaves, creating a murky pond over which an outboard will constantly 'sniff in' malodious vapours (Illus. 117a).

One essential is to thoroughly flush through the cooling system with fresh water thus cleaning out corrosive, salty water and any silt. Smaller engines are usually placed in a test tank, even if the craft has only been used in fresh waters, and run up for some ten minutes or so at tickover (Illus. 117b). It is best not to put the more powerful units into gear as the thrust tends to force all the water out of the tank. Outboard engineers overcome this hazard by fitting test wheels to simulate the loading of a propeller (Illus. 117c). For those of us to whom this piece of equipment is not available, it is obligatory to remember that any outboard motor run out of the water must have the propeller removed in order to save the possibility of accidents. On the other hand where a propeller has been removed, and the engine is put into gear, it is important not to overrev the unit as the propeller may well act as a governor. Larger engines are often tested by clamping a water adaptor plate to the intakes (Illus. 117d).

Whilst in the tank (or whatever) and running, remove the cowl and squirt an upper cylinder lubricant into the carburettor air intake until the engine starts to choke on the oil rich mixture. At that point stop the engine,

117b Tank testing

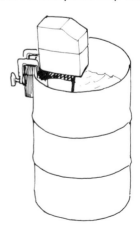

and remove the plugs, loosely screwing in place some old plugs or push in position oil soaked rags. Have the plugs sand-blasted, checking that they operate under pressure, and store in a dry place. NOTE when re-commissioning the engine, it is absolutely vital to turn the engine over with no impediment in the plug holes in order to avert 'hydraulicing'. This is to expel any oil left in the bores thus avoiding the danger of the cylinder walls bursting on the compression stroke.

Spray the powerhead with an inhibiting oil, paying especial attention to the ignition system; grease the various control levers, the relevant grease points, as

117c Test wheels

117d Water intake adaptor plates

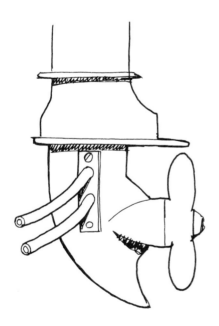

117e General outboard motor service points

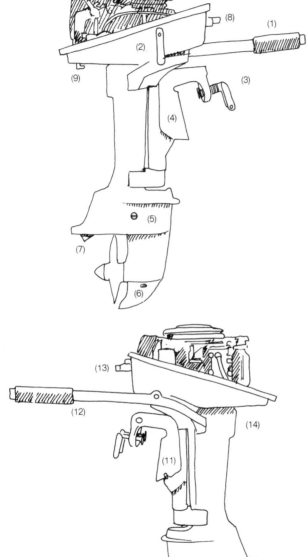

(1) Throttle control (2) Gear lever (3) Clamp body screws

(4) Body swivel (5) Oil level screw (6) Oil drain & fill screw

(7) Exhaust outlet (8) Choke & fuel cut off (9) Powerhead cover latch

(10) Cooling water intake (11) Motor angle adjustment rod

(12) Steering handle (13) Recoil starter handle

(14) 'Tell-tale' cooling water indicator

well as the gear, throttle and choke controls; ensure the clamping body swivel and the tilt reverse lock are well greased and drain off the outboard leg and refill with the correct lubricant (Illus. 117e).

Remove the propeller, check the drive shaft is free from, for instance, nylon line, replace the propeller shaft drive pin and clean up the leading edges of the propeller blades. If these are badly damaged, replace the propeller or send it away for rebuilding and repair. An out-of-balance propeller can cause a lot of vibration with resultant shaft and oil seal wear, so act early rather than repent later, in leisure!

Touch in scratched surfaces with a spray can paint recommended by the manufacturer — do not paint with antifouling. Be careful not to cover up external, galvanic anti-corrosion fittings and replace sacrificial anodes fitted in the cooling waterways.

Check the fuel system from the tank which, if separate, connects to the engine by a dual pipe with push-on connectors, all the way through to the engine mounted, fuel filter fitted on the side of the fuel pump (Illus. 118a). The small, rubber sealing 'O' rings of the fuel lines require replacing if any sign of 'wear and tear' is evident (Illus. 118b). Swill out the fuel tank, a procedure made

Illustration 118 Outboard motor fuel systems

118a Fuel pipes & filler

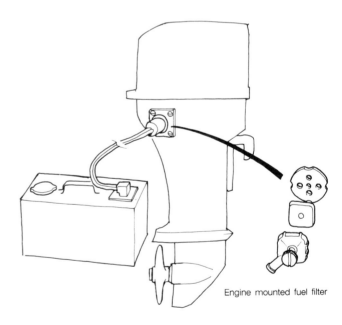

Engine mounted fuel filter

118b Fuel line 'O' rings

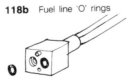

easier by removing the casting screwed on to the tank top and usually containing the fuel gauge and petrol fuel line connections (Illus. 118c). Exercise care when cleaning the tank filter at the end of the fuel pipe pick up and check the float cork of the fuel gauge is in good order. Unused fuel must be disposed of as it does not overwinter very well. Why not use it in the family saloon? That is as long as not so much two-stroke mixture is introduced at one time that it will it upset the car's performance.

Before refitting the powerhead cover, inspect the pull start cord for fraying and hope that it is in good condition. Why hope? Because the job of replacing the wretched thing is one of those time consuming tasks

118c Fuel tanks

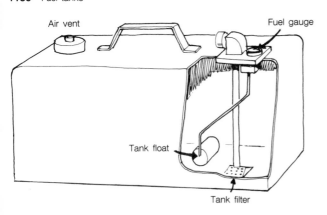

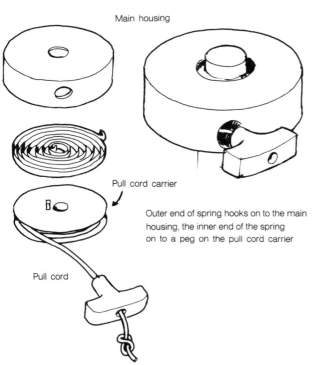

Illustration 119 Pull start recoil mechanism

involving a coiled spring. Need I say more! To replace the cord, remove the carrier beneath which the recoil mechanism lurks, sorry, is fitted! The cord is fed through a hole in the carrier casting and wound on to a rotating, grooved wheel. This wheel is tensioned by a clocklike coil spring, which is wound up as the starter cord is pulled out, thus achieving the required recoil (Illus. 119). An owner should be prepared for an interesting few hours — and might consider sending the family and household pets to sympathetic relations when it is intended to carry out the job!

INBOARD ENGINES

To winterize, inboard engines require the various engine, gearbox and reduction box oils drained and replaced with the relevant inhibiting, overwintering oils. Run the engine and put into gear in order to warm up the existing lubricants, allowing some ten or more minutes to elapse before stopping the engine and draining off the oils. Different installations determine the ease of this task. A tray may be fitted into which the engine oil can be drained and emptied whilst other units require the oil to be evacuated through the dipstick tube. Professionally marinised engines may have been fitted with pumps to the various drain points (one can dream, can't one!) (Illus. 120). After refilling with

Illustration 120 Engine trays & drain pumps

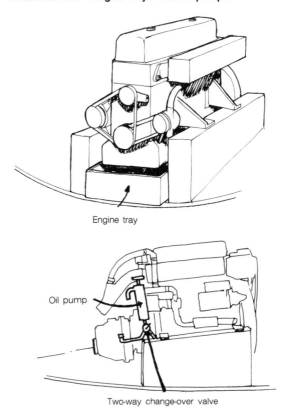

inhibiting oils, briefly run the engine and engage the gears to allow the new lubricants to 'reach all the parts other oils . . . .' After all this draining and filling, wash out the engine sump drain tray using a suitable detergent to break down any oily sludge.

Do not change the engine oil filter until recommissioning and then only after recharging with fresh oil. The older type filter elements are usually held in place by a long bolt through an outer container while the more modern, throw-away cartridge canister filters may require a belt or strap tool to remove the unit. Whichever type of filter is fitted, the knack involves ensuring that the oil filter body sealing ring is correctly in place and does not squeeze out of its retaining groove when the filter body is being finally tightened down (Illus. 121). On starting the engine it is vital to check the oil tightness of this item.

Illustration 121   Oil filters

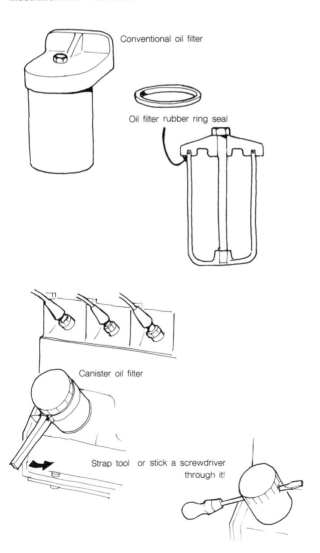

Conventional oil filter

Oil filter rubber ring seal

Canister oil filter

Strap tool   or stick a screwdriver through it!

Naturally there are certain grey areas where an owner must make up his mind how far to go. The perfectionist would remove, for instance, the starter and alternator/dynamo to overwinter in dry conditions, but this is not absolutely necessary as long as they are sprayed with an inhibiting oil.

Assuming the unit is not air cooled, despite the fact that the engine coolant is to be completely emptied, there are quite often cavities, nooks and crannies in the engine block casting that do not completely drain down. Depending on the particular cooling system — raw water or closed circuit — prior to draining place a measured quantity of antifreeze in the header tank and or disconnect the water pump inlet hose from the thru' hull water strainer and place it into a bucket of antifreeze mix. Then run the engine so the solution can percolate to every part of the circuit (Illus. 122a). Incidentally, do not empty the coolant water systems until all the necessary oil and fuel treatments have been completed. At this stage, carefully inspect the cooling water pipes and clips and renew where necessary. Check the manufacturer's manual to ascertain if and where sacrificial anodes are fitted into the engine's cooling water arrangement and replace. An almost always forgotten, but potentially dangerous component are the engine block, cooling water core plugs (Illus

Illustration 122   Water cooling systems

122a   Antifreezing the system

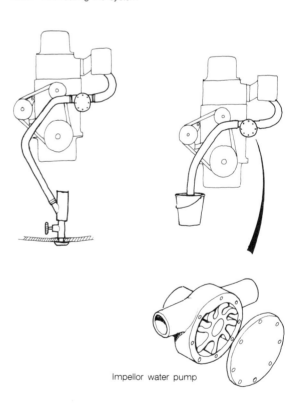

Impellor water pump

122b). These dished blanking plates are often made of steel, more especially where the engine is based on a commercial engine unit, whilst purpose built marine engines may have brass ones fitted. Whatever, steel core plugs resemble fifth columnist, silent sleepers, well hidden away and slowly rusting. A gentle tap with the peen head end of a hammer should indicate the soundness of the article.

The wide variety of differing cooling system layouts almost defies description and depends upon a craft's designed use and the engine size, amongst other considerations! The two basic categories are direct and indirect cooling. Direct cooling water may be pumped through either or both a transmission and engine oil cooler and, after circulating around the engine, be expelled directly overboard, in the case of a dry exhaust system, or via the exhaust in a water cooled exhaust layout. Indirect cooling installations pump 'raw' water through the heat exchanger of a closed engine circuit after which it is discharged but . . . Inland Waterways craft, fitted with engines not exceeding some 20hp, have developed a variation on the heat exchanger theme by dispensing with the raw water circuit, simply pumping the closed circuit coolant via either externally mounted water pipes — keel cooling, or fabricated tanks (with internal water courses) welded to the below water-line hull side — swim or skin tanks.

The essential thing is to painstakingly trace the various pipes and ascertain which system is that *in situ* on any particular engine installation — and the best of luck!

Examine the ductings of air cooled engine's and, if fabric, patch or replace where worn or torn. The engine air passageways must be cleared of fluff, twigs and any other bits and pieces that have been sucked into the system.

122b Core plugs

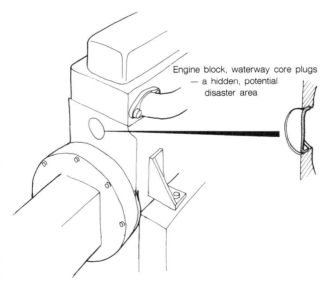

Engine block, waterway core plugs — a hidden, potential disaster area

A couple of relatively inexpensive items that ought to be replaced, regardless of their 'state of health', are the various pulley belts used to drive the alternator/dynamo and water pump and the thermostat, if one is fitted (Illus. 122c). The efficacy of a thermostat can be checked by pouring boiling water over the bellows valve which should open in front of your very eyes!

122c Drive belts & thermostats

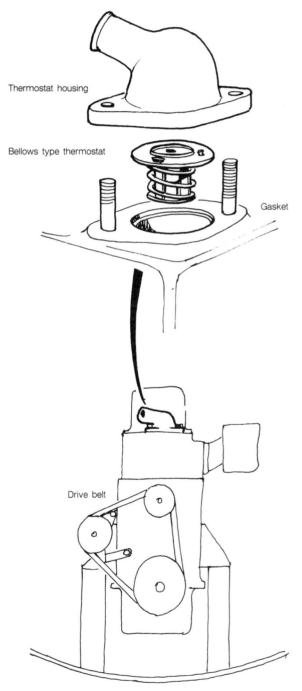

Thermostat housing

Bellows type thermostat

Gasket

Drive belt

This also is an excellent time to inspect the water pump, which nine times out of ten will be a Jabso unit, and remove the impeller for the period of the lay-up (Illus. 122a). Any sign of wear and throw it away, remembering to obtain a replacement!

Probably the most common cause of engine failure is contaminated fuel, so change all the filters when re-commissioning the craft. If there is only an engine mounted filter why not fit an extra one in the feed line? I prefer the type that can be drained while the engine is running (Illus. 123a). Expensive, but well worthwhile especially if the cost is weighed against the possibility of a river weir or sea headland hoving into view during inclement conditions and the engine cuts out! Illustration 123b sketches a couple of typical fuel tank installations and particular points to inspect. A meritorious tip is to lightly grease the threads of the fuel tank filler cap thus deterring the ingress of water.

The exhaust system, be it wet or dry, must be examined from end to end. They tend to be ignored, on the out of sight out of mind basis, but this is not a wise course of action. The exhaust can be the root of serious engine malfunction. The most important matter is to ensure that there are no blockages or impedances to the exhaust gases, thus causing back pressure, which can cause a lot of problems. No doubt readers remember the childhood dodge of sticking a potato in the exhaust pipe of a motor car and recall that this had a tendency to cause a general state of immobilisation. The reason being that if the engine cannot 'breathe out' it will not work! Faults in boat exhaust systems usually result in less immediate but no less effective consequences than the potato! Added to which it must not be forgotten that water cooled exhaust pipes that develop a leak are probably one of

the most effective methods of filling the bilges, apart from opening a seacock! With the increasing use of flexible exhaust pipe, it is essential to inspect the inside of the hose. It is not unknown for the pipe to collapse internally, thus causing a back pressure, often initially imperceptible, which escalates in effect, occasioning strange engine behaviour. Collapsed silencer internals have a similar effect. Diesel engines experience a fall off in delivered power and the back pressure can upset

123b 'Typical' fuel tank installations

Saddle tanks

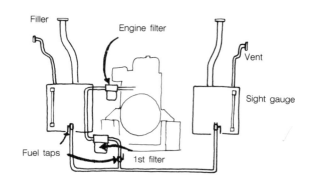

Inland Waterway, stern mounted tank

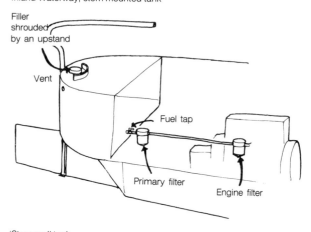

Illustration 123 Fuel systems

123a Water separator fuel filter

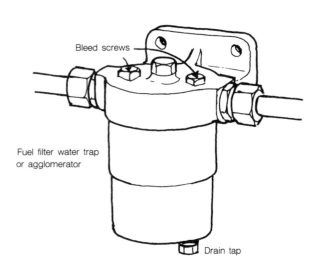

'Strapped' tank

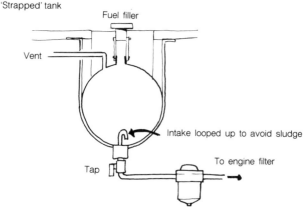

the injectors delivery of fuel over a period of time, choking up the cylinders and manifolds with soggy black carbon deposits of unburnt diesel. Petrol engines evince the signs more immediately, experiencing starting and running problems. They run free, but when the load is put on, falter. In carrying out the winter service, check all flexible exhaust pipe runs are double clipped with stainless steel clips.

Although, as stressed previously, this book is not intended as any more than a maintenance manual, here and there a minor improvement can make an enormous difference to safety and or comfort. In the case of an exhaust close to the water-line, it is almost mandatory

Illustration 124   Exhaust systems

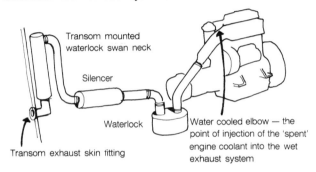

Transom mounted waterlock swan neck

Silencer

Waterlock

Water cooled elbow — the point of injection of the 'spent' engine coolant into the wet exhaust system

Transom exhaust skin fitting

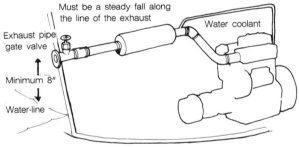

Must be a steady fall along the line of the exhaust

Water coolant

Exhaust pipe gate valve

Minimum 8"

Water-line

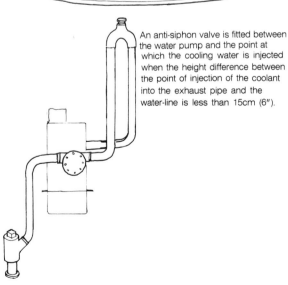

An anti-siphon valve is fitted between the water pump and the point at which the cooling water is injected when the height difference between the point of injection of the coolant into the exhaust pipe and the water-line is less than 15cm (6").

to have a gate valve fitted to the thru' hull skin fitting, if only so that a fault in the line can be quickly isolated (Illus. 124).

Two particular examples I remember highlight the 'curse of the exhaust'. One involved a Stuart Turner two stroke engine, the performance of which slowly became worse and worse, despite constant attention to the electrics and general state of tune, until the unit simply would not run in gear. It was only at a later date that the problem was diagnosed as a collapsed silencer. The other revolved around a diesel engine on which an injector went on the blink. The consequent trickle of unburnt diesel fuel slowly gummed up the exhaust causing accelerating back pressure, which resulted in an increasing build up of coke, which led to more back pressure . . . . I will not bore readers with all the details but in the end the whole exhaust had to be thrown away.

Marine engines often manage to operate in the most hostile environment known to the internal combustion unit. One element required by the engine is lots and lots of air in order to aspirate. So why not give the motive power a treat and change the air filter, which has probably gathered quantities of bedding fluff, human, dog and cat hairs as well as that strange cotton waste type of material that gathers in every crevice on a boat. Incidentally these substances also congregate, as if mutually attracted, around the end of the bilge pump suction pipes.

An oft neglected fitting are the engine mounts. Where the engine is solidly mounted then it is a comparatively simple matter to check the engine holding down bolts. If there is any lack of 'fastness power' due to the bolts thread in the engine beds becoming worn refer to **Sterngear**, Chapter Seven and Illustration 102. The rubber bonded mounts of flexibly mounted engines can become slack and soft due to the presence of hot oil and should be given the 'once over' whilst in commission to ensure they are not allowing too much 'freedom of movement'.

Apart from the detail above, common to both types of engine, there are particular points concerning each.

Diesel Engines

The fuel system must be protected if only to save cash in the long run. The injectors and pumps are very expensive to replace and most damage is caused by the presence of water in the fuel, especially where contaminated diesel is left to corrode away over the winter. To winterize, disconnect the fuel supply pipe from the fuel tanks and place in a container holding a mix of diesel fuel and inhibiting fuel oil. Run the engine to allow the mixture to permeate throughout, thus protecting the diesel fuel pump and injectors (if they are to receive no other attention). A major overhaul necessitates their removal and reconditioning at a specialists. Once the fuel run has been 'broken' by disconnecting any part of the supply, it is quite likely that the system will require bleeding in order to restart. No, not as in blood . . . (Illus. 125). Remove the injectors to storage, squirt some oil down the cylinder bores and turn the engine over by hand a few times to allow the oil to spread about.

Illustration 125   Bleeding a diesel system

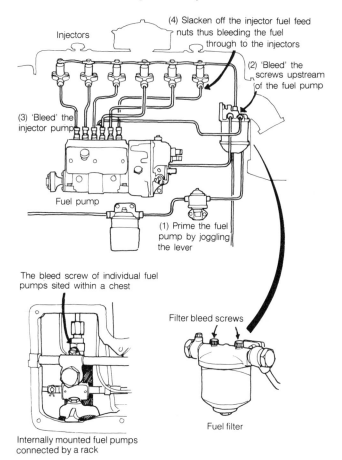

(4) Slacken off the injector fuel feed nuts thus bleeding the fuel through to the injectors

Injectors

(2) 'Bleed' the screws upstream of the fuel pump

(3) 'Bleed' the injector pump

Fuel pump

(1) Prime the fuel pump by joggling the lever

The bleed screw of individual fuel pumps sited within a chest

Internally mounted fuel pumps connected by a rack

Filter bleed screws

Fuel filter

Petrol Engines

To ensure the carburettor and upper works of the pistons and valve gear are well lubricated for the winter, run the engine and squirt some upper cylinder lubrication into the carburettor intake. As soon as this oil rich mixture commences to choke the engine, switch off, after which drain the fuel from the tank(s), fuel pipes and carburettor. Remove the sparking plugs, replacing them with oily rags, and have them sand-blasted, tested and stored until re-commissioning. A disadvantage of draining off the petrol is that a form of lacquer may be left in the carburettor, which can block the jets when the unit is put back into service, but a good wash-out with petrol cures this. Where a mechanical petrol pump is fitted, remove the petrol pump bowl, wash out, removing any sediment and lightly, very lightly, spray the rubber diaphragm of the pump with inhibiting oil

(Illus. 126). When re-commissioning the engine, DO NOT forget to spin the engine over a number of times with the plugs removed thus ensuring that 'hydraulicing' does not occur (*See* the Outboard Engine section of this Chapter).

Marine petrol engines used to be universally fitted with a magneto, but a distributor and coil are now order of the day. Service the distributor prior to spraying the high tension electrics and cables with an inhibiting oil. After removing the distributor cap, clean the contact breaker points with a special file. The wife or girlfriend's emery board suffices as long as the dust is carefully blown away. If the points are badly pitted replace them (Illus 127a) after which reset the gap (usually between

Illustration 126   Cleaning the petrol pump bowl

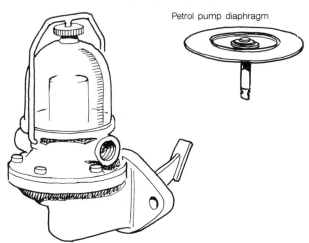

Petrol pump diaphragm

Illustration 127   A petrol engine distributor

127a   The distributor body

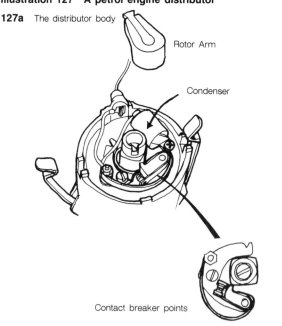

Rotor Arm

Condenser

Contact breaker points

20 and 25 thou.). The metal faces inset in the distributor cap must be scraped and sandpapered clean of any contamination, as must the metal face of the rotor (Illus. 127b). Before reassembling, very lightly oil the pad and cam face of the distributor shaft, and remove the glaze from the central spring pressured, distributor cap mounted, high tension connection. As part of the re-commissioning, fit a new condenser. The state of the spark can be checked by removing an individual

127b Distributor cap

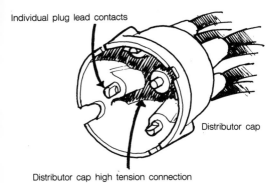

Individual plug lead contacts

Distributor cap

Distributor cap high tension connection

127c Testing the efficacy of the sparking plug

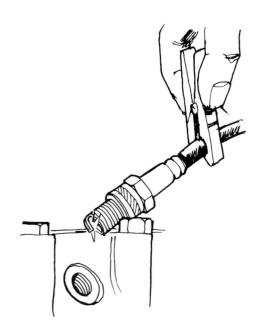

sparking plug and positioning the end about 6mm (¼″) away from a clean area of the engine block. Then have the engine turned over. The spark should be strong and healthy. To save receiving a powerful shock, hold the lead with insulated pliers or a clothes peg (Illus. 127c).

INBOARD/OUTBOARD LEGS & SAILDRIVES

As distinct from conventional sterngear, these 'hybrids' are serviced and overhauled more in line with standard, 'bottom end' outboard motor practices, as covered at the beginning of this Chapter and to which refer for an indication of cooling water, lubricating oil, greasing and propeller procedures. The sacrificial anode is usually in the form of a ring fitted behind the propeller.

A very important point to check in respect of an inboard/outboard leg is that the rubber 'boot', or bellows and associated clips for the drive/thru' hull joint, and any exhaust system, are in good fettle. (Illus. 128a).

Illustration 128   Inboard/outboard & saildrives

128a Inboard/outboard drive

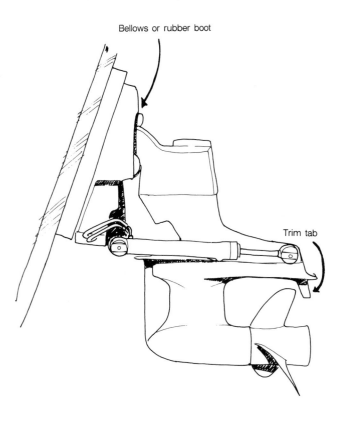

Bellows or rubber boot

Trim tab

Inspect the trim tab, which may also double up as a sacrificial anode, and its set. Adjustment of the trim tab angle to the outdrive body helps compensate for any steering bias.

The saildrive, being thru' hull, as distinct from thru' transom mounted, requires the rubber seal of the hull to unit flange inspected and changed if necessary (Illus. 128b).

128b Sail drive

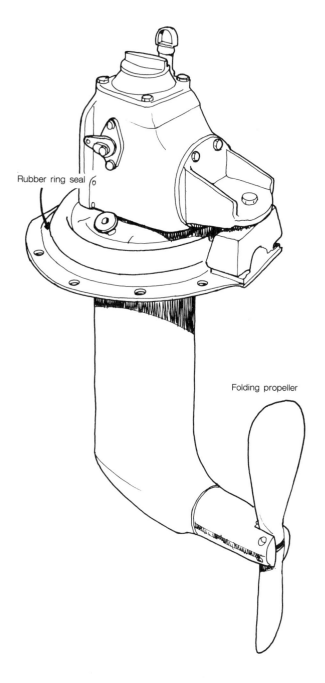

Rubber ring seal

Folding propeller

Illus. 129 ENGINE OVERHAUL CHECK LIST

Note the particular engine manufacturer's schedules must be followed to the most insignificant comma!
Only use the specified oils

Prior to decommissioning the engine for the winter lay-up, compile a defects list of the various faults, niggles, malfunctions and unacceptable points.
Do check the coolant water is coursing freely

A. Petrol Engines	Action	Diesel Engines
x	Apply a proprietary cleaner and wash off.	x
	Sparks	
x	Check:-	
	Timing	
	High tension leads	N/A
	Coil	
x	Remove sparking plugs and replace with clean, oily rags.	
	Lubricating Oils	
x	1. Run the engine to usual working temperature and then drain the engine, gearbox and reduction box oils.	x
x	2. Change the oil filter. (When re-commissioning).	x
x	3. Fill the engine, gearbox and reduction box with overwinter, inhibiting oils.	x
x	4. Briefly run the engine to circulate the inhibiting oils. (This can be left out as the following actions will, in any case, involve some running of the engine).	x
	Cooling System	
x EITHER	A. **Raw Water Cooled**	x
	1. Remove the inlet pipe from the seacock and place in a bucket containing a solution of fresh water mixed with antifreeze.	
	2. Run the engine to allow the solution to permeate throughout the system including the exhaust, if water cooled.	

Fuel System (Diesel)

N/A — Remove the fuel pipe from the fuel tank and insert the end into a container holding a mix of fuel oil and fuel inhibiting oil. — x

3. Stop the engine and completely drain the cooling water from the engine, water pump and exhaust system.

4. Remove the water pump impeller.

5. Check the hoses and hose clips.

6. Check the thermostat is operating.

7. Replace any engine fitted anodes.

8. Adjust or replace the water pump drive belt.

x OR — **B. Closed Circuit Cooling** — x

1. Drain the closed circuit side of the system and replace with an antifreeze solution.

2. Then proceed as in A1 to:-

Fuel System (Diesel)

N/A — Remove the fuel pipe from the fuel tank and insert the end into a container holding a mix of fuel oil and fuel inhibiting oil. — x

3. Not only drain the engine but the closed circuit system.

4. Remove the water pump impeller(s).

Fuel System (Petrol)

x — 1. Switch off at the tank — N/A

2. Drain the system completely

Fuel System (General)

x — 1. Change the fuel filters and clean the sediment trap. — x

x — 2. Clean out the fuel lift pump — x

N/A — 3. Remove injectors and have them serviced by specialists — x

4. Spray the injector pump with inhibiting oil — x

x — 5. Inspect the fuel pipe runs. Replace suspect piping and ensure the pipes are clipped and or taped up clear of obstructions, chafe points and moving parts. — x

x — 6. Ensure the fuel tank(s) are securely fastened and that no wear of the outer skin has taken place due to vibration or chafe. — x

Electrics (generating)

x — Spray with inhibiting oil the:-
Starter
Alternator/dynamo/magneto
or
Dynastart
Fuse boxes
Current control boxes — x

x — Remove the battery for charging — x

x — Check & adjust or replace the drive belt — x

Aspiration

x — Remove the air filter and place a clean, oily rag in the inlet. — x

Exhaust System

x — Inspect the entire run, which must be clean and clear of any obstructions, including:- — x

1. Rubber hoses. Squeeze. If there is any indication of collapse, softness or cracking of the hoses replace them.

2. Metal pipe. Remove the asbestos tape lagging and gently tap. Suspect pipe must be replaced.

2. Exhaust box/waterlocks. Ensure they are 'sound'.

3. Pipe clips/nuts. Replace if suspect. Pipe clips must be stainless steel and doubled up.

General

x — Check engine holding down bolts and mountings — x

x — Check tappet clearances (reset after re-commissioning) — x

x — Place lubricating oils in the cylinder bores — x

x — Grease/lubricate/oil control linkages — x

x — Adjust drive belt(s) tension or replace if worn or cracked — x

x — Check engine electrical connections and spray with an inhibiting oil. — x

x — Engine compartment insulation must be secure — x

Illus. 129 (cont.)

B. Outboard Engines (not exceeding say 40 hp)	**Action**	**Inboard/Outboard legs & Saildrives**
x	Run up the engine, squirting some upper cylinder lubricant into the air intake until the unit starts to choke on the over-rich mixture — then switch off.	Note. For engine details See above

Gearcase

x — With the air vent screw released, drain the oil, flush and refill with replacement oil. — x

Cooling system

x — Having checked the cooling water is flowing from the 'tell-tale':- — x

x — have the water pump impeller changed by a specialist. — N/A

Electrics

Check the:-

x 1. Starter pull cord/rewind
or the
Starter motor and pinion

2. Dynamo
or the   N/A
Magneto

3. Any drive belts

4. Timing

x Remove the sparking plugs and have
them cleaned and tested.   See
x Place clean, oily rags in the plug holes   above
x Reset the contact breaker points (if fitted)

Fuel System

x Drain the carburettor and clean, paying
special attention to the jets.

x Fuel tank:-

1. Empty

2. Clean   See
above
3. Check the float

x Inspect the fuel lines, end connections
and their 'O' rings.

Grease, lubricate & inhibit

x Grease and lubricate the control joints,   See
linkages, levers and nipples as well as   above
the throttle & gear controls and the
tilt/raising mechanism.

x Grease and lubricate the motor clamps   N/A
x Spray the powerhead with inhibiting oil   N/A

Aspiration

x Place a clean, oily rag in the air intake   See
above

Propeller

x Inspect the state of the blades, clean   x
and have rebuilt or replaced as
necessary

x Remove and, as relevant, inspect the   x
locknut cap and split pin, the locknut
and tab washer, splines/rubber bush or
sheer pin, thrust washer and anodic ring

x Grease the splines   x

Body

x Touch up damaged paintwork   x
x Replace external anode   x
N/A Check trim tab is set fair and secure   x

Steering Linkage

x Inspect and grease   x

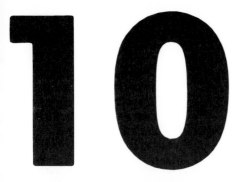

10

ADHESIVES, FILLERS, METAL COATINGS, SEALANTS, PAINTING HINTS & SPECIFICS

Adhesives and sealants probably require some elaboration:

ADHESIVES

The subject and range of glues is a sticky minefield (sorry!) and a little knowledge can be dangerous, so the advice and details given are categorical and without supportive dissertation.

Resorcinol Formaldehyde: The best timber to timber glue, browny red in colour and requires a setting temperature of about 50°F (10°C).

Urea Formaldehyde: Provides a good timber to timber adhesion as long as the timbers are well clamped. Sets clear or pale white in colour and requires a setting temperature of about 40°F (5°C).

Epoxies: The best all round adhesive for wood to GRP, ferrocement and metal adhesion but sets slowly at low temperatures. Beware of very fast setting brands.

Impact: These are the adhesives best suited for sticking plastic laminates to plywood, vinyls, foam-backed headlinings and composition deck coverings to timber and GRP. Strong pressure is required to keep the surfaces together and to stop 'bubbling'. Impact adhesives are petroleum based and give off fumes which can be hazardous in confined spaces.

FILLERS

As with all other preparations, any filler used must be compatible with separate treatments taking place. In the main the conventional stoppers have been replaced by a range of epoxy products. These are fine where they are painted over but colour matching becomes a matter of importance when the finish is clear varnish. One answer is to mix the fine sanding dust of the particular timber into a clear filler and 'spot in' with a stain that matches the surrounds as closely as possible. Where a lot of filling and stopping is required it may well be necessary to stain the whole of the surface concerned. Certainly the modern day stains are excellent and produce a uniform colour finish.

METAL COATINGS

Most modern bolt on deck fittings are cast aluminium or stainless steel. In the past ferrous metal fittings had to be galvanised or painted but current techniques have brought other coatings into the boat owner's orbit. These include metal spraying or sheradising, which results in a very pleasant finish to, for instance, tabernacles and internal mast support tubes. Galvanising is the least expensive method and can be applied cold, as a paint, or as a hot dipped coating, after an acid bath. Unless refurbishing an older craft, galvanising is possibly rather more applicable to anchors and anchor chains.

A voyage through the *Yellow Pages*, or enquiries made to the *Local Chamber of Commerce*, should yield the names and addresses of a number of companies able to undertake refurbishment of fittings with a variety of finishes.

SEALANTS

For most 'bedding' operations (and why not) I strongly recommend the use of a general purpose, cartridge contained, silicone sealant to give a long life, flexible, gasket type joint above and below the water-line. This type of product protects surfaces from suffering hard spots created when bolting down deck and thru' hull skin fittings tight against the shell. It is vital to match sealants to any primers or solvents being used. A mis-match could have the effect of totally nullifying a particular compound's efficacy so, due to the complexities involved, I have taken the (relatively unusual) step of recommending just two companies' products (*See* Chapter Twelve).

If sealants are a 'sticky' area then paints are a morass of often, conflicting information. To overcome this I have based my information and advice on the products of one company pre-eminent in the yachting field — *International Yacht Paints*. The decision was based not only on their all encompassing product range but their comprehensive and informative back-up literature*

PAINTING HINTS

Paint manufacturers produce a welter of information based on their own product range, but the basic fundamentals for any good finish must be a dry, clean and dust free surface, as well as correct preparation.

One indispensable, time saving task that few, if any,

manuals remind an owner to carry out, is to mark or measure the actual water-line immediately a boat has been removed from the water. That is prior to the tell-tale algae and scum line being washed off.

The following are in the nature of jottings to short-circuit the plethora of data available.

One of the first steps is to throw away all the old paints, brushes, sealants and stoppers that have been lurking about, hidden in a locker or on some shelf since last year. Why kid yourself? They are probably no good, rigid, dead, mort and generally useless.

In addition to the purchase of a range of items including brushes, rollers, masking tape, mutton cloth, various grades of sandpaper, wet and dry paper, a sanding block, a scraper or two, an orbital sander, goggles and a face mask, make a Tak-Rag. This is a cheese or mutton cloth damped out with warm water and lightly soaked in a thinned down varnish mix. It wipes surfaces very clean of dust.

Of the three power sanders usually available, do not use the disc type as it tends to dig in and only use a belt sander on continuous, fairly flat surfaces. The orbital sander is the least likely to cause damage and can achieve a fine surface finish. (Illus. 130a).

Cleaning solutions, other than various proprietary fluids, include carbon tetrachloride and the antique furniture trade's concoction of equal parts of methylated spirits, paraffin and vinegar. Apart from these it is worth noting that oxalic acid removes blackening of timber and mahogany keeps its indigenous colour much longer when treated with linseed oil, initially raw.

To heat up a tin of paint, place it in a bowl of hot water, which is much safer than applying a blowlamp.

Although it may seem astonishingly obvious, clean, prepare and paint from the top downwards, thus saving double work by having to clean hull paintwork more than once. Right-handers should work clockwise (or right to left) round a boat, thus brushing from left to right into the existing work (Illus. 130b).

When masking up for clean edges to paintwork (Illus. 130c), do not leave the tape in position for more than the time it takes the paint to go tacky, otherwise it can prove very difficult to remove, especially if it becomes wet. On the other hand try to remove the tape too quickly and the paint peels off with it. That's life!

Bottom painting can be executed with a paint roller. The slightly dimpled look to the finish hardly matters on all but high performance craft. And do throw away rollers after use, particularly when they have been used for antifouling or black varnish (an inexpensive steel boat bottom finish).

Where applying a number of layers of paint, more

---

* I would reiterate that I have no connection with any company listed in this book, other than a normal commercial one as a partner of a small marine business, nor have I received any 'freebies' — yet! Furthermore that a particular manufacturer is not listed or mentioned does not infer any criticism of that company.

Illustration 130   Sander's and a painter's direction

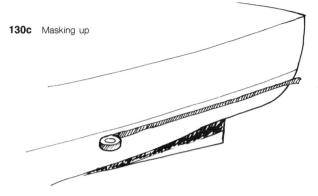

130c   Masking up

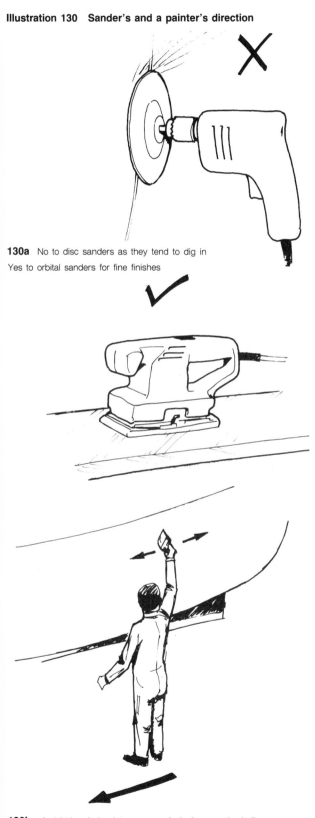

130a   No to disc sanders as they tend to dig in
Yes to orbital sanders for fine finishes

130b   A right-handed painter moves clockwise round a hull

especially primers, it is usual to alternate the colours and note them down in the ship's log (what's that?). At a future date, when carrying out painting maintenance, this record enables an owner to know how many coats of paint are left.

Teak Oil Vis-a-Vis Varnish

For finishes below decks, I am a devotee of teak oiling as much of the woodwork as possible. In the long run it saves the beastly job of stripping off varnish (of which more later) and remains relatively easy to freshen up during the winter. No, not later, let's deal with the great varnish problem now. Proprietary varnish strippers tend to stain the original woodwork. A once neat dodge, but now becoming commonplace, is to use a hand-held, hot air blower. It is necessary to keep the nozzle of the hot air gun close to the varnish work and follow up with a smooth scraper, which lifts the varnish off, once it has heated up. For the final finishing of hardwoods, prior to the last wet and dry papering and varnishing, professionals use a honed, flat steel blade, as a fine scraper ('dum' scraping) which is the 'bees knees'. If the preferred finish is varnish, and the timber has badly weathered, it is probably best to stain the woodwork. Some fillers have a stain finish, thus killing two jobs with one brushing (if you see what I mean). Experts mix the initial coat of varnish with up to 50% thinners and the next few coats with progressively less thinners. In between applications a very light wet and dry 'paper stroking' is carried out and the surface wiped off with the tak-rag prior to applying the next coat of varnish. The final, three to five coats (?) are unthinned and the last is brushed on with as few strokes as possible and all in one direction only.

Teak oil requires the same initial surface treatment as varnish but is infinitely easier to apply, requiring say three coats, the first thinned out some 20%. As pointed out teak oil does not lift and 'bloom' as easily as varnish.

Certainly varnish, and most paints for that matter, should not be applied on any day when the night temperature is likely to drop dramatically, as moisture precipitation may occur and 'blooming' afflict the painstaking efforts. As a last word on this subject, if my advice is anything to go by, do not use a polyurethane varnish for exterior work — there have been, and no doubt will continue to be, so many foul-ups, despite instructions seemingly being followed to the last letter.

Deck Painting

This requires some care and detailed preparation. Scrub the area to be painted with a proprietary boat cleaning agent or a detergent after which wash with copious quantities of fresh water. When the surface has dried circumscribe the deck to be painted with masking tape, ensuring that the corners are rounded, not sharp angles. Do not paint right up to the cabin-side, toe-rails, handrails or deck fittings. It looks a lot more professional to mask up leaving an inch or so clear around them (Illus. 131a). If the deck is GRP, and has not been painted before, degrease and apply a coat of glassfibre primer prior to applying the first coat of deck paint.

Deck paint can be purchased with the non-slip constituent 'built in' but should an owner require to add a little more, then a flour shaker or sugar sifter filled with 'budgie' cage sand (silver sand) does the trick.

Composition Coverings

Certain portions of the deck may require additional protection in order to cope with heavy footed traffic and composition deck coverings can provide an attractive finish. One company's products, made of cork, rubber and a 'mystery' ingredient, is particularly good looking and comes in 1200mm x 900mm (4ft x 3ft) rectangles. Rather than apply it in solid sheets it looks better, and works out cheaper, to lay it in defined cut-out shapes, leaving small areas of deck showing.

Before leaving the subject of composite deck coverings, they are stuck down with a contact adhesive, so do obey the instructions and place weights on the cut-outs whilst the adhesive sets, otherwise it tends to bubble. (Illus. 131b).

Canvas covered decks are dealt with in Chapter Six.

To sum up:

DO NOT — burn off antifouling.
    — burn paint off GRP craft.
    — scorch timber when burning off.
    — smoke when painting or preparing surfaces.
    — use TBT antifoulings that may still be lying about. They are now illegal
DO   — follow the product directions and safety instructions
    — wear a face mask when rubbing down any area of paintwork
    — wear goggles and gloves when necessary

    — ensure adequate ventilation throughout the boat when painting the interior.
    — use paint strippers sparingly on timber and plywood craft. (this is an idiosyncrasy of mine).
    — flat down enamel/topcoats between applications.

The above are general notes. There follows more detailed extracts in respect of painting the six shell materials covered in this book. These assume that the hull and deck have been correctly painted in the past. Note that quantity calculations are dealt with at the end of the Chapter and that the number of applications mentioned hereunder is an average.

GRP

Topsides.

I have never found repainting GRP topsides a particularly worthwhile exercise as in no time at all they begin to look like cracked nail varnish, but there you go. If the decision is made to go ahead, rub down with wet and dry paper of about 240 grade, fill any blemishes and fair in, wash, allow to dry and apply a coat of glassfibre primer. Follow this with a matched undercoat smoothed down with a 320-400 grade wet and dry paper and two applications of topcoat suitable for the job.

Deck Paint

See previous copy in this Chapter.

Hulls

a). If the present antifouling is in a good state of repair, rub down with wet and dry paper of about 240 grade, wash thoroughly and allow the hull to dry prior to applying at least two coats of antifouling. Owners who are not sure what brand of paint has been previously used, and if it will be compatible with a different manufacturer's product, should apply a barrier coat.

b). If the antifouling is worn away in places, degrease with a multipurpose cleaner and degreaser, fill any imperfections with an epoxy filler, fair off, touch in with one coat of antifouling primer and blend in, when dry, using a fine wet and dry paper of between 120-320 grade. Apply a further two coats of antifouling.

c). Antifouling that is in a bad state may require complete removal. There are a number of practical methods including:

 (1) Dry Sanding — very hard, back breaking work requiring a lot of sandpaper, of about 60-80 grade, and a scraper.

 (2) Paint stripper — when used must be manufactured for the purpose. After the waste has been scraped away thoroughly wash the hull.

 (3) Sandblasting — requires the use of a

subcontractor, as the equipment is expensive and specialist. It does not break your back but will dent your bank balance.

After which proceed as in b). above.

d). An alternative painting programme, especially where osmosis protection is in mind, involves applying a two-pack, solventless, clear epoxy. Once all previous paintwork has been removed, the surface should be cleaned and degreased with a multipurpose cleaner and degreaser, followed by a careful rub down with a 180-220 wet and dry paper, after which wash down the

surface. Then apply one coat of epoxy primer with a brush or roller, allowing to dry prior to filling, where necessary, with an epoxy resin filler; rub down lightly with a fine 280-320 grade wet and dry paper and clean off with clean, fresh water. Apply a second coat of epoxy primer followed by a pigmentary coat of epoxy primer and three coats of antifouling. Depending on the instructions and time lapses, the last coat of epoxy primer may have to be followed by a straightforward glassfibre primer before the antifoulings are brushed or rollered on. Phew!

Boot Topping

This water-line stripe is best applied on to the antifouling priming coats. The easiest method is to prepare and prime the hull up to the top of the planned boot topping line, then paint in the boot topping, antifouling up to the bottom of the boot topping. Naturally use masking tape to delineate the paint parameters (*See* Illus. 131).

Bilges

Clean out and apply a multipurpose cleaner and degreaser after which wash and allow to dry completely before treating with a bilge paint. On the other hand it is now considered advisable to treat GRP hulls from the inside out, as it were, and process bilges similarly to the hull's exterior. If this course of action is chosen, it is necessary to apply a multipurpose cleaner and degreaser, rub down (or flat out) with a 180-200 grade wet and dry paper, clean off with water, allow to dry and then paint with two coats of epoxy primer, the second being pigmented.

STEEL

Cosmetic Attention

When localised painting is taking place, allow for hand or power tool wire brushing and grinding to clean back

Illustration 131 Deck covering

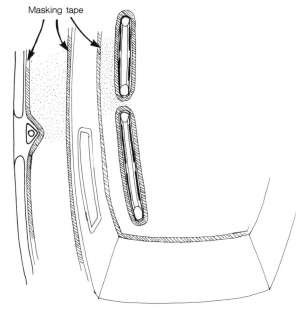

131a Deck masking & painting

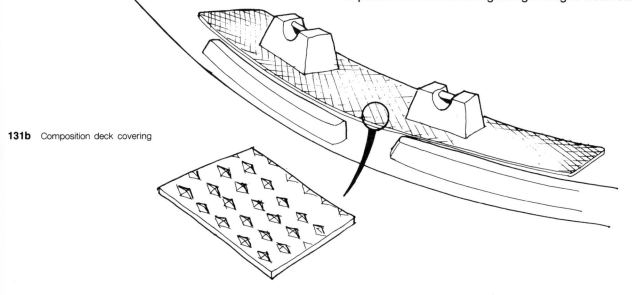

131b Composition deck covering

to bare, shiny metal. AND DO wear goggles — it is very macho without but may well necessitate a visit to the eye department of the nearest hospital!

Above Water-line
After thoroughly dusting off, speedily apply a coat of metallic based yacht primer, fill with epoxy filler and rub down as necessary. Ensure the surface is dry and then build up further coats of yacht primer, fairing into the surrounding area followed by an undercoat and one or two topcoats.

Below Water-line
Follow the *Above Water-line* schedule but substitute an underwater primer and apply some five coats prior to antifouling.

Major Repaint
Probably best achieved by sand blasting overall, cleaning localised areas with a wire brush and disc sander. Pay particular attention to cleaning all welds and removing any mill scale still present.
Then:-

Topsides
Apply one coat of metallic based primer, fill where necessary with a trowel cement, rub down and wash followed by three more coats of primer, one of undercoat and two of gloss yacht enamel.
Or:-

Below Water-line
Apply five coats of suitable underwater primer, followed by two coats of the selected antifouling.
   Incidentally I am a great devotee of Black Varnish for the underwater of steel hulls.

Decks
Follow the *Topsides* schedule to and including the last coat of primer after which apply several coats of deck paint.

Bilges
Follow the *Topsides* schedule (presumably not bothering to fill any imperfections) to and including the last coat of primer after which slap on two coats of bilge paint.

PLYWOOD & TIMBER

The following descriptions cover craft that both flex — (clinker and carvel built boats) and those categorised as rigid (plywood, double diagonal and moulded boats). Note that treatment of varnish is dealt with elsewhere in this Chapter.

Cosmetic Attention
Wooden boat paintwork requires the topcoat paint surface to be rubbed down with 240 grade sandpaper. Gouges, indents and irregular surfaces can be stopped

up with an epoxy filler, rubbed down, faired in, undercoated and finished with a topcoat or two. Where it is necessary to go back to bare wood in places, apply a coat of primer prior to the undercoat.

Major Repaint
It is necessary to burn or paint strip off all the old paint and sand down the surface. To remove the worst of the burnt off and stubborn paint use a 80-120 grade sandpaper followed by a further sanding down with 180-220 grade sandpaper. Erase all traces of sandpaper dust and make sure the surface is dry, wiping down with a tak-rag. Only 'oily' timbers, which include teak and iroko, require an application of thinners to counteract the natural oils. Timber craft kept in fresh water greatly benefit from being treated with a wood preservative inside and out prior to any other paint applications. The first coat of wood primer should be thinned out to the point where it is rather wishy-washy, followed by two coats of unthinned primer. Then trowel cement, where necessary, and sand back with a 280-320 grade paper after which thoroughly clean off.

Then:-

Topsides
Apply another coat of primer, one undercoat and two topcoats.
Or:-
Below Water-line
Apply two coats of primer after which trowel cement any further imperfections, sand with wet and dry paper followed by two coats of antifouling.

Decks
As for *Topsides* but substitute two coats of deck paint for the undercoat and topcoat.
Or:-

Bilges
Apply two coats of primer and two coats of bilge paint.

FERROCEMENT

Hulls
Any old paint that comes to hand cannot be employed on a ferro craft, due to the high alkaline content of the mortar used in the construction. This restricts paints to those based on epoxy coatings (or chlorinated rubber). If the paintwork only needs a rub down, then a few coats of two-pack epoxy primer, faired in where necessary with an epoxy resin filler between the coats of the primer, and a final two coats of antifouling will suffice.

   On the other hand, where the paintwork is to be removed in localised spots or completely, 'stone' the hull with a constantly wetted, medium grade carborundum stone followed by a sanding down with 180 grade wet and dry paper. Wire ends showing through must be punched in and stopped with a filler after which etch the hull with a solution of one part phosphoric acid to four parts of water, applied with a large stiff distemper brush or broom. Then wash the surface and allow to dry for a week. From hereon apply one coat of epoxy primer with a brush or roller, allowing to dry completely prior to filling, where necessary, with an epoxy resin filler; rub down lightly with a fine 280-320 grade wet and dry paper and wash with clean, fresh water. Apply a second coat of epoxy primer followed by a pigmentary coat of epoxy primer and three coats of antifouling. Depending on the instructions and time lapses, the last coat of epoxy primer may have to be followed by a straightforward primer before the antifoulings are brushed or rollered on.

Hull Freeboard & Topsides
Proceed as for the *Hull* but follow the epoxy primer with an undercoat and two coats of gloss paint (in place of the antifouling), lightly flattening down between each coat.

Decks
Proceed as for the *Hull*, but apply only two coats of epoxy primer followed by one coat of undercoat and two of deck paint, the first of which must be applied between three and seven hours of the last coat of epoxy primer, depending on the temperature at the time. If there is a greater interval of time, apply a coat of glassfibre etch primer to give a good key for the next coat of paint.

Bilges
Do not paint internally, especially with an epoxy coat, at the same time as externally painting — blistering may well occur. Initially treat the internal areas with a phosphoric acid/water mix, then apply a 15% thinned coat of epoxy primer followed by three undiluted coats of primer.

ALUMINIUM

Generally aluminium requires thoroughly degreasing. This can be achieved by either:
(a) low pressure, aluminium oxide grit blasting followed by an immediate application of an epoxy primer, to which undercoat can be directly applied. Then proceed as appropriate below.
Or:-
(b) rub down with a fine to medium abrasive followed by painstakingly cleaning with a cloth soaked in a multipurpose cleaner and degreasing agent. After the prescribed time the surfaces must be thoroughly washed with fresh water, allowing to dry prior to applying a coat of self etch primer.
Then:-

Topsides
Follow the above with three coats of alloy primer. Fill, where necessary, with a trowel cement between the second and third coats of the primer after which apply two coats of undercoat and one or two coats of gloss yacht enamel.
Or:-

Below Water-line
Follow the above with five coats of suitable underwater primer and two coats of antifouling.
Or:-

Decks
Follow the above with two coats of deck paint.
Or:-

Bilges
Follow the above with two coats of bilge paint.

CAST IRON KEELS

See Chapter Two for preparatory treatment. Apply five coats of metallic primer followed by two coats of antifouling.

QUANTITIES

As a general indication of the amounts of paint required the empirical formulae that follow give a guide.

Topsides:
The area (in square meters) = (overall length + beam) × (2 × the average freeboard).
Decks:
The area = (overall length + beam) × ¾ — (coachroof, cockpit and hatches).
Underwater:
Racing Craft. The area = water-line length × (beam + draft) × ½
Cruisers. The area = water-line length × (beam + draft) × ¾.
Motor Sailers. The area = water-line length × (beam + draft).

Use the tables below to give the approximate requirements

	m^2 per 750 ml tin
Primers: Glass fibre	7½
Wood	7½
Steel (2 pack)	10
Undercoats	7½
Topcoats/enamels/gloss:	8
Antifoulings:	6
Varnish:	7½
Deck paint	7

250 mls = 0.005 galls;   500 mls = 0.11 galls; 1 litre = 0.22 galls;   2½ litres = 0.55 galls; 5 litres = 1.1 galls.

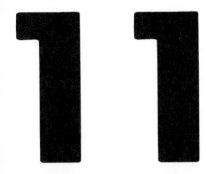

COMMISSIONING, LAUNCHING & JOTTINGS

The impending date of a vessel's launch, so long ago back in the autumn, when brave thoughts and words were probably proclaimed over several pints, gathers pace with alarming alacrity. There is a marked similarity to the start of the autumn school term — it seemed so far off at the start of the summer holiday and there was so much time . . . Many planned improvements will not have been carried out, and even some of the essential, remedial work may have been left undone!

COMMISSIONING

Two weeks before the launch date, if everything must be left to the last minute, tend to the following:-

Seacocks
Wander round and close them all including the engine cooling, galley, WC and vanitory unit inlets and outlets. Failure to do so can lead to an embarrassing chain of events, usually in the deepest water available!

Batteries
Ensure they are fully charged and topped up with distilled water. Although to be deprecated for everyday use, it may be an idea to have a can of *Easy-Start* to hand in case the engine proves obdurate. I say it is to be deplored to make a habit of using engine 'encouragers' but I am assured by plant contractors, who should know, that engines get an appetite for the stuff, becoming hooked. Well there you go!

Engines
The power unit must be re-commissioned, not forgetting to:-

flush out any inhibitor in the fuel line; change the inhibiting lubricating oils for the 'real thing'; turn the engine over a number of times to get rid of oil in the cylinder bores and check sparking plugs or injectors are not just finger tight (they make a spectacular missile if ejected under pressure!).

Ensure that fuel pipes, fuel tank drain plugs, fuel filter bowls and engine oil filters (and their 'O' sealing rings) are all in place and securely tightened. Adjust the tension of the various water pump and charging drive belts. Oh, do make sure there is some fuel in the tanks and , in the case of diesel engines, that the fuel is bled through to the injectors (*See* Chapter Nine & Illus. 125).

Domestic Water Supply
This may well have been uncoupled in the Autumn, so will require re-connection after removing the bungs or corks (that should have been pushed into loose pipe ends). Replace any old pipe clips with new, stainless steel ones and flush the water tank through several times. Ensure items removed for winter storage are put back and re-connected.

Bottled Gas
Check that all the connections are coupled and there are no leaks. If the gas bottles were removed for storage, make sure the large neoprene washer has not been misplaced from the gas bottle to regulator connecting nut.

Domestic & Navigation Lamps
Each electrically 'driven' item must be re-connected and light tubes, bulbs and fuses be refitted.

Grease
Smear the battery terminals with petroleum jelly, charge the sterntube and the rudder post grease caps.

Bilge Pumps
Ensure the pumps have been reassembled. Launching a timber built craft may well necessitate pumping some water into the bilges and recaulking the odd seam that shows up leaks. If the craft has been bank stored for a period of time, it is a wise plan to keep the craft in the crane slings as well as having a large, sludge gulper pump available. The timbers may require a week or so to completely 'take-up'.

Antifouling
Have some paint and a brush to hand in order to touch-in where hull supports have precluded access.

Deck Fittings
Deck stanchions and their accompanying guard wires should be laid along the side decks to save the crane strops tearing them out by the roots when lifting (Illus. 132a). Attach guard wires to the pulpit and pushpit with lashings which can, in emergency, be cut away (Illus. 132b) and lash D shackle pins in position (Illus. 132c).

Ground Tackle & Safety Equipment
All too often the availability of fenders (and their ropes) and mooring warps are forgotten, let alone their condition assessed. While checking out the aforesaid items why not look over the mooring chain as well as the main and kedge anchors? The fire extinguishers, first aid box and flares require, as is relevant, the once-over, replacing, servicing and or topping up.

Sailing Yachts
The mast must be 'dressed'. This at least allows some time in which to replace worn sheaves, clevis pins, toggles and snagged standing rigging, all of which should have been attended to in the Autumn. Put the masthead light bulb back and check the unit works — rather now than later, that is when the spar is in position and the light is an impossible 30 foot up! If any standing rigging has been replaced, have the odd toggle to hand, in case (hush my mouth) it has been made too short. And do have plenty of split pins available.

LAUNCHING

Once launched the following may act as a memory jogger:-

When the craft has settled in the water, carefully proceed from stem to stern, checking out the water tightness of all the thru' hull skin fittings. Turn over the engine, gingerly at first and operate the throttle and gear mechanisms. With the engine running and in gear, inspect the propeller shaft for alignment and water tightness. If the shaft appears to be out of line or the inboard sterntube bearing heats up unacceptably (too hot to touch), then the line up must be reset. Fill the inboard stern gland greaser (if this has not already been carried out — as it should have been) and give a few turns. Ensure that forward movement of the gear lever, or control, results in forward motion (not reverse!)

Outboard motors require the angle of installation or rake set up to ensure the propeller is efficiently driving the boat (Illus. 132d).

Does the craft lie on its designed water-line once the water and fuel tanks are topped up and the ground tackle is all in place? If not, add some trim ballast and or move the ballast to correct.

AND BEST WISHES.

Perhaps it will not go amiss to sketch an 'iron topsail' (engine) starting procedure just in case nervous exhaustion numbs the brain cells and panic sets in because the wretched thing will not start. I have known owners emulate John Cleese and start beating the offending lump . . . . .

1. Verify there is fuel in the tanks.
2. Turn on the cooling water intake valve or seacock.
3. Turn on the battery master switch.
4. Check engine/gearbox levels.
5. Inspect the battery fluid levels.
6. Turn the ignition switch on. Diesels may require pre-heat for the prescribed time .
7. Start the engine.

Illustration 132 Launching tips

132a Stanchions

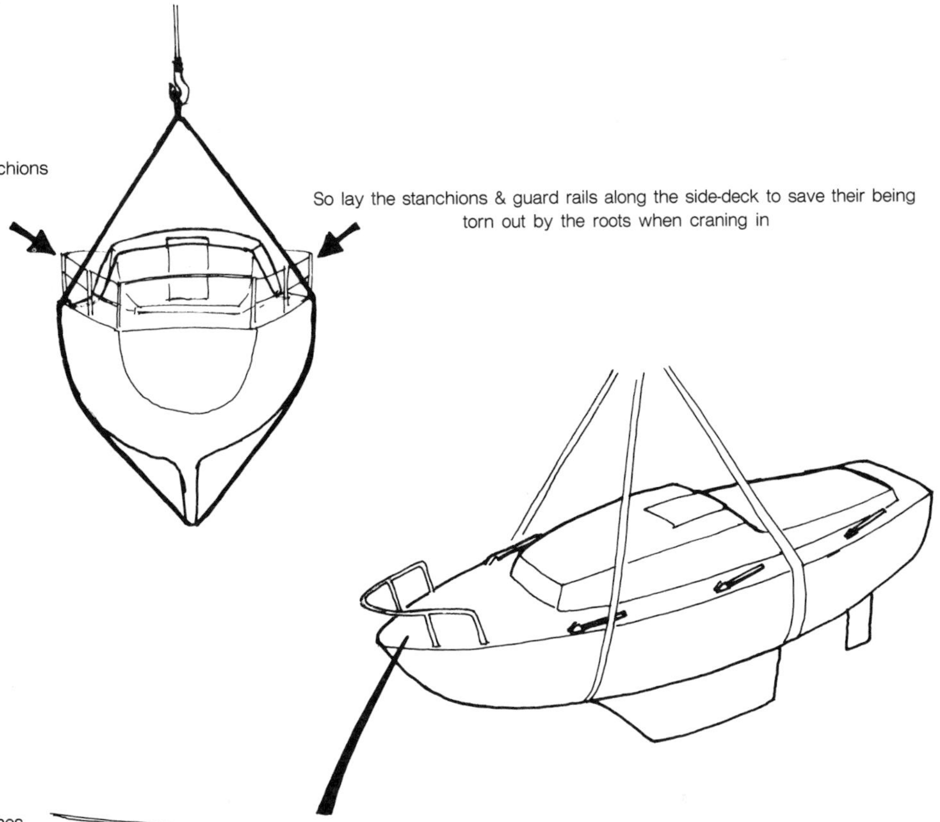

So lay the stanchions & guard rails along the side-deck to save their being torn out by the roots when craning in

132b Guard rails/lifelines

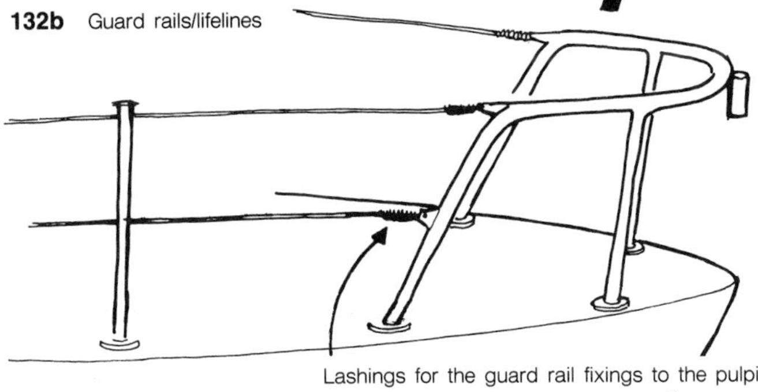

Lashings for the guard rail fixings to the pulpit & pushpit

132c A 'lashed' D shackle

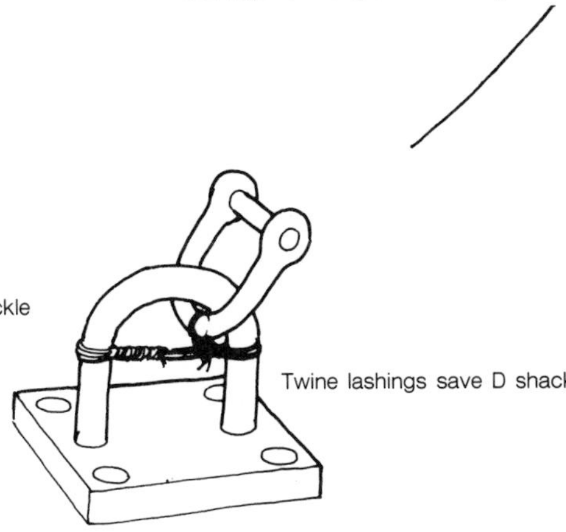

Twine lashings save D shackles being lost overboard

132d An outboard motor angle of installation

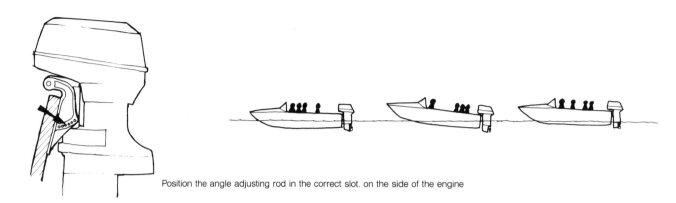

Position the angle adjusting rod in the correct slot. on the side of the engine

8. If a unit is water cooled ensure that coolant water is flowing. If not, stop the engine, by operating the engine stop control. (DO NOT SWITCH OFF THE IGNITION FIRST*) and then switch off the ignition switch. Lack of cooling water can be caused by blocked inlet/filter/strainer. Turn off the inlet seacock, remove the strainer and clean it in a bucket of water, replace and start again. NOTE these strictures do not apply to keel cooling and swim tank systems.

9. Check the gear and throttle controls are moving 'sweetly'.

10. Verify the fuel lines are not leaking and, in respect of petrol engines, the ignition system is not arcing or 'floating about'.

11. Make sure the oil filter seal is not leaking.

To end this Chapter, a plea to seagoing skippers to ensure their radar reflector is correctly positioned and that navigation lights are correctly positioned, working and in such a position as to be clearly seen. The necessity for this was very forcibly brought home to me when I was privileged to experience a 48 hour passage on one of 'Her Majesty's grey hulled messengers of death' — more prosaically a destroyer. It would be a salutary lesson to all boat owners to observe the difficulties experienced by the Bridge during a fast night passage, especially in the confines of the English Channel.

*Note that when wishing to stop engine's fitted with an alternator, it is essential that the ignition switch is left in the 'on' position, and the engine stop button is pulled, pressed or whatever or throttle released, if no stop button is fitted. Once the engine has stopped then switch off the ignition. This procedure protects the engine's alternator from open-circuiting and the resultant damage.

12

TABLES, CONVERSION FORMULAE & USEFUL NAMES & ADDRESSES

TABLES

Hose Clips

Pipe clips are extremely confusingly sized by the various manufacturers and the list below will be of some help in sorting out the ridiculous situation. Use ONLY stainless steel clips.

000	⅜″ - ½″	9 - 13mm
M00	⅜″ - ⅝″	9 - 16mm
00	½″ - ¾″	13 - 19mm
0	⅝″ - ⅞″	16 - 22mm
0X	¾″ - 1″	19 - 25mm
1A	⅞″ - 1⅛″	22 - 28mm
1	1″ - 1⅜″	25 - 35mm
1X	1⅛″ - 1⅝″	28 - 41mm
2A	1¼″ - 1⅞″	32 - 48mm
2	1½″ - 2⅛″	38 - 54mm
2X	1¾″ - 2⅜″	44 - 60mm
3	2″ - 2¾″	50 - 70mm
3X	2⅜″ - 3⅛″	60 - 80mm

Machine Screws

Due to standardisation over recent years, the metric equivalent of the machine screws listed below should be used as imperial sizes may be more than double the cost.

British Standard	Approximate Metric Thread equivalent	Clearance Drill Size	75% Tap Thread Drill Size
$\frac{3}{16}$″ (0.1875)	M5	$\frac{7}{32}$″	$\frac{3}{32}$″
¼″ (0.25)	M6	$\frac{17}{64}$″	$\frac{7}{32}$″
$\frac{5}{16}$″ (0.3125)	M8	⅜″	$\frac{17}{64}$″
⅜″ (0.375)	M10	$\frac{7}{16}$″	$\frac{21}{64}$″
½″ (0.5)	M12	$\frac{9}{16}$″	$\frac{7}{16}$″

Metal & Wire Gauge Equivalents

It is useful to have the tables to hand as there is nothing more infuriating than being unable to communicate with a supplier or to have gauge numbers with no way of converting them to really useful equivalents, such as thickness. This usually occurs at a weekend according to Murphy's Law.

Metal Gauge Number	Imperial Thickness inches	Metric mm
1	0.3	7.61
2	0.276	7.00
3	0.252	6.39
4	0.232	5.88
5	0.212	5.38
6	0.192	4.87
7	0.176	4.46
8	0.160	4.06
9	0.144	3.66
10	0.128	3.25
11	0.116	2.94
12	0.104	2.64
13	0.092	2.34
14	0.080	2.00
15	0.072	1.83
16	0.064	1.62
17	0.056	1.42
18	0.048	1.22
19	0.040	1.01
20	0.036	0.91
21	0.032	0.81
22	0.028	0.71
23	0.024	0.61
24	0.022	0.56
25	0.020	0.51
26	0.018	0.46
27	0.016	0.41
28	0.014	0.36
29	0.013	0.33
30	0.012	0.30

Standard Wire Gauge	Imperial Thickness inches	Metric mm
30	0.0124	0.314
29	0.0136	0.345
28	0.0148	0.375
27	0.0164	0.416
26	0.018	0.457
25	0.020	0.508
24	0.022	0.558
23	0.024	0.609
22	0.028	0.711
21	0.032	0.812
20	0.036	0.914
19	0.040	1.016

Standard Wire Gauge	Imperial Thickness inches	Metric mm
18	0.048	1.219
17	0.056	1.422
16	0.064	1.625
15	0.072	1.828
14	0.080	2.032
13	0.092	2.336
12	0.104	2.640
11	0.116	2.946
10	0.128	3.251
9	0.144	3.657
8	0.160	4.064
7	0.176	4.470
6	0.192	4.876
5	0.212	5.384
4	0.232	5.892
3	0.252	6.400
2	0.276	7.010
1	0.300	7.620
0	0.324	8.229
2/0	0.348	8.839
3/0	0.372	9.448
4/0	0.400	10.16
5/0	0.432	10.97
6/0	0.464	11.8
7/0	0.500	12.70

Nobility Table

Least noble	Material	Voltage potential
	Magnesium alloy	− 1.6
	Zinc	− 1.10
	Galvanised iron	− 1.05
	Aluminium	− 0.75
	Mild steel	− 0.70
	Cast iron	− 0.65
	Lead	− 0.55
	Brass*	− 0.27-0.29
	Magnese bronze	− 0.27
	Copper-Nickel	− 0.25
	Silicon bronze	− 0.18
	Monel*	− 0.08-0.20
	Stainless Steel*	− 0.05-0.20

Most noble

* The actual nobility depends upon the exact alloy composition of the metal.

To eliminate corrosion in sea-water it would be necessary to achieve a voltage difference of only 0.20 volts — so anodic protection is the answer.

Water pipe equivalents:-

3/8″	12mm)		3/4″	22mm)	not inter-
1/2″	15mm)	inter-	1 1/4″	35mm)	changeable &
1″	28mm)	changeable	1 1/2″	42mm)	require a
2″	54mm)				conversion coupling

NOTE Gas & fuel pipe sizes are measured in Imperial sizes.

Plywood board equivalents:-

1/8″	4mm
1/4″	6mm
3/8″	9mm
1/2″	12mm
3/4″	18mm

Sandpaper grades:-

60-20	Very abrasive and used to remove burnt off paintwork. Scores the surface.
180-200	Abrasive and used to prepare wood for a coat of primer.
220	Used to prepare a surface for an undercoat.
280-320	Used to prepare a surface for a topcoat or a first coat of varnish.
400	Used to cut back the first topcoat or a subsequent application of varnish.
400-600	Used to remove blemishes in the topcoat of enamel paint or varnish.

Skin fitting equivalents:-

1/2″	13mm
3/4″	19mm
1″	25mm
1 1/4″	32mm
1 1/2″	38mm
2″	50mm

Timber thickness approx:-

1/2″	13mm
5/8″	16mm
3/4″	19mm
7/8″	22mm
1″	25mm
1 1/4″	32mm
1 1/2″	38mm
1 3/4″	44mm
2″	50mm
2 1/2″	63mm
3″	75mm
4″	100mm
5″	125mm
6″	150mm

Note the above sizes are for sawn timber. Planed timber looses about 1 1/2 mm ($\frac{1}{16}$″) per planed surface, so a board ordered at 25 mm (1″) planed thickness finishes up at about 22 mm (7/8″)

Woodscrew drilling sizes:-

		Screw gauges* 6	8	10	12	14
Softwoods.	pilot drill	—	$\frac{1}{16}$″	$\frac{5}{64}$″	$\frac{5}{64}$″	$\frac{7}{64}$″
	clearance drill	—	$\frac{3}{32}$″	$\frac{5}{32}$″	$\frac{5}{32}$″	$\frac{7}{32}$″
Hardwoods.	pilot drill	$\frac{5}{64}$″	$\frac{3}{32}$″	1/8″	1/8″	$\frac{5}{32}$″
	clearance drill	$\frac{5}{32}$″	$\frac{3}{16}$″	$\frac{7}{32}$″	1/4″	1/4″

*To ascertain a screw's gauge measure the diameter of the head of the screw, using a ruler marked up in sixteenths (of an inch). Multiply the measurement by two and subtract two from the result.

USEFUL CONVERSION FORMULAE & TABLES

To convert Pounds (lb) to Kilogrammes (kg) multiply by 0.4536 and kilogrammes to pounds multiply by 2.205

Water 1 litre weighs 1.00 kg/2.2 lb.
1 gallon weighs 4.53 kg/10 lb.

Gallons to litres: Multiply by 4.546
Litres to gallons: Multiply by 0.22
1 cu ft holds 6 1/4 gallons and weighs 62.3lb

To convert cubic feet to cubic metres multiply by 0.028

The central figure in the table represents either of the two outside columns, as the case may be i.e. 1 gallon = 4.546 litres or 1 litre = 0.22 gallons.

Litres		Gallons
4.546	1	0.220
9.092	2	0.440
13.638	3	0.660
18.184	4	0.880
22.730	5	1.100
27.276	6	1.320
31.822	7	1.540
36.368	8	1.760
40.914	9	1.980

Petrol 1 litre weighs 0.73 kg/1.61 lb.
1 gallon weighs 3.36 kg/7.4 lb.

Diesel 1 litre weighs 0.84 kg/1.85 lb
1 gallon weighs 3.86 kg/8.5 lb.

Electrics
Amps equals watts divided by volts.

Cable/Current Requirements

Possible Item	Current requirement in amps (approx)	Conductor specification in mm		Cable Ref.* Numbers	
		Single core	Twin Core	Single core	Twin core
Gauge lamps	6-8	14/0.30	2x14/0.30	PV2a76/1	PV2a 76/2
Interior lamps	9-12	21/0.30	2x21/0.30	PV2b76/1	PV2b 76/2
Larger lamps (such as search lights)	17.5	28/0.30	2x28/0.30	PV376/1	PV3 76/2
Battery supply	27.5	44/0.30	2x44/0.30	PV3a76/1	PV3a 76/2
Dynamo	42	84/0.30	—	PV3b12/1	—
Alternator	60	120/0.30	—	PV3c12/1	—
Starter motors	135	266/0.30	—	PV336/1	—
	170	37/0.90	—	PV436/1	—
Electric winch	300	61/0.90	—	PV536/1	—

*These are *Ripaults* reference numbers.

Measurements

To convert inches to centimetres (cm) multiply by 2.54 and centimetres to inches multiply by 0.393

1 inch = 25.4 millimetres (mm)
1 foot = 30.48 centimetres (cm)
1 yard = 0.9144 metre (m)
1 mile = 1.6093 kilometres (km)
1 millimetre = 0.03937 inch
1 centimetre = 0.0328 foot (ft)
1 metre = 1.094 yards (yd)
1 kilometre = 0.62137 mile

The central figure in the table represents either of the two outside columns, as the case may be i.e. 1 inch = 2.54 centimetres or 1cm = 0.394 inches.

Centimetres		Inches
2.540	1	0.394
5.080	2	0.787
7.620	3	1.181
10.160	4	1.575
12.700	5	1.969
15.240	6	2.362
17.780	7	2.756
20.320	8	3.150
22.860	9	3.543

Metres		Yards
0.914	1	1.094
1.829	2	2.187
2.743	3	3.281
3.658	4	4.374
4.572	5	5.468
5.486	6	6.562
6.401	7	7.655
7.315	8	8.749
8.230	9	9.843

Speed

To convert knots to miles per hour, multiply by 1.15

Distance

To convert miles to kilometres multiply by 1.609 and kilometres to miles multiply by 0.621

Temperature

To convert centigrade to Fahrenheit divide by 5, multiply by 9 and add 32. To convert Fahrenheit to centigrade deduct 32, divide by 9 and multiply by 5.

Easy Conversions

Metres into yards . . . add one-tenth
Yards into metres . . . deduct one-tenth
Kilometres into miles . . . multiply by 5 and divide by 8
Miles into kilometres . . . multiply by 8 and divide by 5
Litres into pints . . . multiply by 7 and divide by 4
Pints into litres . . . multiply by 4 and divide by 7
Litres into gallons . . . multiply by 2 and divide by 9
Gallons into litres . . . multiply by 9 and divide by 2
Kilogrammes into pounds . . . divide by 9 and multiply by 20
Pounds into kilogrammes . . . divide by 20 and multiply by 9

USEFUL NAMES & ADDRESSES

Chapter One
Trailer-parts & information:

*Indespension Ltd, Mechanical Services Ltd., Belmont Rd, Bolton, Lancs. Tel. (0204) 58434.

Chapter Two
Keel bolt X-Ray:

X-Ray Marine Ltd, Gatehampton Manor, Goring on Thames, Reading, RG8 9LU. Tel. (0491) 874031.

Chapter Three
Water & bilge pumps; pressure water systems:

*Munster Simms Engineering Ltd, Old Belfast Rd, Bangor, Co. Down, N. Ireland, BT19 1LT Tel. (0247) 461531.

Bottled gas:

Calor Gas Ltd, Appleton Park, Riding Court Rd, Datchet, Slough, SL3 9JG. Tel. (0753) 40000.

Calor gas fitting & appliances: caravan galley fittings & chemical toilets:

Joy & King, 6 Wooburn Industrial Park, Wooburn Green, High Wycombe, Bucks. HP10 0PF. Tel. (06285) 30686.

Toilets:-
chemical:

Sowester, South Western Marine Factors Ltd, PO Box 4, 43 Pottery Rd, Poole, Dorset BH14 8RE. Tel. (0202) 745414.

seagoing toilets & gate valves

Simpson-Lawrence (apply to head office for the closest depot). 218-228 Edmiston Drive, Glasgow, G51 2YT Tel: (041) 427 5331/8.

Chapter Four
Masts & spars:

*Kemp Masts Ltd, St. Margarets Lane, Titchfield, Fareham, Hants. PO14 4BG. Tel. (0329) 41900.

Deck fittings:

Simpson-Lawrence & South Western Marine Factors. *See* above for address.

Chapter Five
Freeing agents, inhibiting & penetrating oils:

Silicone sprays such as *WD40, Rust-Eze* & *Plus Gas.*

Chapter Six
Gelcoat protection & osmosis treatment:

*International Paints, Yacht Division, 24-30 Canute Rd, Southampton, SO9 3AS. Tel. (0703) 226722

*SP Systems, Structural Polymer Systems Ltd, Love Lane, Cowes, Isle of Wight, PO31 7EU. Tel. (0983) 298451.

GRP supplies:

Strand Glassfibre Ltd, (apply to head office for the closest depot).

Brentway Trading Estate, Brentford, Middx. TW8 8ER. Tel. 01 568 7191. Local suppliers & boat builders.

Fastenings & caulking cotton:

Simpson-Lawrence. *See* above for address.

Cold castable resin/iron ballast system:

Barton Abrasives Ltd, Bagnall St, Great Bridge, Tipton, West Midlands, DY4 7BS. Tel. 021 557 9441.

Chapter Seven
Morse & Teleflex cables:

South Western Marine Factors Ltd, Controls Dept, 5/7 Uddens Industrial Estate, Ferndown, Dorset BH21 7LF. Tel. (0202) 892542

Sterngear & other engineering supplies:

Carvel Developments, Bedford Engineering Works, Houghton Rd, Bedford. Tel. (0243) 54781

T. Norris (Ind) Ltd, 6 Wood Lane, Isleworth, Middx. Tel. 01 560 3453.

Propeller rebuilding: Steel Developments Ltd, 238 Merton Road, Southfields, London SW18 5JQ. Tel. 01 874 7059

Propeller shaft (out of line) couplings: Halyard Marine Ltd, 2 Portsmouth Centre, Quartremaine Rd, Portsmouth, Hants. PO3 5QT. Tel (0705) 671641.

Galvanic/anodic protection: M.G. Duff Marine Ltd, Chichester Yacht Basin, Birdham, West Sussex PO20 7EW. Tel. (0243) 512777.

Chapter Eight

Wiring: Local auto-electrical factors.

Electric cables & connectors: *Ripaults Ltd, Southbury Rd, Enfield, Middx. EN1 1UE. Tel. 01 804 8181.

Wiring & marine electrical electrical supplies: E.C. Smith & Sons (Marine Factors) Ltd, Units H & J, Kingsway Industrial Estate,

Kingsway, Luton, Beds. LU1 1LP. Tel. (0582) 29721.

Marine electrical fittings: Simpson-Lawrence & South Western Marine Factors. See above for addresses.

Chapter Nine

Engine water coolant pumps: *Cleghorn Waring & Co. (Pumps) Ltd, 9-15 Hitchin St, Baldock, Herts. SG7 6AH. Tel. (0462) 893838.

Indirect engine cooling: E.J. Bowman (Birmingham) Ltd, Chester St, Birmingham, B6 4AP. Tel. (021) 359 5401.

Engine exhaust systems: A.N. Wallis & Co, (W H Den Ouden), Greasley St, Bulwell, Nottingham, Notts. NG6 8NJ. Tel. (0602) 271154.

Engine electrical equipment: *Lucas Marine Ltd, Frimley Rd, Camberley, Surrey, GU16 5EU. Tel. (0276) 63252.

Chapter Ten

Adhesives & fillers: Simpson-Lawrence & South Western Marine Factors. See above for addresses.

Sealants: Adshead Ratcliffe & Co. Ltd, Derby Rd, Belper, Derbyshire DE5 1WJ. Tel. (0773) 826661.

*Ralli-Bondite Ltd, Arnside Rd, Waterlooville, Hants. PO7 7UJ. Tel. (0705) 251321.

Paints: *International Paints. *See* above for address.

Composition deck covering: James Walker & Co. Ltd, Lion Works, Hoe Bridge, Woking, Surrey. GU22 8AP. Tel. (04862) 5951.

* The companies marked with an asterisk have been very helpful and in some instances have given a great deal of assistance.

General

Sell's Marine Market — The Boating Fact Finder, 55 High St, Epsom, Surrey KT19 8DW. Tel. (03727) 26376.

British Waterways Board, Melbury House, Melbury Terrace, London NW1. Tel. 01 262 6711.

Inland Waterways Association, 114 Regents Park Rd, London NW1 8UQ. Tel. 01 586 2510.

R.Y.A., Victoria Way, Woking, Surrey GU21 1EQ. Tel. (04862) 5022.

Thames Water Authority, Thames Conservancy, Nugent House, Vastern Rd, Reading RG1 8DB. Tel. (0734) 593333.

INDEX

INDEX

INDEX

INDEX

INDEX

INDEX

INDEX

INDEX

INDEX

INDEX

INDEX

INDEX